To Fly Korea's Skies

To Fly Korea's Skies
An Autobiography

First published   December 2013
English edition   March 1, 2016

Written by Kim Shin
Translated by Keedon Kwon
Edited by Sung-Yoon Lee

Publisher Han Chul-hee
Published in Korea by Dolbegae Publishers

Registered August 25, 1979 No. 406-2003-018
Address 532-4 Pajubookcity Munbal-li Gyoha-eup, Paju-si, Gyeonggi-do, Korea 10881
Tel (+82) 31-955-5020
Fax (+82) 31-955-5050
Website www.dolbegae.co.kr
E-mail book@dolbegae.co.kr

Editorial Director Lee Kyoung-A
Book Design Lee Eun-jeong, Park Jeong-young
Cover Design Kimjindesign
Printing Hanyoung P&B
Bookbinding Kyungil P&B

ISBN 978-89-7199-709-3 03910

To Fly Korea's Skies

An Autobiography

Kim Shin

Dolbegae Publishers

Foreword

Over my long lifetime, I have met numerous people and lived through countless events. In retrospect, I've lived much of my life through periods of war and suffering: World War II and the Second Sino-Japanese War, the anti-Japanese Korean War of Independence, the Chinese Civil War, and the Korean War. Meanwhile, the joy of Korean liberation from Japanese colonialism was short-lived, and our nation once again had to endure the deep scars of war and national division. I was born in 1922. To my generation of Koreans, history was just another name for tribulation.

But, in spite of the trials and tribulations, we did not lose hope. Amid the ruins of war, with our bare hands and through blood and sweat we rebuilt everything. We worked really hard, we acquired knowledge diligently, and we made steady progress. That is why much of the outside world calls our contemporary history a miracle of industrialization and democratization. Indeed, modern Korean history is a miracle, but not one enabled by chance. Rather, it was built by the indomitable spirit of our patriotic martyrs who, in their fight for freedom and independence, gave it all—in Korea itself, Manchuria, Shanghai, Chongqing, Russia's Maritime Province, Siberia, and in the United States. That rarified spirit of independence is the foundation of the Korean miracle.

Born the son of an independence fighter, I saw and experienced up close the struggles of Korean patriots and martyrs. Much of boyhood and adolescence were cast in anxiety and loneliness, as one might feel walking through a pitch-black night, unable to see even an inch ahead. At the same time, as I was surrounded by many elders who embodied the spirit of righteousness, I was able to take pride in myself and not relinquish the thin thread of hope I held onto.

As with most other families of independence fighters, my own family was unable to enjoy to the full love and warmth of being a family. Death always lurked around the corner, and the fear and stress of imminent arrest were omnipresent in our lives. I have no memory of my mother, who died when I was but an infant. And I have only few early, intimate memories of my father, whom I could see only once in a while. Even after Korea's liberation in 1945, I was able to live with my father for not even two years. I lost my grandmother who loved me and cared for me so dearly in a foreign land while on the run. And my older brother died all too young, before he could witness Korea's independence.

Even after liberation, my family had to lead a cautious and muted life as if walking on thin ice. To be family members of Paikbum Kim Koo was at times a source of great pride and self-esteem, but it was also a heavy burden that constantly weighed on our shoulders. It meant always having to put the public interest before individual interest and never to deviate from that principle of life. It occasionally meant our every move would be watched and monitored and, at other times, a constraint under which our every word and act would be scrutinized and dramatized.

Hence, in spite of my long-held desire to tell the story of my life in a book, I could only be very cautious. Nonetheless, I finally mustered up the courage to reveal my life in a book for no other reason than the hope that the extraordinary life stories of independence fighters and their family may, even in some small way, touch the hearts of many people. Moreover, I must admit that in sharing my experiences in the founding of the Republic of Korea Air Force and its development in its formative years, my participation in the Korean War, and my career as the Chief of Staff of the Air Force, Ambassador to the Republic of China, and Minister of Transportation, I am hoping to shed light on modern Korean history.

I wish to stress one point here. When Korea was liberated, I was receiving flight training in the Chinese Air Force. As I was preparing to return to Korea, my father told me to stay and continue with my training. As a result, I became virtually the only Korean to have completed full flight training in the U.S. Air Force. It was thanks to my father's acumen in realizing the strategic importance of air power and the potential of aviation sector. For a Korean of that era, I was a rare individual with expertise in the field of aviation, and this knowledge base eventually became the axis and foundation of my life. In this regard, I can only be infinitely grateful to my father— famous independence fighter or not—but as any son would be to his own father for his guidance.

I have lived my life with pride, the pride of an officer of the Republic of Korea Air Force who has defended the skies of his nation. I keep in my heart always an overwhelming sense of debt and respect for my fellow comrades, both my seniors and juniors in the Air Force, and especially for those who paid the ultimate sacrifice in the service of their nation. I will donate the entire proceeds from the sale of this book to Haneul Sarang Jaedan (Love for the Skies Foundation), a non-profit organization established to support the families of Air Force pilots who died in the line of duty.

To leave an accurate record, I have made every effort to recall the past as faithfully as possible and have cross-checked as much relevant data and information as I could. But I fear there are omissions and errors here and there. There is bound to be some gap between an individual's personal memory, his story, and history. I seek the reader's understanding on these and bear sole responsibility for them.

Fall, 2013
Kim Shin

Table of Contents

The Tragedy of War and the Maelstrom of Revolution

Part 4.

Republic of Korea Ambassador to the Republic of China

Acknowledgement

1. Author's recollections and narration have been extensively cross-checked for factual accuracy; however, there may still remain some inconsistencies.
2. The period the author addresses in this book is from the year of his birth in 1922 to the year of the publication of the Chinese translation of *Paikbum Ilji*: Kim Koo's Autobiography, in 1994.
3. Chinese names of persons, geographical locations, and other proper nouns are transliterated mainly in Chinese pinyin. Some names of schools, institutions, pre-1911 proper nouns are transliterated in Korean-style. Most Korean names are transliterated in modern Korean style, except for those well known in original form, e.g., Kim Koo, Syngman Rhee, Kim Il Sung, Park Chung Hee, Roh Tae Woo, etc.

In tribute to all the heroes who struggled on behalf of Korean independence in Shanghai, Nanjing, Chongqing, and other foreign places, and to the heroes of the Republic of Korea Air Force who paid the ultimate sacrifice in defending their country's skies.

Part 1

Trees that Grow in the Land of Separation

Chapter 1

The Patriot-in-Exile's Infant Son

Under Grandmother's Loving Care

I was born to Kim Koo, father, and Choi Jun Rye, mother, as their second son, in Shanghai, China, on September 21, 1922. At the time, my father was 47 years-old. I had three older sisters, who all died at a young age from diseases. My father left An-ak, Hwanghae Province, Korea, on March 29, 1919, and arrived in Shanghai on April 13. My mother came to Shanghai in August 1920 with my older brother, In, who was four years older than I. In 1922, my paternal grandmother, Kwak Nak Won, also joined us in Shanghai.

When my mother gave birth to me, she was in very poor health. But she couldn't just lie in bed and rest as my grandmother was working hard doing all sorts of odd jobs around the house. Grandma felt sorry for her daughter-in-law, who was in frail condition and struggling to recover from giving birth, whereas the daughter-in-law, that is, my mother, felt terrible seeing her old mother-in-law working so hard. One day, my mother tried to help while she was still quite feeble from childbirth. She fell down the staircase carrying a big pale of water. She broke her ribs from the fall and one of the broken ribs

My mother's tomb From the left are me, my father, grandmother, and brother. The inscription on the tombstone is the work of Kim Du-bong, written exclusively in Korean phonetics, with my mother's date of birth inscribed according to the Dan-gun calendar, and her date of birth in accordance with the length of time passed since the founding of the Korean Provisional Government.

punctured her lung. As a result, she was hospitalized in a Western hospital in Shanghai's Hongkou district. At the time my mother told my grandmother,

"You are too frail to raise that baby by yourself. He should be entrusted to an orphanage."

Madam Kim Sun-ae, the wife of the famous independence fighter Kim Kyu-sik, wrapped me around a blanket and took me to my mother at the hospital, so that my mother could see me at least one more time. But I was unable to be by her side at the moment of her death.

On January 1, 1924, grandma and Madam Kim took my brother and me by the arm and rushed to the hospital to see mother. However, by the time we got there, she had already passed away.

Mother had said that she wished to see her sons one last time, but it was not meant to be. How can anyone truly understand the pain and angst my mother must have felt in the last moments of her life. Only Kim Eui-han and his wife, Jeong Jeong-hwa, were at my mother's side at her last breath. It was exceedingly difficult for my father to visit her in the hospital, as Hongkou was a city overrun by the Japanese. After my mother died, I was indeed sent to an orphanage as my mother had suggested to grandma. However, my grandmother took me back home when the first opportunity arose. Later, I would be sent to an orphanage twice more, but grandmother would do her best to retrieve me and take me home. That I did not grow up an orphan I owe entirely to my tenacious and caring grandmother.

While still living, my mother would often ask grandmother, who was over-extending herself taking care of me, to give up on raising me. It was easier to care for my older brother, as by then he could walk by himself. But as I was but a suckling, mother knew it would be much harder to take care of me. Mother was always very concerned for grandma in trying to raise me by herself. When I consider that a mother's love for her child is the most powerful sentiment in the world, I can only imagine how heart-wrenching it must have been for her to insist that I be sent to an orphanage. And it must have been tough on my father, too, seeing his infant son grow up without a mother. At the time Park Eun-sik lived next door. Park's daughter-in-law, that is, the wife of Park Si-chang, was Choi Yun-sin, the daughter of Choi Jung-ho. Ms. Choi would come by from time to time and help grandmother out, but we obviously could not depend on her solely.

Whenever I see blazing charcoal fire I think of my grandmother and long to see her. Perhaps it was because she experienced much hardship due to the daring activities of her only son, but her love for grandchildren was extraordinary. Whenever I would wake up and cry in the middle of the night she would try to pacify me by slipping her own dry nipple in my mouth. When that would not work, she would start a charcoal fire to heat up some water so she could feed me warm water. Once the water warmed up, she would put out the charcoal right away by pouring water over it, as we needed to save on the charcoal. When I would wake up and cry again in the middle of the night she would light the charcoal again. It was not a simple task to light up again wet charcoal.

The water that grandmother fed me was not just plain drinking water. At the time in China, one could not drink plain water, as plain water meant contaminated muddy water. The Chinese would get water from the river and pour it into a big jar, add aluminum sulfate into the jar to purify the water, and then boil it before drinking it. In Shanghai there were many shops that sold water purified in this way. A big coin could buy a big kettle filled with purified water and a bag of brown sugar. Grandmother gave me purified water with brown sugar added to it.

The Travails of a Stateless People

At the time I was born the reality that Korean independence fighters in Shanghai faced was quite grim. Some even succumbed to Japanese

Ahn Tae-guk's Funeral   My father stands on the right-hand side of the photo in a lighter suit that the rest, wearing a mustache.

schemes and became Japanese collaborators. With time, more and more people gave up and left the resistance movement, unable to cope with extreme poverty and hunger. Until the establishment of the Korean Provisional Government in 1919, the situation that the independence fighters faced had not been too bad. For example, Ahn Tae-guk, who had established the Sinminhoe with Ahn Chang-ho and Yang Gi-tak in 1907 and had been imprisoned in 1911 for his leading role in the "105 Men Incident," finally sought refuge in Shanghai after having spent some time in Manchuria. Ahn died of an illness in 1920. The outfits worn by those gathered at Ahn funeral at the International Cemetery suggest their lives were not so dire.

However, soon thereafter the lives of the Korean defectors

deteriorated precipitously. In the aftermath of the crushing defeat of Japanese troops by the Korean Independence Army in the Battle of Cheongsanri in October 1920, the Japanese authorities became ever more frantic to destroy the Korean Independence Army and other anti-Japanese resistance organizations. Japan's pressure grew so stifling that the future looked bleak. Amid the darkness some left Shanghai and acquired Chinese citizenship in order to become a peddler just to survive. Others changed their name in order to evade the constant surveillance of the Japanese military.

Under such circumstances the independence fighters and organizations became divided and disorganized. A popular saying even went around, that those who stood their ground and stuck by the Korean Provisional Government were either crazy or had given up on their lives. One day my grandmother came back from the birthday party of an elderly woman whose son had once been an independence fighter but had given up on the movement. It turned out that the son had prepared a fairly lavish party for his mother, as the family's lot had gradually improved. Upon return home grandmother said to father, "Some do a good job of parenting their children and looking after their family...Are you saying there is hope for the Korean Provisional Government or not? You have brought on me a lot of hardship. Are you now intending to make your own children suffer as well?"

My father replied, "I shall never leave the Korean Provisional Government even at the cost of death!"

Grandmother yelled in indignation, "Is that really an appropriate thing to say to your mother? Roll up your pants and fetch the cane!"

My father was in his fifties at the time, but had to obey his mother. It wasn't that grandma was irate at my father's resolve to protect the Korean Provisional Government until the bitter end. Rather, she was unable to suppress her anguish and anger at the hopeless future that the Korean Provisional Government seemed to face, on top of having to raise two small grandchildren and take care of the household by herself.

Just then, Maria Cho, the mother of the famous independence fighter Ahn Jung-geun, stopped by. Ms. Cho and grandma were well acquainted with each other, from the time my father had sought shelter at the house of Ahn Tae-hun in Chunggye, Sincheon, in 1895. Maria Cho would occasionally bring food over, well aware that we struggled to make ends meet. As expected, she brought food for us, and was astonished at the sight of my father being whipped on his calves by grandma.

"Oh, my! Your son's over fifty, and you're still resorting to corporal punishment?"

As Ms. Cho insisted that she stop, grandma backed down as if she couldn't resist. Ms. Cho, in apparent disbelief, asked father, "Considering that you are still caned by your mother at your current age, how often were you punished like this when you were young?

Father replied, "Well, since I've not kept a record, I really can't remember."

Ok Kwan-bin. He was a graduate of Pyongyang Daeseong School and known for his oratorical skills. He was arrested in the 1911 "105 Men Incident" and served time under the Japanese. Thereafter, Ok was involved in the activities of Heungsadan, an enlightenment organization, and also in the Korean Provisional Government. However, later he became a Japanese collaborator and fed intelligence on the Korean Provisional Government to the Japanese authorities. Once he became successful in business he would bribe the Japanese and increasingly slander Korean independence fighters. He also posed as a leader in Shanghai's overseas Korean business community.

Ok's cousin, Ok Sung-bin, taught English at Daeseong School upon finishing his studies at Soongsil School. He, too, was arrested and tried for his own involvement in the "105 Men Incident," and later, moved to Shanghai. He went into business with his cousin, Ok Kwan-bin, and in the mid-1920s assumed the role of surveillance police officer in charge of ethnic Koreans for the administrative office in Shanghai's French concession. The administrative office in the French concession began to cooperate with the Japanese in keeping an eye on and tracking down Korean independence fighters in the aftermath of the patriotic act of resistance by Yun Bong-Gil in Shanghai's Hongkou Park on April 29, 1932.

Yi Seong-gu. He had thrown a bomb at the Japanese Consulate in Shanghai in 1925 and was a special member of the Korean Laborer-Soldier Association, an anti-Japanese Korean organization based in Shanghai. In 1933 Yi had an appointment to meet Ok Sung-bin in front of a pharmacy in the French concession. The moment Yi arrived on the scene, he was arrested by Japanese policemen who had been staking out the premise. Yi was forcibly taken to Korea and tried and jailed. He died in a prison in Seoul from the after effects of severe torture.

Ok Kwan-bin and Ok Sung-bin were eventually shot and killed

by members of the Southern China Korean Youth League (Namhwa Hanin Cheongnyeon Yeonmaeng; anarchist anti-Japanese movement active in the 1930s), respectively, on August 1 and December 18, 1933. That they had given up on anti-Japanese independence movement and gone into business could be condoned; but that they had become collaborators with the Japanese and betrayed their former comrades could not be forgiven. Independence movement by definition means a small power resisting against a big power. It was this fighting spirit that enabled Korean independence fighters to carry on the fight against the very powerful Japan until the end. One could call such dogged determination foolhardy or unrealistic. But it was this belief in the justness of their cause that drove the few who remained with the Korean Provisional Government to bear it out until the end.

When we lived in Yongqingfang in Shanghai, there was a waste dump on the edge of the town. Grandma couldn't bring herself to go through the heaps of trash during the day, but at night she would rummage through the waste field. Among the trash she would find scraps of vegetable ends discarded by the Chinese. Grandma would gather those scraps, preserve them in salt, and cook them. She had to, in order to live--or, rather, in order to fight against Imperial Japan for independence.

Grandmother's Prayers

In the midst of such travails, one day grandma decided to return to Korea. She was able to make up her mind because she had friends in An-ak, Hwanghae Province. An-ak was where we had lived before resettling in Shanghai. It was also a place where my father's friends, Kim Hong-ryang, Kim Yong-jin, and Kim Yong-je, were all influential community leaders. In 1908 father had worked as a teacher in Yangsan School, An-ak, which had been established by the Kim family, upon the invitation by Kim Yong-je.

My father enjoyed a good reputation for he had proved himself an effective arbitrator whenever there was a dispute within the Kim family. He had also worked as a supervisor at the Kim family's Dongsanpyeong Farm from 1917 until his defection to China in 1919. During this time, my father prohibited tenant farmers from gambling and restricted their alcohol consumption. He also took the initiative to enlighten and educate the public by establishing schools. He was able to reform the troubled Dongsanpyeong Farm and help the Kim family, therefore, he had a very good relationship with the Kims.

I returned to Korea with my grandmother in November 1925, when I was about four years-old. Later I enrolled in Ansin School, An-ak, where my mother had once worked as a teacher. Opened in 1920 as an annex to Guitdam-gil Church, Ansin School was the very first private school in An-ak town. The Kim family provided us with a thatch-roofed bungalow to live in, and also arranged for me tuition waiver. While we lived in An-ak grandma would often shed tears, thinking of my big brother whom she had left behind in Shanghai.

On the Eve of Return to Korea, with Grandma
This photo was printed in the *Dong-A Ilbo* on November 6, 1925,
together with an article titled "Even in Death, to My fatherland."

"I wonder in which corner of Shanghai your brother is these days, whether he is able to find food to eat...I can hardly chew and swallow food, thinking of him."

Grandma would lament like this and cry at mealtimes. She often wrote my father saying that she would also raise her eldest grandson herself. In the end, in September 1927, my brother also joined us in An-ak. In school, my brother and I were boys without mom or dad. My brother eventually graduated from Ansin School and enrolled at Soongsil School, a Christian school in Pyongyang, in March 1931. Meanwhile, whenever a new teacher came to Ansin School, I would be reprimanded for not paying the monthly tuition.

"Grandma, my teacher demands that I bring the monthly tuition to school," I would say, running to her in tears. Each time, grandma took up the issue with a member of the Kim family.

"I thought I didn't have to pay the monthly tuition. What's going on?"

In these situations, it was the Kims who would be flustered.

"Maybe there's a new teacher who's unaware of the situation. Please don't worry."

The first word a newborn learns to say is "mama" or "dada." However, I could not even conceive of the word "mama," let alone "dada," during my boyhood years. The very first word that I spoke was "grandma." And most of my early memories revolve around grandma. By circumstance, grandma was thrust into the position of raising her grandsons and she constantly worried about our schooling. Whenever she would meet one of my teachers, she would say,

"If necessary, please beat my grandsons just short of crippling them, and set them straight."

With other kinds at school, whenever one was caned on the calves by a teacher, his father would complain. But in my case, grandma would plead with my teacher to be relentless and knock sense into me. Her requests were met without fail. For offenses that merited just one blow in the case of other kids, I would receive two or three.

Next to Ansin School was a school established by the Japanese called Sim Sang Elementary School. On had to be a graduate of Sim Sang Elementary School in order to preen about in front of others or be appointed to some clerkship. On the other hand, Ansin School lacked that kind of cachet. Yet, it was a truly a Korean nationalist school.

One day, all students were summoned together to raise the Japanese flag and sing a Japanese song to congratulate the Japanese emperor on the occasion of the birth of his son. We were obliged to celebrate the birth of Akihito (born on December 23, 1933), the son of Emperor Hirohito. On this occasion, some upper classmen proposed changing the words of the song we were to sing. In place of the phrase "From ancient times His Majesty Emperor Tenji," we sang at the top of our lungs a profane word, as instructed by our upperclassmen.

"Stupid idiot!"

Soon, the Japanese police, visibly shocked, came and made quite a fuss, cursing at us. All of a sudden I grew afraid. We made the excuse that we sang along out of peer pressure without knowing what we were saying. Ansin School was constantly under the watch of the police, as was my family. It was impossible to hide that my father was an independence fighter. All letters addressed to us from Shanghai were censored. The police would routinely show up at our home, too.

"Hello grandma. How are you these days? How's your health?"

The police would keep my family under surveillance under the pretext of asking after my grandma's health. They even sent us rice cakes on Japanese national holidays and other celebratory occasions. The Japanese police often made conciliatory remarks. "You must have many worries providing such small kids with formal education. But have no worries. When they graduate, we could take them to Japan and enroll them in one of the Japanese Imperial universities. So, grandma, have no worries at all."

Whenever a letter from my father came, the Japanese police would ratchet up its charm offensive. They would tell grandma if she could persuade her son to return to Korea, the Japanese authorities would give him a high ranking position in the Governor General's office. Grandma always ignored such schemes. On each Japanese holiday, every house had to hoist the Japanese national flag. But we never did.

"Everyone else has put up the Japanese national flag. Grandma, you should as well," they would pester her. Finally, she got fed up and told me, "Draw a black circle on a sheet of newspaper with ink and put it up on the front gate."

I obeyed and made a black circular blob on a piece of newspaper and hung it up on the front gate. When the Japanese police saw it, they brought their own national flag and put it up in place of mine.

Grandma was a devout Christian. Having few people around to trust and depend on, she would attend church with extra zeal. I accompanied her to church on Sundays. To this day I occasionally sing the hymns we sang back then and reminisce.

One day I asked her, "Grandma, what do you pray for?"

"I pray for the early collapse of the Japanese rascals and consequent liberation for Korea," she said.

Grandma's prayers were the same as my father's great wish. At the church service grandma would give me three *jeon* for the collection plate. While we were struggling to eat three meals a day other children around me would frequently buy candy. Whenever I saw my peers' cheeks bloat up with candy in their mouth and drips of sugar-tinged saliva running down their mouth, my heart ached with envy. I donated just two *jeon* and bought candy with the rest.

While children of relatively affluent parents would often be seen eating fruits like apples and bananas, all I could do was watch them eat. As young as I was, I was too proud to ask for a bite. But such was my desire to taste the fruit, I would pick up the banana skin others had discarded and eat it. I also relished eating the apple skin others had peeled off and thrown away. The first time I tasted fruit in my life, it was, properly speaking, the skin of the fruit.

In midwinter it grew so cold that grandma brought into the room a charcoal brazier. She had to make sure that all the smoke had died out before bringing the brazier into the room. But one time she was so concerned that my brother and I would be cold she brought the brazier in while the charcoal was still emitting smoke. She passed out from the fumes. A neighbor, the father of Choi Chang-han, came and carried grandma out in haste, leaving the door wide open. He dribbled into grandma's mouth salty water from pickling radish.

Fortunately, grandma regained her consciousness. All the while, my brother and I watched and trembled in fear.

To Dream My Lifelong Dream on a School Trip

It was either in fourth grade or fifth grade at Ansin School. My entire class was going on a five-day school trip to Pyongyang. The expense for the trip was 3 won per person. It was a very large sum for grandma. Well aware of our financial situation, I gave up on going on the trip without hesitation. I was the only one in my class who could not afford to go.

Ansin School was co-ed. My assigned partner in class was Kim Deok-ryang, the daughter of Kim Yong-dae. Doek-ryang told her father that I could not afford to go on the field trip. One night, Mr. Kim came to our house and called on grandma. She was sewing under a dimly lit lantern. In order to save on oil, grandma would add salt to the oil and light the lantern only very dimly. It was dark inside, and I was reading under the dim light. Mr. Kim said to grandma, "Such dim light will damage your grandson's eyesight."

"What can we do? We must save. What brings you here in the middle of the night?" she asked.

Mr. Kim said it would not be good for Shin to be left out of the school trip when everyone else was going. He left with grandma 3 won.

In Pyongyang we visited places like Moranbong and Nak Rrang Museum. We also visited military installations like the Japanese

Aviation Corps at Mirim Airport and the 77th Regiment of the Japanese Army. The Japanese authorities intentionally showed us such military facilities in an attempt to impress us.

What did impress me the most was the Mirim Airport. In those days, the main aircraft of the Japanese Aviation Corps was the biplane. Our hosts even showed us planes in flight. Those planes were not flying very fast, so we would see clearly the pilots sitting in the cockpit. I was struck by the handsome image of the pilot, with his long muffler fluttering in the wind and big aviator glasses. I was smitten by that image. And I decided right there and then that I would become a pilot one day!

When I became the Chief of Staff of the Air Force, the head-quarters of the Air Force was in Yoido. Once each year, I invited twenty to thirty elementary school students to ride on a military transport plane and flew them to the air space of Incheon and back. My subordinates would ask why I was doing such a thing. I replied that I wanted to provide the children with an unforgettable dream, as I had experienced myself at that age.

One day in the early 1980s I was flying on Korean Air headed for the United States. In mid-air, all of a sudden, I became curious as to who the chief pilot may be. I posed that question to a flight attendant, and she asked why I was asking such a question. I replied that I knew there were many commercial airliner pilots who had formerly been in the air force, army, and navy, and that I was just curious as to know which branch of the military the captain was from. The flight attendant told me that the captain was a former air force pilot. I asked for his name, which the flight attendant told me.

Then I gave her my business card and asked her to pass it on to the captain.

"This is my name. Could you give this to the captain and tell him I am seated right here?"

A few minutes later the captain approached me. He told me that when he was a grade school student in Seoul, he had a chance to ride on a military plane during the annual "Air Force Day" celebrations. From that day on, he firmed up his dream to become a pilot. He served in the air force as a fighter pilot, and upon leaving the service he joined Korean Air. I was pleased to hear and see that my efforts had come to fruition.

Another occasion that firmed up my will to become a pilot was witnessing the Japanese air raid of Nanjing in 1937. Later, with each flight of the Korean Provisional Government, as we ran from one town to another, to Wuhan, Changsha, Guangzhou, Liuzhou, and Chongqing, I witnessed first-hand indiscriminate aerial bombardment by the Japanese. My blood boiled watching so many lives killed by so few planes. I thought of becoming a pilot and seeking revenge by bombing Japan. When I was a student at Southwest United University (Xinan Lianhe Daxue; 西南聯合大學), many students volunteered for the military crying out that it was time to put down our brush and take up arms. I volunteered for the air force without hesitation.

In retrospect, it was Kim Yong-dae who made it possible for me to dream for the first time of becoming a pilot. He was a wealthy resident of Hwanghae Province. Later, in the wake of the outbreak of the Korean War, Mr. Kim fled to the South with his family without a penny to their name. One day Mr. Kim came to see me with his family at the air force base in Sacheon. I did all I could at the time to ensure that Mr. Kim and his family would be safely transported to Busan. And I helped his children to find jobs. I was so gratified that I could be of some help to someone who had given me so much in my youth.

Escape to China

From 1928 on, father would regularly write letters to overseas Koreans in Hawaii and other places and make a plea for assistance. Many came together and lent their support to the Korean Provisional Government. At the time, Koreans in Hawaii were migrant laborers who had gone to work on the plantations. They sent to the Korean Provisional Government a portion of their hard-earned money by toiling away in the fields all day under the scorching sun.

January 8, 1932. The Korean patriot Yi Bong-Chang threw a grenade at the emperor's procession in Tokyo. The emperor was returning home from observing a military parade. Later the same year, on April 29, the Korean patriot Yun Bong-Gil threw a bomb at a platform of Japanese officials gathered in Shanghai's Hongkou Park to celebrate the emperor's birthday. Things changed quickly after it became known that both these acts of resistance were masterminded by my father, Kim Koo. The Chinese government and the public could not conceal their astonishment. Soon thereafter, the Guomindang, Chinese Nationalist Government, buoyed by such daring acts, started to lend assistance to the Korean Provisional

Government, even as wary of the Japanese as it was.

Now, my father had a new cause for serious concern. He grew concerned of the possibility of the Japanese taking my brother and me hostage and forcibly making us into collaborators. Father decided to have the family move to China, which was relatively safer. But there were few safe routes. In the end, father decided on seeking official travel permits rather than have us escape in secret.

My family filed an official application for travel permit at the local police station. The police station in turn received a travel permit from the provincial administrative office in Haeju. Soon, grandma packed for the trip and dispensed with all our possessions. However, the Governor-General Police Bureau prevented us from departing Korea.

Grandma grew indignant and yelled, "You, rascals! One day you say we are approved to travel. The next day you say we cannot. How dare you toy around with us! Do you think you can survive over the long-term after taking over our country by force?"

Grandma even passed out, so enraged was she. It was early November, 1933. The Japanese police had us move into a tile-roofed house near Ansin School when we convinced them that we had no house to return to. They kept their watch on us constantly. In the end, the only way for us to depart for China was to secretly escape. We planned our escape with the help of Minister Kim Seon-ryang, Mr. Choi Chang-han, and a few others. It was early January, 1934, and Mr. Choi had by then returned to An-ak without luck after having left for Nanjing in late 1933 to study there.

On March 19, 1934, grandma and I rode in a car with Minister Kim Seon-ryang for Sincheon. There, we took the train and met up with Choi Chang-han on the train. We spent one night in a motel in Pyongyang. The next day, Minister Kim brought my brother, In, from the dormitory of Soongsil School. Grandma, In, Mr. Choi, and I took the train, passing through Andong (today known as Dandong), and headed for Fengtian (today Shenyang). On the train a Japanese military officer asked grandma where she was headed.

"The father of these children has a small business in Fengtian. He misses his children so much I am taking them to him."

After several tries, we finally made contact with folks in Fengtian who were to help us. We arrived at Dalian on the morning of March 21. In Dalian we were once again inspected by the Japanese, but managed to get through when my brother said, "I am taking my baby brother and grandma to leave them with our relatives in Weihaiwei." We left Dalian on a boat the evening of March 21 and arrived at Weihaiwei the afternoon of March 22. Mr. Cho Se-hun, the son-in-law of Ahn Jeong-geun, the brother of the famous Korean patriot Ahn Jung-geun, led us to safely check into an inn.

That night we left again on a boat and arrived at a dock in Hwangputan in Shanghai. We spent one night in Ahn Gong-geun's house, which was in the French concession. The next day we took the train to Jiaxing and headed for Eom Hangseop's house. I grew more and more excited at the thought of soon seeing my father, whose face I could barely remember. My heart beat faster at the sheer thought that I was getting closer and closer to him.

Chapter 2

The Nanjing Years and the Outbreak of the Second Sino-Japanese War

Yun Bong-Gil's Patriotic Deed and the Start of the Arduous March

At the time we arrived in Jiaxing to be reunited with my father in 1934, the Korean Provisional Government faced a dire situation. In the aftermath of Yun Bong-Gil's patriotic act against the Japanese in Shanghai on April 29, 1932, Japan revamped its efforts to arrest my father and other officials of the Korean Provisional Government. My father had planned for Yun's Bong-Gil's attack and other operations in order to revive the Korean Provisional Government. The Korean Provisional Government faced an existential crisis in the mid- to late-1920s, but since restructuring itself from a premiership to a parliamentary system of collective leadership, the Korean Provisional Government was able to preserve itself.

Just when a semblance of stability had been restored, the government-in-exile faced greater machinations by the Japanese. As a result, some were bought over by the Japanese, while others fled for the United States. Others with lesser means tried to stay out of view and made ends meet as a street vendor, while those who were originally from Manchuria went back home. Yi Dong-nyeong, one of the leaders, said of this situation,

"Once there were so many people. Now they've all scampered and only a few remain. The few who remain persevere regardless of prospects for success, only because we got our feet wet in the first place."

My father had not even shared with Yi Dong-nyeong any specifics regarding Yun Bong-Gil's act. All he had said was that he was planning for something that would shock the world. And Mr. Yi had told dad, "I am sure you know what you are doing. Do as you deem fit, and take account for it." Father established the Korean Youth Patriots Corps for the purpose of assassinating Japanese officials. The Corps was under the auspices of the Korean Provisional Government, but father intentionally made it appear like a separate organization. Until the very last minute before the act, father made sure to keep the plan a secret.

Japan began a massive-scale search from the early morning of April 30. Father sought refuge in the house of George Fitch, an American administrator at the YMCA in Shanghai, together with Kim Cheol, Ahn Gong-geun, and Eom Hangseop. But soon thereafter, father decided to claim responsibility for the attack as the Japanese authorities were arresting Koreans indiscriminately. Ahn Gong-geun said that they should hold off on the announcement as it may put the Korean Provisional Government leadership in danger. But father could not bear to see innocent Koreans who had nothing to do with the attack rounded up and put in jail. Once he made up his mind, he asked Eom Hangseop to write the first draft of the statement. Thereafter, through the good offices of Mrs. Fitch, my father issued the statement through an American wire service in the name of the Korean Youth Patriots Corps.

Mrs. Fitch made several calls to her contacts to help father publish the statement. Unbeknownst to her, however, the French authorities had wire-tapped her phone line and were listening in. The Japanese authorities had caught wind and started a surveillance operation on the Fitch's house by sending men, for example, disguised as electric technicians. Once my father's statement had been issued, father and his colleagues could no longer stay in the Fitch's house. On May 14, 1932, Dr. Fitch, with his wife in the car, took my father, Park Chan-ik, Eom Hangseop, and Ahn Gong-geun to the border between the French concession and Chinese territory. The four on the run crossed into Chinese territory with the Fitches looking on behind them and headed for Jiaxing by train.

My First Reunion with Father in Nine Years

The Chinese Nationalist Government, Guomindang, had Chen Guo-fu assist my father and his entourage. Chen's secretary, Xiao Zeng, contacted Chu Fu-cheng, who in turn arranged for them to stay in Jiaxing. Chu Fu-cheng, Dean of the Law Department at Shangai University, was an influential figure in the Guomindang. He was from an elite family in Zhejiang.

Chu Feng-chang, Chu's first son, had studied in the U.S. Upon

Posthumous National Founding Award Ceremony in Honor of Chu Fu-cheng
Chu's grandson accepted the award in honor of Chu, who died in 1948, at a ceremony in Jiaxing.

return home he ran a cotton yarn factory for a while, and thereafter worked as a technology manager at a paper mill. At the time, Yi Dong-nyeong, Yi Si-yeong, Kim Eui-han, and Eom Hangseop's family members had already taken shelter in Chu Feng-chang's closed down cotton yarn factory. It was also the first place of refuge for my father and his colleagues upon arrival in Jiaxing. Each of Chu Fu-cheng's family members helped key figures of the Korean Provisional Government and their family by providing them with shelter.

In April 1934, upon our escape from Korea, my grandmother, brother, and I, too, hid ourselves in Jiaxing. Our hiding place was a two-storied house with a spacious garden. My father came from Nanjing to see grandma and me not long after we arrived in Jiaxing. At the time, Nanjing was the capital of the Guomindang government

Family reunion in 1934 I saw father only sporadically in Nanjing. This is one of very few family photos taken.

and was thus relatively out of Japan's reach. My brother, who had come to Jiaxing together with grandma and me, had gone off to Nanjing. Thus, when father finally visited, only grandma and I were there to greet him.

As soon as my father arrived at our hide-out, grandma hastily called for me. It was the first time in nine years that I was seeing my own father. But it was basically the first time I was really seeing him face to face, as the last time I had seen him was when I was barely a toddler. I entered the room where my father was waiting. There stood a man with a fairly dark complexion, his face dotted with a few age spots.

"Look at you! You've grown so much" my father said to me stroking my head.

Many emotions came over me at that moment. I had learned the word "grandma" before learning the words "mama" and "dada." Such was my fate that warm feelings between family members could seldom be enjoyed or expressed. Such was the fate of the independence fighters and their families that they had to conceal entirely their personal anguish and suppress their desires. These were the harsh realities that constantly hovered above us.

At the time, Japan had put a bounty of 600,000 *dayang* on my father. A *dayang* was a silver coin and was worth 300 bronze coins. It was the largest bounty ever put on an individual in all of Japanese history. The initial bounty was 200,000 *dayang*, but soon Japan's Ministry of Foreign Affairs, the Japanese Government General of Korea, and the Occupation Forces Headquarters in Shanghai banded together to set a joint bounty of 600,000 *dayang*. Grandma, unaware of this serious situation, said to father,

"It's about time for you to take charge of rearing your own sons."

My father was in no position to do so. In fact, he had taken a great risk to come and see us. As a huge bounty had been set, there were not only pro-Japanese Korean collaborators but also Chinese and even Westerners on the lookout for my father.

A Life of Hiding in Nanjing

After a few months in Jiaxing grandma and I headed out for Nanjing. It was a long journey by train, passing through Hangzhou and Shanghai before finally reaching Nanjing. Once in Nanjing, we stayed in General Kim Hong-il's house. General Kim had served as a manager in a weapons factory of the Chinese Army in Shanghai, then as the Chief of the General Staff Office of the General Headquarters of the Nineteenth Army Group, and later as the Chief of Staff of the General Headquarters of the Korean Liberation Army. He lived a bit better off than most officials in the Korean Provisional Government. In time, I became friends with his son, Kim Yong-jae.

In May 1933, my father met Chiang Kai-Shek, and the two men agreed to open a special class for Koreans at the Luoyang branch of the Chinese Central Army Academy. Accordingly, 90 Koreans received military training from February 1934 to the spring of 1935. In December 1934 my father established the Counter-Intelligence Corps of the Korean Liberation Army centering on the Korean recruits at the Academy. Korean students in Nanjing Central University also joined the Corps headquartered in 1 Gaogangli, Mujiangying, Nanjing.

Father ran the Korean Counter-Intelligence Corps Preliminary Training Camp at two buildings in Dongguantou, Nanjing, from February 1935 onwards. This camp ran until spring 1936. Father tried to get the trainees of the camp to enter the Chinese Central Army Academy, but the Chinese government did not allow it for fear of Japan's objection.

My brother, In, was among the youngest out of the youths gathered at Dongguantou. I still remember Yi Jae-hyeon, Kim Won-yeong, and Na Tae-seop. Among the Korean recruits there were spies who had been co-opted by the Japanese army. One day, a Korean trainee was spinning on a horizontal bar when money fell out of his pocket. It was a roll of five *yuan* bills issued by the Central Bank.

At the time, different regions used different currencies. While provinces like Zhejiang and Jiangsu used the currency of the central government, the Chinese warlords in Hubei, Hunan, Guangdong, Guangxi, Fujian, etc. issued their own currencies. Furthermore, the weapons used by warlords also varied by region, from French, American, to British, etc. While apparently standing united under the Chinese national flag, in reality the warlords were busy enriching themselves.

Moreover, the warlords put most of the tax money into their own pockets. The common cause of the anti-Japanese resistance did bring the warlords closer together, but before this need arose, each province under a particular warlord virtually acted as a separate country. The warlords lived large, with each man often having more than ten concubines. To maintain such a lifestyle, they needed money. Since they could not print money at will, they tended to spend taxes collected for personal use. Some even extracted the equivalent of twenty years of taxes all at once.

At any rate, five *yuan* was not a small sum. Moreover, as it was a roll of five *yuan* bills, it was a considerable amount of money. The Korean recruit in question ran away that night for fear of blowing his identity. The truth was, where there were Koreans, there were Japanese spies. Some of the Korean recruits at the Army Academy later became commissioned officers in the North Korean People's Army. When I escorted my father to Pyongyang in 1948, I attended a dinner party hosted by Kim Il Sung. At the back of the party hall, there stood servicemen quite a few of whom I recognized. They were acquaintances from my Nanjing years. I gave them a friendly knowing look, but none of them responded.

Grandma and I lived apart from my father in Nanjing as we had in Jiaxing. But unlike in Jiaxing, father would stop by from time to time. Grandma and I had to move several times in Nanjing. We moved from General Kim Hong-il's house to the vacation home of Xiao Zeng, near the gymnasium of the Nanjing Diyi Park. But it was not a suitable place for us to hide in as people would constantly stop by. One day, Gu Zheng-lun, the commander of the Garrison Headquarters in Nanjing, made an earnest appeal to my father.

"The Japanese are threatening us for helping you and your family. We have to be extra careful."

Soon, grandma and I moved once again, this time to a small house in Malujie. It was quite shabby, but quite suitable to hide ourselves in. When we needed to contact my father, we would stop by an inn near the Qinhuai River. Ahn Gyeong-geun had been staying there for some time disguised as a Chinese man. When grandma told him that she needed to see my father for whatever reason, Ahn would deliver her message to someone else, who would in turn pass it on to another person, and so on. Before the message reached my father, it would have passed through three or four persons. Once he received the message, father would drop by in the middle of the night, only to stay for a short while.

Grandma had to take care of household chores by herself, as old and frail as she was. She could not hire a maid, as to do so may tip off the Japanese military clues on my father's whereabouts. Father, unable to ignore his own frail mother overextending herself, reached out to Jeong Jeong-hwa, Kim Eui-han's wife, for help. Madam Jeong came to our house with her son Kim Ja-dong in September 1935 and stayed with us for close to a year, helping my grandma out. But grandma felt so guilty about Ms. Jeong being away from her own husband, one day she said,

"Enough! Please go back now. Who am I to separate a young couple like you and your husband! This is not right."

Grandma stubbornly pushed Ms. Jeong out, telling her to go home to her husband. In the end, as much as Ms. Jeong meant well, she could not oppose my stubborn, and well-meaning, grandma.

The Second Sino-Japanese War

There was an airport next to Diyi Park in downtown Nanjing. The airport was called the Minggugong (Ming Palace) Airport, as it was located on the site of an old palace in Ming China. It was mostly German airplanes that took off from and landed at this airport. German airplanes called Junkers would take off from Berlin, pass through Soviet air space and over Xinjiang before arriving in Nanjing. Junkers were mainly used as passenger planes, and flew between Berlin and Nanjing once a week.

With the onset of war, the Minggugong Airport was turned into a military air base. On the occasion of Chiang Kai-Shek's fiftieth birthday, the Chinese people somehow raised funds by individual contribution and presented him with 68 warplanes. This was called the "presentation of airplanes to wish him a long life." The congratulatory ceremony for Chiang fiftieth birthday was held in Xiaolingwei. Boy Scouts from all over the country gathered and performed a march. Chiang Kai-Shek took the rostrum not in a general's uniform but in that of a generalissimo. I, too, participated in the event as a Boy Scout. That was the first time I saw Chiang Kai-Shek. It was October 31, 1936.

The air force did a flyover in two formations in which one formation flew in the shape of "zhong" (中) and the other in the shape of "zheng" (正). 'Zhongzheng' was Chiang Kai-Shek's given name. He wore aviator glasses and got into one of the presented planes. The fighter he boarded was a Hawk model, with non-retractable wheels. At the time, Chinese warplanes were vastly inferior to Japanese. Moreover, China would not even make full use of the inferior fleet in its possession due to fuel shortage. As a result, the Japanese Air Force belittled the Chinese Air Force. For example, during the Japanese bombing of Chengdu, a Japanese pilot landed his bomber at the Chengdu Air Base, proceeded to tear off all the Chinese flags hoisted on the base, and casually took off into the air.

Chiang Kai-Shek had tried to prepare for the Japanese invasion long before Chinese public became wary of an imminent invasion. However, the warlords throughout China would not cooperate. In order to address this problem, Chiang formed a brotherhood alliance with Zhang Xueliang, Zhang Zuolin's son, and Northwestern warlord Feng Yuxiang and Yan Xishan.

However, on December 12, 1936, the Xian Incident struck. Chiang Kai-Shek, who was visiting Zhang Xueliang in Xian, was arrested and locked by Zhang's bodyguards over differences on how to respond to the mounting Japanese aggression and as complaints against Chiang by Chinese troops mounted. Chiang had not treated Zhang's Northeastern troops well. While taking particular care of the central army under his direct control, Chiang had discriminated against the Manchurian Army, the Western Northern Army, and the Sichuan Army.

Zhang Xueliang's Manchurian Army, while discontent was brewing, had been ordered by Chiang Kai-Shek to destroy the Communist Party. The Manchurian Army, already as disgruntled as it was against Chiang, thought, "Why should we Chinese fight each other? We should fight the Japanese." During such a discord, the Chinese Communist Party had infiltrated the Nationalist forces through underground organizations. It put forth the argument to Zhang Xueliang that "compatriots should not fight each other." Persuaded by the argument, Zhang had Chiang Kai-Shek incarcerated. The Communist Party made Chiang promise not to engage it in a civil war, but to cooperate with it to fight against Japan. The result was the Guomindang-Communist United Front.

Following the Xian Incident, the Lugou (Marco Polo) Bridge Incident took place. Japanese troops attacked Chinese troops near the Lugou Bridge located in a southwestern suburb of Beijing on July 7, 1937. This marked the full-scale outbreak of the Second Sino-Japanese War. The Japanese Army launched a full-scale attack on the Huabei area, including Beijing and Tianjin, on July 28. It attacked Shanghai on August 13 and occupied it in early November. It went on to occupy Nanjing on December 13. Japan expected to sweep through China in just two or three months. Yet, the Chinese Army's resistance was strong, and the war dragged on as the frontlines expanded across China.

My School Life in Nanjing

Although I had finished fifth grade in Korea, I started all over from first grade in Nanjing because I could not speak or write in Chinese. But math was a different matter. During exam periods, students in my grade as well as students in higher grades would ask me to help them with math problems.

My school was named Dazhongqiao Elementary School. Kim Ja-dong was in this school, too. I changed my name to Guan Shin to conceal my identity and disguised myself as a Japanese boy. At this school I focused mostly on learning Chinese, as I had already completed all other subjects in Korea. All I needed was a better grasp on Chinese. I graduated from the elementary school in two years, and entered Anhui Middle School.

When I was in middle school, the Japanese conducted indiscriminate bombing on Nanjing. The bombers had mainly taken off from the Japanese Naval Air Force based in Jeju Island in Korea. Some took off from bases in Taiwan. The Japanese flag was painted on the wings of the bombers. As the flag looked like a circular black plaster on a sheet of paper with the color being the only difference, the Chinese called it "plaster flag."

I vividly saw the Japanese war planes bomb the city. Three planes formed a team; three teams formed an air fleet; and three fleets formed a larger air fleet. The Chinese came to realize that now there was no distinction between the warfront and the rear. One day during a bombing raid, my father came early in the morning to check on us.

"Mother, are you all right?"

She answered "Yes," nonchalantly.

Still concerned, he asked another question.

"How did you cope last night?"

She again answered insouciantly,

"I felt the house shake up and down a little."

She had sufficiently strong nerves to make little of the bombings. When we lived in Liuzhou, there was a time when an air raid siren blasted through the central part of the city. I said to grandma, quite concerned, "Everybody is getting out. You should, too."

She replied without even blinking, "I won't. You go on."

I could not obey her, of course. I said, "How in the world can I go out alone and leave you behind?"

Grandma was stubborn to the end. Sometimes, I had no choice but to leave her behind and seek a bomb shelter by myself. When Anhui Middle School moved to Tunxi to the south of Anhui due to the air raids, I sought refuge there by myself. By then, I had little difficulty living alone without grandma as I could converse in Chinese. My intention was to stay there for a short while just to avoid Japan's air raids. But, as the war went on, I ended up staying longer than I had imagined.

Chapter 3

Oh! My Grandmother

My Father, Kim Koo, is Shot

In November 1937, a month before Nanjing fell to the Japanese troops, officials of the Korean Provisional Government decided to gather in Dongguantou and then relocate together to Wuhan. Our family could not move together with them. At the time of the decision to relocate to Wuhan, father suggested to grandma leaving me behind in Tunxi. He tried to persuade her, "Because Shin is away from Nanjing and can take care of himself and speak Chinese, he can come whenever we tell him to come. So, you should go ahead and leave without him."

She stubbornly refused. "If Shin doesn't go, neither do I."

My father, unable to persuade her, called for me in a hurry. So, when others were escaping Nanjing to go further south, I went the opposite way, north toward Nanjing. Grandma, father, I, and Ahn Gong-geun's family all boarded a British ship at Xiaguan in the Yangzi valley and headed for Wuhan. After staying in Wuhan for a few days, my family took a train to Changsha, where we stayed for about seven months. When we set out for Changsha, Ahn's family, which had been with us the entire time, did not come with us. I learned later that there was discord between Ahn Gong-geun and my father at the time.

When we had headed for Wuhan, Ahn had not brought along Madam Kim A-ryeo, the wife of the patriotic martyr Ahn Jung-guen and Ahn's own sister-in-law, from Shanghai. My father grew angry and said to Ahn, "How could you possibly leave behind in a place occupied by Japanese invaders the wife of the martyr who sacrificed his life for the sake of our country?" I personally do not think that Ahn had meant to leave her behind, but that circumstances in Shanghai might have precluded her from leaving the city. In any case, after this incident, the relationship between the Ahn family and my father gradually grew more and more distant. The Ahns eventually refused to join us when we relocated, first, to Changsha, and then Guangzhou.

In Changsha, we lived in a place called Mayuanling. At first, we could not settle down in any one place together. So many refugees had flooded into Wuhan and Changsha, it was very difficult to find housing where all of us could live together. Grandma and I lived by ourselves in a house near a market place. Later, we got hold of a house in Mayuanling where all of us finally could live together. Near our house was the Xiangya Clinic.

In Changsha, there were frequently active discussions on the unification of the various Korean political factions. On May 6, 1938, the Korean People's Party headed by my father, the Joseon Revolutionary Party headed by Ji Cheong-cheon (known as Yi Cheong-cheon during his exile in China), and the Reconstruction of the Korean Independence Party faction headed by Jo So-ang held a meeting to discuss the unification of the parties at Nanmuting. Nanmuting, which had been the office of high officials during the Qing period, was a two-storied wooden building that the Joseon Revolutionary Party had been using as its headquarters. During the meeting, the Joseon Revolutionary Party member Yi Un-hwan rushed in and opened fire.

My father Kim Koo, Hyeon Ik-cheol, Ryu Dong-ryeol, and Ji Cheong-cheon were all shot. Hyeon unfortunately died on site, while Ji escaped with just a light wound. My father and Ryu, however, were severely injured. The Chinese police arrested Yi Un-hwan. They also arrested Gang Chang-je and Park Chang-se as the masterminds behind the attack crime. In the confusion that followed, however, Gang and Park were released, while Yi was able to run away. Though some have said that these men had committed the crime out of disgruntlement against their victims, I believe it was a political act of terror in an attempt to prevent the political unification.

My father, with a bullet lodged in his chest, was in critical condition. He fell into a state of unconsciousness and was hospitalized for a month. When he was taken to the Xiangya Clinic, doctors simply took him as a lost cause and gave up on him. They judged that he had no chance of surviving and just left him lying in the emergency room. Only when they saw that he was still breathing even after a few days, did they begin treating him in earnest. Chiang Kai-Shek, upon hearing the news, told Zhang Zhizhong, his close associate and the governor of Hunan Province, to do everything he could to save my father. Zhang visited the hospital to ask after my father's health.

Although my father escaped death by virtue of Chiang's help, the doctors were unable to dislodge the bullet. As a result, father was temporarily paralyzed, as the bullet in his chest blocked his blood circulation. Fortunately, with time he recovered enough to move about on his own without difficulty. My father avidly practiced calligraphy and left many handwritten scripts. Among them several scripts feature a visible tremor in the brush stroke, the result of his unsteady hand from the gun wound.

I did not visit father once while he was hospitalized, for fear that doing so might alert grandma to the truth that he had suffered a serious gunshot. Although I did not go and see my father at the hospital, I was kept fully apprised of his condition. But I could not tell grandma what had happened, lest the shock and grief be too much for her to handle.

The Tiger Grandmother Who Silenced Even the Elders

When my father had recovered enough to be able to move about on his own, he visited grandma. Far from welcoming him, she gave him a scolding.

"Does it make sense that you were shot by your own compatriot rather than by the Japanese rascals? What did you screw up so badly as to allow something like this to happen?"

Grandma had known everything all along. One day, when we lived in Jiaxing, as her birthday approached, several ladies brought her many birthday gifts to please her. Grandma's face tightened up and she asked in an annoyed tone,

"What's this?"

The ladies cautiously replied, "We have brought you gifts as you've endured so much hardship and since your birthday is just around the corner."

Grandma bellowed, "To whom do we owe the fact that we are able to live a decent life without going hungry? Are we not living like this by feeding off the blood of the martyr Yun Bong-Gil? How could you possibly buy and bring all of these things!"

Storming at them, she threw all the gifts out of the door. The ladies all just sat there trembling in fear. Her anger melted away a little bit only after Madam Jeong Jeong-hwa, who knew grandma well, swore that they would never do something so thoughtless like this again and desperately begged for forgiveness. Thereafter, the Korean ladies began to call my grandma "tiger grandmother." She was equally stern with father. My father could not live together with grandma and me even in Changsha. She would tell father, "How dare you even think about living with me when duty calls and you must tend to the affairs of our nation?"

Knowing her single-minded personality, father visited his mother only occasionally until she passed away in Chongqing. During the Changsha years, folks associated with the Korean Provisional Government people saw my grandma struggling with household chores by herself and helped us out a lot. Among others, Ms. Kim Hyo-suk, the oldest daughter of Kim Bung-jun, offered her the greatest help. Unfortunately, Kim Bung-jun was later abducted to North Korea during the Korean War and died there. Ms. Kim's husband was Song Myeon-su, who would be active in the Korean Liberation Army. Ms. Kim's younger sister, Kim Jeong-suk, too, would become was a member of the Korean Liberation Army, as would also her husband, Go Si-bok, and her older brother, Kim Deok-mok.

Thinking of Ms. Kim Hyo-suk, I am overcome with many emotions. I once met with her in Taiwan when I served as the Ambassador of the Republic of Korea to Taiwan. She visited Taiwan as a missionary on behalf of the Unification Church. She was trying to leverage the fact that the Chief Secretary of the Presidential Office at the time had graduated from Zhongshan University in Guangdong, of which she, too, was a graduate. But the Taiwanese government was quite wary of her missionary activities, and even suspected that the Unification Church might have been a cover for a communist faction.

I asked her to come in to see me and explained to her straight-forwardly, "You'd better go back to Korea because the Chinese people do not take kindly religions like the Unification Church, as they are of a different nature from the established religions."

She went back to Korea before long, though I am not sure that it was because she followed my advice or because she had run into difficulty propagating the Unification Church. Later, when I served as Minister of Transportation, she worked in the library of the Railroad Bureau in Yongsan, which was under the auspices of the Ministry of Transportation. Whenever she saw me, she would tell me that I ought to write a biography of my grandmother without delay. She told me that she was collecting sources to write my grandmother's biography herself. However, she was unable to complete it before she died in L.A.

in 2003.

Grandma never had formal education and could not read or write well. But she spoke more articulately than many educated people. Often, even learned men would be speechless in her presence, such was the force and logic with which she spoke. Even Korean elders like Yi Dong-nyeong and Yi Si-yeong dared not talk back to grandma. She never felt small even in the company of elder statesmen, and said all that she wanted to say.

"You old men, just let it be and get out. You should let young people come in and take over. Why are you old men still meddling in their jobs while giving them nothing but empty advice?"

This was how grandma blamed the elders whenever they interfered with the affairs of young people. The elders would never grow angry at grandma. Instead, they just took it and smiled.

When grandma and I first came to Changsha, it was very hot. I enjoyed swimming day and night in the Xiang River. In Changsha I felt relatively at peace with myself, my body and mind somewhat relaxed. But such comforts did not last, as Changsha, too, would soon become a dangerous place. The governor of Hunan Zhang Zhizhong ordered that the city be scorched and burned. It was part of the scorched earth strategy to leave nothing for the invading Japanese Army. But the strategy did more harm to the Chinese than the Japanese. For this, Zhang was later subjected to considerable criticism.

Our family had to be on the run once more. This time, it was to Guangzhou. We left in July 1938, traveling by train. The train made innumerable stops along the way as it was not a regular passenger train. When it became very hot, I climbed on the roof of the train. It was a very dangerous act, but I did not care as I was by then a hot-blooded seventeen year-old.

One day, I fell asleep on the roof of the train. After a while, grandma searched every corner of the train looking for me. Oblivious to it all, I climbed down from the roof after a long nap. When I finally showed up, grandma laughed out heartily instead of scolding me, as my face was pitch black, showered with train smoke whenever the train passed through a tunnel.

When we arrived in Guangzhou on July 17, 1938, Chae Won-gae, then a member of the Chinese Army, came in a car to pick us up. Originally from Yeongwon in South Pyeongan Province, Chae would later join the Korean Liberation Army and become a division commander in the Republic of Korea Army after Korea's liberation in 1945. He drove grandma, father, and me to the Asia Inn.

Among those who had moved to Guangzhou at the time I remember Yi Jun-sik, Kim Bung-jun, Song Myeon-su, Kim Hyo-suk, Kim Jeong-suk, and Yang U-jo. When the Korean Provisional Government relocated in Guangzhou, Yi, as a Chinese Army officer, along with Chae, provided great help in setting up its office in Dongshanbaiyuan. Song later became an Office of Strategic Services (OSS)-trained member of the Korean Liberation Army.

Yang, who had studied in America when he was young, worked mainly in the Korean Independence Party, serving as a Provisional Assemblyman and Propaganda Committee member in the Korean Provisional Government, among other things. Yang's wife, Choi Seon-hwa, was a graduate of Ewha Woman's College and a learned intellectual. She started to assist the Korean Provisional Government as she participated in the Young Korean Academy and taught at Ewha Woman's University from the mid-1950s on. As far as I can remember, Yang was relatively well off because he owned some property in Hong Kong and Guangdong.

The Asia Inn had hotel-level facilities. It even had separate shower rooms. There were also many young guests staying at the inn. Among others, I remember Ro Tae-jun who was the second son of Ro Baek-lin, former Prime Minister of the Korean Provisional Government, and who participated in the anti-Japanese war affiliated with the 13th Chinese Army and later took an active role in the Korean Liberation Army. At the inn were many people who lived with us in Mayuanling, but there were also many new people from other places who had gathered there.

Northeast of the Asia Inn flowed the Zhu River. When we arrived in Guangzhou the weather was very hot and humid. I swam in the river often to cool off. When I went swimming, I would bring some change and buy some food from the boats passing by. I spent quite some time in the river each time I went. At least while I was swimming, I could forget about our hard reality for a while.

Continuously on the Run

Chiang Kai-Shek announced moving the seat of government to Chongqing in late 1937. He used the word *"peidu"* for the new capital, which meant provisional or wartime capital. The Korean Provisional

Government had to relocate frequently, too. It moved from Shanghai to Hangzhou in May 1932 (while father sought refuge in Jiaxing) and then to Zhenjiang in November 1935. At the time, most of the key figures of the Provisional Government lived in Nanjing. Nanjing was the main base until the Korean Provisional Government moved again to Changsha, Hunan Province, in November 1937. My father worked mainly in Nanjing as well before the relocation to Changsha.

When the Korean Provisional Government moved yet again from Changsha to Guangzhou, Guangdong, in July 1938, only about ten core members resided within the city limits, while the rest settled in Foshan, about 25 kilometers west of Guangzhou. The Korean Provisional Government's base in Guangzhou and Foshan lasted but a short while, as it relocated yet again to Liuzhou, Guangxi Province, in October 1938. It then moved to Qijiang, located right below Chongqing, Sichuan, in May 1939. The Korean Provisional Government finally settled down in Chongqing in September 1940. My father had already arrived there at the end of October 1938, while my grandmother and I arrived there at the beginning of 1939.

The Shanghai period lasted for thirteen years in the 26 year history of the Korean Provisional Government. In the aftermath of martyr Yun Bong-Gil's act of resistance in 1932, the Korean Provisional Government moved through Hangzhou, Zhenjiang, Changsha, Guangzhou, Liuzhou, Qijiang, and Chongqing over a span of eight years. The Chongqing period lasted five years until Korea's liberation in 1945. Meetings on the political unification of the various Korean factions took place in Changsha. In Qijiang, too, unification talks such as the seven-party and five-party talks were held, but to no avail. When the Korean Provisional Government attempted unification talks with Kim Yak-san's communist faction in Chongqing, it was finally able to succeed because the Guomindang said just as it had formed a united front with the Chinese communists so, too, should the Korean Provisional Government merge with the Korean communists. It also promised unconditional aid in the event the two sides would be united.

The house in which grandma and I lived in Foshan was like a Buddhist temple. Even when other houses nearby would be frequented by visitors, ours was quiet. As we learned later, our house had a big problem. It was infested with termites. Termites gnawed at the wooden structure so much, we almost believed the Chinese people when they told us that termites could also gnaw through silver coins. Ignorance was indeed bliss. We lived in a house which might collapse at any point without a care in the world, not knowing that it was infested with termites.

It was easy to come and go between Guangzhou and Foshan because trains were commonly available. When I wanted to contact the Korean Provisional Government, I would take the train from Foshan to Guangzhou and back. When we moved to Liuzhou after the Foshan years, we took a steam boat up the Xi River. The steam boats used at the time were wooden ships with iron-plated bottoms. The ships did not take on any passengers except for their own crewmen. The passengers would board a wooden boat connected to the steam boat, which could accommodate about twenty passengers. A steam boat typically could tug three or four boats.

The steam boat we took moved very slowly as it went upstream along the winding river. When there was an air raid, it moved even more slowly because it had to hide out by the banks of the river. It proved a month-long journey, so the old people had a hard time, while the young people could endure it. Since Liuzhou had no place for steam boats to drop anchor, we got off a little ways away from the city and traveled to Liuzhou by car. An advance party went to Liuzhou to look for housing here and there. We ended up dispersed in several places throughout Liuzhou.

The elders of the Korean Provisional Government lived together in one of the places. I remember among others Yi Dong-nyeong, Yi Si-yeong, Cha Ri-seok, Song Byeong-jo, and Jo Wan-gu. Many elders who were unaffiliated with the Korean Provisional Government had also come to Liuzhou. I lived together with grandma in a separate small house and carried out liaison work for the Korean Provisional Government. The liaison work suited me well, as it required running to and fro and the ability to speak Chinese.

In February 1939, the Korean Liberation Propaganda Youth Corps was founded in Liuzhou. This organization, which may be said to be the precursor to the Korean Liberation Army, engaged in a great deal of propaganda activities to imbue the younger generation with the will to resist against Japan. As much as I wanted to participate in it, father discouraged me.

"You should take good care of your grandmother for the time being."

My father had told me so because there would have been no one else to take care of my grandmother if something ever happened to me. I wanted to join the Youth Corps, but dutifully followed my father's words.

The Journey from Liuzhou to Chongqing

Grandma and I left Liuzhou for Chongqing before most others in the Korean Provisional Government did. Father wanted to take care of her firsthand as soon as possible in view of her advanced years and deteriorating health. He had already moved to Chongqing at the end of October 1938. Grandma and I traveled in a truck, with grandma, who was unwell, sitting in the passenger's seat next to the driver. She was suffering from a severe sore throat and goiter. Goiter was an endemic disease in the Guangxi region. Natives of this region consumed rock salt which, unlike sea salt, does not contain enough iodine. The lack of dietary iodine made residents of this region susceptible to goiter.

The journey from Liuzhou to Chongqing was rough. When we were traveling from Hechi to Dushan through Luzhai, a Japanese cavalry regiment rapidly advanced through Guilin and Liuzhou to Dushan. The sudden expansion of the war threw the Chinese people into chaos. Just as we arrived in Guiyang via Dushan and Duyun, the fleeing Chinese were flooding into the city. We stayed in Kim Cheol-nam's house for two nights before heading to Zunyi. As grandma was not in good shape, we also stayed in Zunyi for a day.

All I can remember of our travel from Zunyi to Chongqing is the constant downpour. The Chinese have an idiom, "*Shuquanfeiri*" or "Sichuan dogs bark at the sun." It means that dogs in Sichuan are surprised to see the sun and bark at it since all they are used to are clouds, fog, and rain. The road passing through Zunyi was particularly rough. We were supposed to climb up a mountain, but we could only reach the peak after passing through seventy-two sharp turns. It was the same on the way down as well. Local people called the area "*Qishierguaidiaosiya*," or "a cliff with seventy-two turns for hanging oneself."

Beyond this rough patch lay the Yangzi River before reaching Chongqing. Chuqimen was the place where we stayed before crossing the river, and its dockside was called Matou. My father was staying at an inn there. Grandmother and I stayed with my father at the inn for a while and then moved to Kim Hong-seo's residence near the Sunjia Flower Garden. All the while, grandma told the Kims that she felt sorry for imposing on them. Eventually, grandma and I came left their house and found a small place for ourselves.

Just a few months after arriving in Chongqing, grandmother's health took a turn for the worse. My father called in Dr. Yu Jin-dong, who had graduated from Tongji University and worked for a tuberculosis sanatorium in Lushan. After the war broke out, however, he worked in Wanxian, Sichuan. When Dr. Yu arrived in Chongqing, however, my grandmother had already passed away. Instead of treating her, he had to put a shroud on her.

Dr. Yu subsequently settled down in Chongqing and opened a clinic. He participated in the Korean Provisional Government and would go on to become the Surgeon General of the Korean Liberation Army. He returned to Korea following liberation and then went back to China to open a clinic in Nanjing. When the Korean War broke out, the Chinese government declared that ethnic Koreans living north of the Yangzi River had to take up Chinese citizenship, while Koreans in the south could maintain Korean nationality if they wanted to.

In protest of the policy, many Koreans contacted Pyongyang and moved to North Korea. Moreover, the Chinese Communist Party did not look favorably toward former officials of the Korean Provisional Government people, who had close ties to the Guomindang. Dr. Yu went to North Korea in 1957, too. Since he was an alumnus of Kim Il Sung's alma mater, Yuwen Middle School in Jilin, Kim would give Dr. Yu a special stipend. However, Kim's cronies remained wary of their leader's childhood friend. In the end, Dr. Yu was forced to move from Pyongyang to the North Hamgyeong Province, where he died in 1961.

The Death of My Grandmother and Brother

"My days are now numbered. When our country is finally liberated, go to Shanghai to visit your mother's tomb and gather her remains. If her bones have all turned to dust and there are no remains left, wrap up the earth around the area where her head was placed and bring it to Korea for a proper burial. Do the same for me." My grandmother would say these things to me shortly before she passed away.

These words were as good as her will. Only my father and I were sitting by her deathbed when she passed away on April 26, 1939. My grandmother kept calling my name, "Shin! Shin!" Watching grandma's last moments, father knew by intuition almost the exact moment of his mother's death. Since he had watched over many deaths, he could tell when her very last moment on earth was coming. He burst into tears.

"You've passed away now after suffering so many years of hardship, all because of your undutiful son."

Even my father, with nerves of steel, was just a weak man helplessly collapsing before the death of his own mother. He wailed pounding the ground with his bare hands. What makes a person a dutiful son or daughter might be the circumstances in which he or she lives. My father's lifetime wish was Korea's liberation, and this wish made him an undutiful son. After wailing for a while, my father looked up and said to me, "You have served as the dutiful son of my mother on my behalf."

My grandmother was buried in Mt. Heshang. Only a few folks from the Korean Provisional Government could attend the funeral, since most Korean Provisional Government affiliates had yet to arrive in Chongqing and because the few who were there were mostly struggling to get settled in. Those in attendance consisted mostly of folks who had already settled down in Chongqing, the wives of some figures of the Kim Yak-san faction, and Kim Hong-seo. The wartime situation did not allow us to hold a Korean-style funeral, for example, by preparing a colorfully decorated bier. The grave site was also chosen by some old men's rough geomantic evaluation of propitious burial ground.

My brother, In, rushed over to Chongqing after learning of grandma's death. He was engaging in underground operations against

Japan together with Kim Dong-su, Yi Ha-yu, and others in Shanghai, which was occupied by the Japanese Army. As the Japanese Army tightened surveillance, he had to escape first to Hong Kong before making it to Chongqing.

After my grandmother's death, my brother attended Zhongyang (Central) University in Shapingba, Chongqing, as it had become difficult for him to return to Shanghai. I stayed in Guanyin Temple in Qijiang because there was no suitable place for me to stay in. At the time, Guanyin Temple was the base of the Korean Youth Battlefield Operations Corps.

The Battlefield Operations Corps, which was established in 1938, worked on extracting military secrets of the Japanese Army and co-opting those Koreans who were in the Japanese Army. It was incorporated into the Korean Liberation Army in January, 1941. Na Wol-hwan, who led the corps, had been in the Military Police of the Chinese Army and was then affiliated with the Korean anarchist faction. Yi Ha-yu and Yi Jae-hyeon (aka Yi Hae-pyeong) were also in the corps. They rented a room in the Guanyinsi and rallied young people to anti-Japanese activities. At the time, young people with an anarchist affiliation in Chongqing were closer to the Korean Provisional Government than to the communist group.

My brother, In, married Ahn Mi-saeng, the daughter of Ahn Jeong-geun, who was the younger brother of the famous martyr Ahn Jung-geun. At the time, Mr. and Mrs. Ahn Jeong-geun were living in Nanan, Chongqing. My brother and his wife thereafter had their daughter, Kim Hyo-ja. However, she was born when my brother was ill. He had contracted tuberculosis in Chongqing.

At that time, Chongqing was filled with thick coal smoke coming out of homes and factories, and was very humid due to its meteorological and topographical characteristics as a low-pressure basin. Many Koreans in Chongqing lost their lives from tuberculosis. As he lay in his sickbed, my sister-in-law took on the role of the breadwinner. Since she was proficient in English, she was able to get a job in the Bureau of Public Information in Chongqing's British Embassy.

For my brother, no sign of recovery was in sight. The last resort was penicillin. But it was very difficult to find penicillin due to the embargo by the Japanese. What's more, since getting goods in was difficult, those few that made their way in through the embargo were prohibitively expensive. My sister-in-law asked my father to obtain some penicillin.

But my father said with a serious look on his face, "How can I try to save only my son's life when so many comrades have died of the same disease in this city?"

I gather my sister-in-law must have been very resentful of father for this cold-hearted answer. Unfortunately, my brother died at the age of twenty-seven in Chongqing on March 29, 1945, five months before Korea's Liberation. The deaths of my grandmother and brother while fleeing from the Japanese shattered my soul to pieces. For a while, I felt as if I were in the middle of a pitch-black night even during the day. Yet, there were too many deaths spread all around me to just remain grief-stricken.

When people died while fleeing from the Japanese, it was common to bury the deceased on the corner of the road. We buried

Hyeon Ik-cheol, who died from a gunshot at the hands of Yi Un-hwan in Changsha, on a small hill up the curbside. As our car approached the site when we left Changsha, father stopped the car.

"We should at the very least bow before the grave of our comrade, Hyeon."

At the time, father had not completely recovered from his own gun wound. As he tried to climb up the hill, people around us stopped him, lest he should hurt himself.

I could only fulfil grandma's dying wish some ten years later. Upon return from Pyongyang in 1948, father said to me in a serious tone, "The situation in China worries me. You know the best where your grandma is buried. Go quickly and bring back her remains."

At the time China was unraveling due to the civil war between the Guomindang and the Chinese Communists. It was only a matter of time before the Communists would prevail. Father assessed the situation and thought that travel to China would become very restricted once the whole nation was communized. In 1948, I went to China on father's command and gathered the remains of my mother, grandmother, brother, Yi Dong-nyeong, and Cha Ri-seok, and brought them all back to Korea. However, there were so many more remains of fallen Korean independence fighters to find. I meant to return soon thereafter, but in 1949 the Chinese Communists conquered Beijing and travel to China no longer became possible.

As much time has passed, I presume I am now the only person who knows the burial site of so many Koreans on Mt. Heshang. Since it became possible for a Republic of Korea national to visit China, I've visited China on several occasions and requested the local Chongqing authorities to build a monument for Koreans at Mt. Heshang. Upon further thought, however, I realized that the distance and the lack of convenient public transportation to Mt. Heshang would make it difficult for many Koreans to visit. Hence, I requested the Chinese to build a monument on a flat surface north of the Korean Provisional Government office, and the Chinese have given their approval. However, I regret that the monument, due to various reasons, is yet to be built.

Zhongyang University Middle-High School Student
Kim Shin Gang

In the aftermath of my grandmother's death, I registered as an official of the Ministry of Internal Affairs, at a time when Shin Ik-hee was the Minister of Internal Affairs. There were several officials in the ministry at the time. Among them, Shin Sun-ho, the daughter of Shin Geon-sik, Min Yeong-ju, the daughter of Min Pil-ho, who was married to Kim Jun-yeop, and I were all of the same age, born in 1922.

The chief reason I joined the Korean Provisional Government as an official in the Ministry of Internal Affairs was the fact few people in the Korean Provisional Government could speak Chinese. As there was much work related to hosting Chinese guests on special occasions, in particular, the March First Independence Day and Korean Liberation Army Day celebrations, the Korean Provisional Government needed proficient Chinese speakers. Besides receiving and entertaining Chinese guests, I also ran errands for those elders who could not speak Chinese well. I would also take the bank checks that Cha Ri-seok had received from overseas Koreans and exchange them for Chinese currency.

In the wake of grandma's death, I lived with the young anarchists in Guanyin Temple for a while, then moved into the conference room in the Korean Provisional Government office in Wushiyexiang. My father would call me in and send me on errands sending letters here and there. Because the Korean Provisional Government elders lived across town, I had to run lots of errands in this way. By keeping myself busy, I somehow managed to suppress my profound grief over grandma's death.

When I lived in the conference room on the first floor of the Korean Provisional Government office, father lived in his office on the second floor of the same building. So did Cha Ri-seok live in this way, in his own office. As Japan's bombing of Chongqing intensified, we moved to Tuqiao, in the suburbs of Chongqing. The Kim Yak-san faction did not need to move at first as it had already settled in the Sunjia Flower Garden, some distance from the heart of Chongqing. However, this area, too, would come under fire later.

After working for the Korean Provisional Government for a while, I entered Zhongyang University Middle-High School in Qingmuguan, which was somewhat distant from Chongqing. Because the city was bombed day and night, all the schools in the city were relocated to the suburbs. I entered the school as a middle school second grader in 1939 and attended it for five years until the third year of my high school course. The school building was a make-do structure built by

Zhongyang University Middle-High School near Chongqing
I am second from left in the back row. Due to a series of illnesses, I was emaciated at the time.

tying giant bamboo logs together, plastered together with earth and lime, and roofed with straws. It was flanked by male quarters on one side and female quarters on the other side.

Officials of the Chinese Ministry of Education had also come down to Qingmuguan. Also present were many refugee students from various regions such as Manchuria, Huabei, Shandong, etc. As a result of negotiations with the ministry, Koreans were permitted to study in Chinese schools. The Chinese government regarded those Koreans who fought against Japan as comrades and treated Korean students equally as Chinese students. When I entered Zhongyang University Middle-High School, I was the only Korean. Two or three years later, other Korean students came. Kim Jeong-pyeong, the son of Kim Cheol-nam, who was a section chief in the Air Defense General Control Department of the Chinese Army, enrolled at this time. In 1943 when I graduated, there were about ten Koreans at this school.

When I was attending Zhongyang University Middle-High School, the Chinese Communist Party used to have those students trained in the Communist Youth Organization infiltrate schools of Guomindang affiliation. It was not easy to identify those communist students who had disguised themselves as refugee students. The Communist Party distributed the *Xinhua Ribao* (*Xinhua Daily*), the party's main propaganda newspaper, for free in Chongqing. The *Xinhua Daily* was a newspaper that Zhou Enlai had established in Wuhan in January 1938. Zhou persuaded the Guomindang government into letting him distribute the newspaper, saying, "We have engaged in the anti-Japanese struggle, too, so wouldn't it be all right to distribute the Communist newspaper?" I would say that the Communist Party was a cut above the Guomindang in its overall strategy.

The Guomindang's student and youth organization was the Sunwenist (Three Principle of the People) Youth Organization. Every summer, the Chinese government opened the organization's camps to train students. All students in my school were part of the organization. In the summer, we would go out in Beibei, Chongqing, and engage in many athletic activities. As I was a good swimmer, I was awarded certificates of merit several times. When I visited my father in Chongqing later carrying these certificates, he was very proud of me.

At the time, we students called our school meal "*babaofan*" (literally, eight delicacy meal). Traditionally, *babaofan* was a delicious dish that was made by steaming various ingredients together, similar to Korea's sweet steamed rice with nuts and jujubes. But we facetiously called our school mean *babaofan*, because it contained various items such as unhusked grains, rocks, and sometimes even rat droppings in the rice.

Very often, the school meals had gone bad by the time they were served to us, as our meal had been cooked from what was left over after distributions to the army. However, we had no choice but to eat them, as they were the only thing we could eat. The side dishes we ate most of the time were crunchy preserved vegetables called *zhacai* and preserved hot peppers. Sichuan hot peppers were very spicy, indeed. A single preserved hot pepper was enough to stand up to a bowl of rice.

Students would go through a brief military-style procedure before meal. They would stand still at the command of "attention!" while the principal would take his seat at the far end of the room. Students would take their seat upon the command of "sit!" The principal would then be the first one to pick up his chopsticks and take the first bite, followed by everyone else. About once a month, pork or chicken would be served. On these occasions, as soon as the principal lifted his chopsticks to his mouth, a war of rattling chopsticks would begin.

I went through all four seasons on a single big coat. I came to be well known in my school for it. Rumors spread around. "That Korean guy doesn't have any clothes." I wore a Korean overcoat underneath the main coat. My shoes were military boots that a Japanese solider had used. They were so big that they rattled around my feet all the time. But I was not one bit embarrassed, for we were all struggling through war and the lot of the refugee students was about the same.

At school, I used the alias Kim Shin Gang. This practice was influenced by my brother. My brother, Kim In, used "Kim Dong San" as his alias, after Dongsanpyeong in An-ak, Hwanghae Province, where he was born. I adopted mine from Singang (Shenjiang in Chinese pronunciation), another name for Shanghai, where I was born. I asked the school to change my name to my real name, Kim Shin, only shortly before graduation. Even today, my Chinese alumni know me as Kim Shin Gang.

When school went on break, students returned to their families nearby, while I had no place in particular to go. I just wandered around the empty school before reluctantly deciding to go to Chongqing. It was not an easy trip from Qingmuguan to Chongqing. Although buses were available, I chose to take rough roads on foot with my friends to save money. We left at dawn carrying a few pairs of straw shoes over our shoulders. We ate meat on our way with the money we saved by not taking the bus. We also bought liquor to go with meat. Chinese liquor was so strong that we very often fell asleep drunk, only to awake in the middle of the night. We would then continue our journey to Chongqing by night.

When I would visit my father in Chongqing, he would tell me to go back to school soon. There was nothing I could do for him, while he was busy all the time. Sometimes, I went to Qijiang instead but could not stay there for long because there was not that much for me to do there, either. I was completely alone after my grandmother died. I was pushed to extreme loneliness. No one was around me. My adolescence and early adulthood knew nothing but an unending refugee life, the deaths of my family members, and utter loneliness.

Suffering from Diseases

When I attended Zhongyang University Middle-High School, I received an appendectomy at the Zhongyang University Hospital. The operation was free for refugee students.

Seeing me visibly nervous before the surgery, the doctor said to me, "You are healthy, so there will be no problems."

Then he asked, "Do you have family members to take care of you or visit you?"

When I answered that I did not, he began the operation, explaining surgery procedures to his students. Looking back now, he was giving them an on-the-spot training upon confirming that I had no family to protest on my behalf even if the operation did not end well.

As the operation was a medical training session for the students, it took longer than it might have. I became thirsty. When I asked for water, the doctor just rubbed my lips with a wet cotton ball, telling me that I should not drink water. After the operation, I found out that the surgical scar was two or three times bigger than normal. I had lost so much weight that others said my facial bones were nearly visible. I received another surgery for hernia later. I also suffered from malaria each summer and was liberated from it all when mosquitoes disappeared with the onset of autumn.

After graduation from Zhongyang University Middle-High School, I went on to Xinan Lianhe (West-South United) University, in Kunming, Yunnan Province. The university was a temporary institution set up during the war which existed for eight years from May 1938 to May 1946. It was a combination of the best universities in China such as Beijing University, Qinghua University, and Nankai University. Even under such an extreme wartime situation, the faculty consisted of the best scholars in China. By virtue of having attended this university, to this day I am treated as an alumnus by Beijing, Qinghua, and Nankai Universities.

During the years at Xinan Lianhe University, I was afflicted by bedbugs and lice. I also suffered from typhoid during these years. I almost died from a very high fever, which claimed my hair and eyebrows. Later, when I went to the United States to learn how to fly a warplane, the doctor at the air force hospital asked me a number of questions during a physical exam.

"Have you ever had a surgery?"

"I have had an appendectomy and a herniotomy."

"Have you ever had any serious diseases?"

"I have had malaria."

"How many times?"

"Maybe one hundred times."

"Have you ever had another serious disease besides malaria?" he asked again, speechless and his eyes getting bigger and bigger.

"Yes, I have had typhoid."

"How can you still be alive?" he said, dumbfounded at my words.

I just smiled.

Through this series of serious illnesses I went through, there was no one to take care of me by my side. The one exception was when the Korean doctor, Kim Jwa-gyeong, helped me narrowly escape death, when I contracted typhoid during my United University years. He put me in a tub filled with hot water and massaged me to make me sweat, as I would have died if I had not. Fortunately, drops of sweat soon fell on the rice straw mat placed on the floor thanks to Yunnan's warm climate. On seeing this, he told me that I would live and warned that I should be very careful about what I ate. As my stomach had become extremely weak, oily food could retrigger typhoid, he said.

To make matters worse, however, on the road back to Chongqing after recovering from typhoid, the truck that I was riding in slid on a muddy road in the mountains and hit the roadside slope hard. While the truck was stuck, unable to move an inch, I saw flames of light coming down the hill. They were bandits. They robbed all the passengers in the truck of their clothes, watches, and so on. They tried to take my coat, too.

"I am a student, I have no money, and I am on my way back home after barely recovering from an illness. Have a heart, please," I pleaded.

They ignored my desperate pleas and tried to take my clothes off. I was wearing a jumper with a zipper, and they were unable to forcibly take it off, maybe because they had never seen an item of clothing with zippers. So, they took away just my pocket watch. We spent the night there with our clothes and possessions stolen. As dawn came, automobiles began to pass by.

We shouted for help toward the passing cars. Yet, they did not stop, because it was well known that the area we were in was infested with bandits. After what seemed like hours, we saw military vehicles approaching, and shouted for help. Soldiers got out carrying rifles and asked us what was going on. We told them that we had been robbed and they took us to a place named Luxian. I took a boat there, got off in Hechi, and then headed to Chongqing, although there was no particular place there I could stay in.

Part 2

Our Nation's Dream High in the Blue Sky

Chapter 4

The First Step toward Becoming a Pilot

Entering the Air Force Academy

Upon gaining admission to Xinan Lianhe University, I was required to take a preparatory course for three months before entering the regular program. At the university, I met some key figures who had given critical support leading up to and in the aftermath of martyr Yun Bong-Gil's act of resistance in 1932. I had known of them because father had told me about them following Yun's deed. They included the brothers Zha Liangzhao and Zha Liangjian.

Zha Liangzhao was a prominent figure whom my father had met before he escaped from Shanghai in the wake of Yun Bong-Gil's righteous act. When I entered Xinan Lianhe United University, he was a member of the faculty. Once my father learned of it, he said to me, handing me his business card, "Go and see Professor Zha Liangzhao once you get to Kunming."

I found a brief note written on the business card, which said, "My humble son (*tun er*) is going to your university. Please take good care of him as he is completely lost." The Chinese word "*tun er*" literally means piglet. Chinese people used this word to express humility when they asked favors of others for their children. It was the very first time my father had ever asked another for a favor on my behalf.

Zha Liangjian, Zha Liangzhao's younger brother, was a graduate of School of Law at the University of Michigan, and later became Taiwan's Minister of Judicial Administration. He was a judge and chief court clerk in Shanghai in the mid-1930s and also served as the Chief of the Chongqing Court in 1943 and the Chief of the Shanghai Court in 1945. Zha Liangyong, a journalist and also famous historical and martial arts romance novelist under the penname Jin Yong, came from the same extended family. He was admitted to Xinan Lianhe University, but chose not to attend it. Instead, he entered Chongqing's Central School of Politics in 1944, but subsequently dropped out. The Zha family of Haining, Zhejiang, was a family of prestigious background that had produced prominent talents and officials over generations.

It was around the time that I enrolled in the regular program at Xinan Lianhe University that I contracted typhoid. A few months after recovering from it thanks to Dr. Kim Jwa-gyeong and returning to Chongqing, I made up my mind to join the air force. In fact, I had already once taken the entrance exam for the air force after my graduation from the middle-high school, but had not passed it. Xinan Lianhe University had been my alternative choice.

I passed this time around. I returned to Kunming, on an air force plane that took off from the Shanhuba Airport near the Yangzi River in Chongqing. The Air Force Academy was located in Wujiaba, Kunming.

Initially, the Air Force Academy was located in Jianqiao,

Hangzhou, Zhejiang, but it was relocated to Kunming after the Chiang Kai-Shek army's retreat. The academy moved to Kunming also because U.S. soldiers were stationed there. America sent retired air force veterans to China to support its war against Japan. The group's name was the American Volunteer Group (AVG). The U.S. government sent civilian veterans because its policy forbade official involvement in the Second Sino-Japanese War.

The AVG's nickname was the "Flying Tigers." We called them "*Feihudui*" (flying tiger corps). The commander was General Claire Chennault. He had airplanes brought to India first by ship and then flown to Yunnan. The U.S. assessed that air transportation of supplies was risky due to Japan's blocking of sea routes. Hence, in an attempt to open up a land route, the U.S. built a mountain road through the Himalayas in the Assam region of northeast India. I watched the opening ceremony when I was studying at Xinan Lianhe University. Kunming was the sole lifeline through which China could receive American aid.

Japan, too, opened a land route to transport supplies because American submarines increasingly made sea-borne transportation difficult. The Japanese Army occupied Guilin and extended its supply line towards Changsha, Hengyang, Guangzhou, and Liuzhou, finally succeeding in securing its supply line to Dushan, Guizhou.

Under such circumstances, university students had to take up weapons shouting slogans like "military first" and "victory first." It was in such circumstances that I applied to join the air force.

At the time, a Korean by the name of Jang Seong-cheol, who was a member of the Chinese Air Force, was working on the Kunming

Air Base. He had come to China after receiving pilot training in the Soviet Union. As he drank heavily, however, he gave up flying and served as the manager of the repair factory that oversaw military supplies and supervised the repairmen on the ground. His wife was the daughter of Kim Cheol-nam, who was a section chief in the Air Defense General Control Department of the Chinese Army. Kim Jeong-pyeong, Kim Cheol-nam's son, was my junior in Zhongyang University Middle-High School, as I've mentioned above.

At the Kunming Air Base, I received no particular flight training and only basic military training for close to six months. Although the dream of becoming a pilot progressed more slowly than I had expected, I never faltered even one bit in my determination.

Chiang Kai-Shek's Struggle to Unify the Warlords

When I lived in Nanjing in the mid- to late-1930s, the Chiang Kai-Shek government reinforced its power through the so-called New Life Movement. In particular, it enforced strong policies against opium addiction, which was a big problem in China. Under the new policy, anyone caught smoking opium would be arrested and be forced to end the habit. If the offender still kept smoking and got caught three times or more, he would be shot to death.

Thanks to the New Life Movement, places like Nanjing and Shanghai that were governed by the central government came to have relatively fewer corruption problems in the military and government. On the other hand, the movement did not take root in other regions with their own local knots of power maintained by warlords. As far as opium use was concerned, however, most regions strongly punished it. Wuhan, Changsha, and Guangdong, all places where we have lived at one time or another, completely adhered to a zero tolerance policy on opium.

Even though the Chiang Kai-Shek government ruled Nanjing, Shanghai, Jiangsu, Zhejiang, Anhui, and part of Shandong, it had varying degrees of influence over different regions. Guangdong and Guangxi tended to be strongly opposed to the Chiang government. Japan took advantage of such a situation and, in attempting to divide China, gave arms to warlords such as Yan Xishan and Feng Yuxiang.

Shandong was seized by Han Fuqu, while Manchuria was ruled by Zhang Xueliang, the son of Zhang Zuolin. They flew the banner of the Republic of China but maintained their own armies. The power of the central government did not reach into Chongqing completely, either. In particular, the whole Chaotianmen area, a pier leading to Chongqing, was lawless.

In the summer, boatmen could dock their boats right alongside the piers of Chaotianmen as the river swelled, while they had to walk up from the shore in the winter as the river ebbed. Both sides of the stone steps ascending to Chongqing were lined with opium dens filled with people smoking the drug while lying on their side. While opium was strictly prohibited by the central government, the Chongqing authorities turned a blind eye in order to blackmail operators of opium dens and smokers. Around the dens, there would always be frail and gaunt addicts waiting in line for their turn. They were called "*epian guizi*" or opium ghosts.

The warlords were vile in many other ways as well. They even sometimes extracted twenty years of taxes in advance. They would also abduct pretty women on the street and rape them with impunity. One day, a local leader, whose daughter had been raped by a warlord, presented a petition to Liu Xiang, the governor of Sichuan.

"You high officials are charged with the duty of protecting and loving the people as parents would their own children. Despite your duties, how can you just watch as warlords indiscriminately abuse young women?"

Upon receiving the petition, Liu Xiang realized that he had to take some measures. At the time, he did not directly govern the entire region of Sichuan. It was such a big region that he had divided into four divisions, placing four commanders in charge of each. It was not easy to arrest and punish a divisional commander who commanded many troops and were no different than the warlords themselves. Moreover, Liu Xiang himself was no stranger to corruption and vile practices. After some consideration, he answered the petition as follows.

"Since ancient times, heroes have loved beautiful women."

Such lowly people as they were, the local warlords in Sichuan joined forces to wage the anti-Japanese war when Chiang Kai-Shek came to Chongqing with his central army. Although Sichuan troops were rather good at combat, the Chinese people joked that Sichuan soldiers carried two guns: one, a real gun and the other, an "opium gun."

Opium aside, Sichuan soldiers were actually good in battle. In particular, they were good at mountain warfare since Sichuan had many mountainous areas. During the Korean War, the Capital Division Commander Baek In-yeop once captured many Chinese soldiers and called me in as an interpreter. I found that many of the Chinese soldiers had come from Sichuan. Since Korea is a mountainous country, the Communist government had sent many Sichuan soldiers to participate in the war.

In any case, once Chiang Kai-Shek's central army came to Sichuan and established power, Chiang ordered the removal of all opium dens. Overnight, the dens disappeared. In the aftermath of the arrival of the central government, order was gradually restored to Chongqing.

Japan's Bombing of Chongqing

Japan dropped an enormous amount of bombs over Chongqing. While Japanese bombers took off from Jeju Island and Taiwan when bombing Nanjing, as the battlefront expanded, they took off from an air base in Wuhan for bombing Chongqing. Chongqing had frequent rainfalls in the winter but extended clear days in the spring. When spring came, the Japanese Air Force bombed Chongqing every day. Shibanjie, where the office building of the Korean Provisional Government was located, was also hit. When a bombing raid began, the government sounded sirens and also sent flag signals from hills in case of power failure.

Since Chongqing was a rocky region, a sturdy bomb shelter dug deep could withstand fairly well the bombings. But the shelter we hid in was only half-completed and had only one exit. If the exit was destroyed, we would have had no choice but to be completely trapped inside the shelter. One day, a bomb hit a pile of rocks heaped up next to our shelter. The smell of gunpowder burst inside. Once we got out after the bombing ended, it turned out that the pile of rocks was all gone, leaving behind no trace. The walls of the building next to our shelter had all collapsed. Jo So-ang took pictures standing next to the collapsed walls.

The daily bombings included "fatigue bombing." Fatigue bombing was an endless series of bombings by alternating fleets of bombers that came every ten or twenty minutes. Five or six hours of extended fatigue bombing would leave the survivors on the ground completely exhausted. Chongqing is such a hot part of China that it is known, along with Wuhan and Nanjing, as one of the three "furnace" cities. People died from heat suffocation by staying inside air raid shelters too long during fatigue bombing. The bodies of those who died during the bombings were piled up along the wall of the Jialing River. Just as they began to decompose, they would be carried away in boats to somewhere.

Nighttime raids made our lives particularly miserable. When the power was cut due to bombing, it was difficult to tell when the raid was over, as the sirens could not go off. Flag signals from hills were of no use due to the darkness. The Japanese bombers often dropped poisoned cigarettes during bombing raids. People would pick them up, smoke them, and die. They would also drop propaganda handbills, with various pictures of modernized regions like the Japanese-occupied Manchuria.

The Sunjia Flower Garden and Qijiang were subject to the air raids, too. The Garden did not have any military facilities and was rather distant from Chongqing, but was nonetheless targeted. Qijiang had no military facilities, either. We later came to learn that Japanese intelligence had gathered information that there were Korean Provisional Government officials to be found there. When the Japanese Air Force bombed Qijiang, my father indeed was there. When the bombing raid began, he escaped to a nearby empty tomb. It was a stone tomb and thus served as an air raid shelter. Fortunately, no key figures of the Korean Provisional Government were seriously injured.

Qijiang became the target of air raid because Japanese spies in Chongqing had furnished the intelligence. They sent information about target locations through secret radio communications. We once captured a Japanese spy corresponding by radio like this on the spot. At the time, Yu Jin-dong and his wife, Gang Yeong-pa, were living with their daughter in Kim Hong-seo's house in Sunjia Flower Garden. A domestic helper at the time lost her life in one of the raids. The Chinese government eventually transferred main government organizations to distant suburbs away from the Japanese bombings.

Japan bombed Chongqing using incendiary bombs which produced enormous flames upon hitting the target. Since there were lots of wooden houses in Chongqing, incendiary bombs caused several dozens of fire in a blink of an eye. Many people would come out carrying water buckets to extinguish the fire as the city did not possess fire trucks. Yet, as there were clear limitations to extinguishing fire with bare hands, Chongqing turned into a sea of flames whenever it was bombed.

Later, Japan became the target of the same tactic when the U.S. Air Force dropped incendiary bombs on Tokyo. On March 10, 1945, the U.S. dropped a massive amount of incendiary bombs on Tokyo, in an effort to bring the Pacific War to an end as quickly as possible. About 100,000 people lost their lives as Tokyo, littered with wooden houses, turned into a sea of flames.

The area surrounding the office building of the Korean Provisional Government was bombed several times. But people could escape the bombings relatively safely and conveniently once an air raid shelter was completed. As it had good ventilation and sanitary facilities, it became a rather pleasant haven during the summer months. When I visited it later on, I found that the shelter had been converted into an inn.

As Japan's bombing of Chongqing became severe, the Chinese government considered transferring the capital to the Xikang area. In 1939, the Chinese government combined the eastern area of the Tibetan plateau and the western area of Sichuan to create the Xikang Province. The entire province, which was abolished in 1955, gave China a strategic advantage in waging war against Japan thanks to its mountainous terrain.

The Road to Indian-Administered Lahore

After completing basic military training in the Kunming Air Base, I, together with my colleagues, took an American transport airplane to a U.S. air base in the northeastern region of India. We would be receiving primary flight training. Flight training should take place in a relatively secure place; however, in China, there was no such place at that time. We were headed to Lahore, Punjab in India, which is now Pakistani territory.

To go to Lahore, one had to fly over a long series of peaks that looked like camel humps. Strong updrafts and downdrafts were frequent in this rugged mountainous area. Our airplane would suddenly soar up toward the sky only to suddenly fall down as if it were crashing. Quite frequently, airplanes flying through this area experienced instrument failure or even crashed.

Our transport airplane did not even have safety belts, so each of us had to hold on to whatever we could. If one lost his grip, he could have been bumped around, possibly in a life-threatening situation. Turbulence was not the only danger lurking. Japanese fighters were on the lookout for U.S. transport planes. Due to such considerations, our airplane departed at sunset.

There was a good reason why the Chinese government opted for basic flight training in India. When the Chinese trainees who completed basic military training were sent to the U.S. directly, seven out of ten would fail the pilot entrance exam. The big language barrier aside, the difference in lifestyle also proved to be an impediment. While Americans with only a middle school level of education knew how to drive a car, some of the trainees had never even ridden in a car, let alone know anything about operating machines. Thus, the Chinese government sent trainees to America after having them complete primary flight training in India, in order to save face. Once this program was introduced, the number of successful candidates increased steadily.

We did not go to Lahore directly, but first got off at Chabua base. Constructed in 1939, it served as a major supply base for transporting good to Kunming. Even today, it is used as an Indian air base, as its location makes it a strategic outpost. Chabua felt like a sauna as it was so humid and stifling. Though the local people were not particularly troubled by the hot weather, U.S. soldiers could not stand it. They took off their tops and wore only shorts during the day.

We stayed in the barracks for a few days. One morning, when we woke up, we found that all of the food and shoes supplied by the U.S. army were gone. Monkeys had stolen them. Monkeys also disrupted military engineers when they were paving roads. However, monkeys were not the only animal-related issue we faced. Two American soldiers once went into the woods and disappeared. A search party searched through the woods for a long while before it saw something looking like an old tree wriggling. It was a big snake. When the search party captured it and cut its stomach, they found guns, dog tags, and helmets in its stomach.

We left Chabua by car for Kolkata, where we stayed in temporary U.S. barracks. We then took the train to Lahore. The trip took three days as it was a long journey, crossing the Indian subcontinent from east to northwest.

This train trip allowed me a bit of exposure to Indian culture. The passenger cars of our train were divided into seven classes from the first to the seventh. People of different religions and castes could not take the same car. Passengers took cars predetermined by their caste and could not move from one car to the next. All meals had to be consumed in their predetermined restaurant according to class. We ate combat rations given by the U.S. army. The passenger car we took had relatively good facilities, including air conditioning. When the train stopped at a station, beggar kids rushed over and shouted, "Give me money." We threw them tidbits like biscuits. When we did this, not only children but monkeys also jumped at the food. As humans and monkeys fought each other for biscuits, the station turned into an arena of mayhem.

During the trip, I observed India from a perspective rather different from that of my Chinese colleagues. India was a British colony, just as Korea was Japan's colony. I felt that Great Britain ruled colonial India very intelligently. For example, British people did not take up jobs that entailed potentially cantankerous contact with ordinary Indians, such as traffic police, but entrusted those duties to the Indians themselves. Of course, British people made the key decisions on everything behind the scenes. While the front desk employee in a public office would be an Indian, a British supervisor would make the final decision. From its extensive experience in colonial rule all over the world, Great Britain had become a formidable country that reaped as many benefits as possible while coming into direct contact with their colonized people as little as possible.

Once we arrived at the air base in Lahore, some ten planes flew over us in low-altitude flight to welcome us. The daily temperature range in Lahore was extremely wide. As it was stiflingly hot during the daytime, people working in the army and public offices took about three hours off from work during the day. But for Chinese trainees, who were preparing for war against Japan, there was not even one minute to rest.

Training began in the classroom, as we acquired the basic background facts related to flying, such as meteorology, aerodynamics, motor studies, etc. We had much to learn before actually getting a chance to fly an aircraft. When we did get to fly, we first learned how to take off and land. The instructor would operate an aircraft from the cockpit, while the trainee observed it from the back seat. We did not go very high up at first, and flew at an altitude of only about three hundred meters.

The first thing we practiced in flight was flying in a quadrangular pattern. The instructor flew straight for hundreds of feet and then continually turned to the left. This is called circuit flying. It was very hot, as we were at an altitude where sunlight reflected onto us. Moreover, since the aircraft had no cover, the hot air would hit the trainee's face directly. Circuit flying also made our lips very dry and chapped.

The hot weather made our everyday lives very difficult. We could not sleep well at night. We were given a nap break in the afternoon when the weather made training nearly impossible. In order to be

Lahore Air Force Base
I completed my primary flight training in Lahore, today Pakistani territory. In the first picture I am in the middle. In the background is the gate with the inscription "Chinese Air Force Academy." In the second picture I am second from the left.

able to actually take a nap, we soaked our blankets in water and draped the wet blankets on the windows to stop the hot air from pouring in. Still, we could hardly sleep, it was so hot. Some trainees could not stand the heat and stayed in the shower for an hour or two, which sometimes led them to getting sick.

In these conditions, the overall health of the trainees took a toll. Many of us failed to pass the training regimen due to health problems instead of technical deficiency. I somehow managed to overcome such conditions and to pass the preliminiary flight training.

I was the only Korean there, while all the other trainees were Chinese. In fact, I was only one of two Koreans to receive regular flight training in the U.S. The other was my senior at the Academy Kim Won-yeong (1919-1945). Unfortunately, Kim died from a crash in 1945 and was enshrined in the Aviation Martyrs Cemetery in Nanjing. He was the son of Kim Bo-yeon, who had worked in the Korean Provisional Government and served as a member of the Korean Liberation Propaganda Youth Corps. When he received flight training in America after training in India, he flew a P-40 instead of an F-51.

As I was preparing to go to the U.S. after finishing my primary training, the news of Japan's unconditional surrender broke. Korea's liberation came suddenly just like that. Everyone one of us, American soldiers and all the trainees, got on an aircraft and made a celebratory flight, sharing the joy. One Sunday, I went see a movie in a downtown theater. Images of Japan's unconditional surrender were shown in the news report that aired before the movie started. There were also scenes of Koreans waving the Korean flag and crying

"Hurrah!" in the Capitol plaza. I felt as if my heart would explode any minute. I wanted to race back to Korea as soon as possible. The Chinese trainees, too, expected to go back to China, now that the war was over.

Things turned in an unexpected direction, however. We were ordered to go to the U.S. instead of China or Korea Since the trainees who had completed the preliminary flight training in India were beneficiaries of the U.S. military aid program, we were obliged to go to America and receive further training even if the war was over. As the last group of recipients of the U.S. aid program, we went to America.

Chapter 5

Rigorous Flight Training in America

To America, to Become a Pilot

"It is now time for the Korean Provisional Government to return to Korea. Now that my brother is no longer with us, I shall escort you to Korea," I wrote in a letter to my father.

At the time, deaths during flight training were common. Thus, children with no siblings were not admitted to flight schools. When my brother was alive, I was not an only child and thereby was eligible to enroll in a flight training program. But now that I was the sole surviving child, I intended to go back to my country if father approved. But my father had different ideas.

"Go back to Korea? What are you talking about? Even if our country is liberated, it will take a long time to nurture people of talent like you. Since you already have one foot in the door, you must continue with your training."

His answer was firm. Frankly, I was disappointed at first when I read his letter. Once I came to think of it further, however, he was right, and I had to follow his advice. He always put the future of Korea first, even under the possibility of losing his only son.

Eventually, I made up my mind to go to America with my Chinese colleagues.

A problem arose, however. Since I was a Korean, it was awkward for the Chinese government to guarantee my identity for the purpose of my entry into the U.S. The same problem had forced my senior Kim Won-yeong to disguise himself as a Chinese man when he had entered America. The U.S. authorities then were much more disposed toward accepting his claim since it was wartime. But my case was different. As I was already known to be a Korean, there was no way for me to get around it.

The Chinese Consulate informed the Chinese government of my identity guarantee problem. The central government sent a message, saying, "He is of a family that fought alongside us against Japan. Do not make an issue of it and just guarantee his identity." With my identity guarantee problem thus resolved, I took a train at Lahore for Kolkata and then took a ship to America. The ship, the Liberty, had a 7,000 ton deadweight capacity and transported military supplies. Although the seas were usually calm when the ship passed through the Indian Ocean, they became turbulent once we entered the Atlantic Ocean after passing through the Indian Ocean, then the Red Sea, and then the Mediterranean Sea. Even veteran crew members who had sailed on ships for decades would vomit everything they had eaten.

After crossing the Atlantic Ocean, the ship finally docked in New York at the end of 1945. We entered the Brooklyn port in smaller boats that carried 20 to 25 people each. Ships from India or Southeast Asia had to go through customs, immigration inspection, and quarantine inspection particularly thoroughly because they had a higher probability of carrying pathogenic bacteria from their tropical point of origin. We stayed in the U.S. army barracks while going through all the procedures over seven days. In the restaurant of the base, there were people working wearing clothes with the inscription "POW." They were all German prisoners of war.

Upon completing all the procedures, we went to downtown New York and boarded a train for San Antonio, Texas. The final destination was the Randolph Air Base, 24 kilometers northwest thereof. This base was nicknamed the "West Point of the Air," that is, the military academy of the Air Force. Why did it have such an ambiguous name when it could have just been called the "Air Force Academy"? It was because of the ambiguous status of the Air Force within the U.S. military.

During the Second World War, the U.S. Air Force was part of the Army and the Navy. Thus, it was called the Army Air Force and the Naval Air Force, respectively. It was only after the war was over that the Air Force separated from the Army and the Navy, as its role during the war had increased drastically. The Air Force bombed targets that the artillery brigade could not reach. It was able to cut enemy supply lines and bomb railways, air bases, munitions factories. But the Army wanted to put the Air Force only in the frontlines where it was fighting. Hence, there were often conflicts between the Army and the Air Force. Eventually, the Air Force separated from the Army as the need for an independent strategic air force came to the fore in the wake of the end of the Second World War.

The Randolph Air Base was renowned throughout the world as

a first-rate training base. Trainees from China and South America trained together with Americans. Before we received any training at the base, however, we first had to go through American-style basic training for three months in the San Antonio Air Cadet Center. The basic training was nothing particular. It focused on things like familiarizing oneself with American commands and other basic things American trainees needed to know. The moment we went back to the Randolph Air Base after completing the basic training, my heart swelled with expectation, as I was now that much closer to realizing my dream of becoming a pilot.

Rigorous Training at Randolph Air Base

The training at the Randolph Air Base had three stages: primary, basic, and advanced. Although we had completed primary training in India, we had to start all over again. As we all knew what to do during the primary training phase, our instructors gave us many compliments. The type of aircraft we rode on during the primary and basic training was the PT-17. We had ridden on the PT-13 in India. "PT" stood for Primary Training.

While the PT-13 was started manually, the PT-17 was started automatically using a battery. Except for this difference, the two models were exactly the same in everything including shape, engine, etc. Both had the nickname "Stearman." We rode on the AT-6 after we had graduated from flying the Stearman. "AT" stood for Advanced Training and the plane's nickname was "Texan."

Toward the end of the advanced training, we rode on the fighter aircraft P-51, which was an actual fighter aircraft. Its nickname was "Mustang." After the Air Force was separated from the Army and the Navy, the letter "F" replaced the "P." "F" stood for "Fighter." The bomber was abbreviated as its initial "B," while "RS" stood for "Reconnaissance."

The first thing we learned was how to take off and land. Besides that, we learned a whole variety of other things related to aviation, including motor studies, meteorology, radio control, etc. Only after having learned all of these things did we finally learn aviation techniques. There were many aviation techniques. One was the circular flight where a pilot made one full-turn in the air. A difficult part of the circular flight was keeping the aircraft at a certain fixed altitude. We received a failing grade if our airplane fell by more than fifty feet in altitude as we made the 360 degree circular flight. We also learned how to handle various emergency scenarios. For example, we learned what to do when the engine suddenly stopped– escaping using a parachute or making a forced landing.

Instruction in such basic techniques was followed by advanced techniques like battle techniques formation flight. We also learned how to fly at night which was actually easier than flying during the day. For example, the glow from the sun would make it harder to focus on the runway while landing. But, at night, the bright lights on the runway made the task easy. Take-off was easier at night, too. As there were so many other things to learn besides all this, it took about two and half years to complete the full program.

As far as the Air Force was concerned, more people were killed during training than in combat. According to a U.S. Air Force investigation into the causes of pilot deaths during the Second World War, more pilots were killed during training than in battle, by instrument failure, or by bad weather. Considering such facts, flight training was carried out in a highly strict manner. If trainees made even the slightest mistake, the instructors would harshly scold them, swearing at them. For even the slightest lapse in concentration heightened the probability of an accident.

Until a trainee was able to make a solo flight in a Mustang, an instructor flew with the trainee in the same plane. The instructor took the front seat and the trainee the back seat, and the two controlled the aircraft together. As the yokes were connected, the trainee could learn how to control the aircraft by feeling how the instructor steered, and the instructor could also feel how the trainee was steering. If the trainee made a mistake, the instructor sometimes would hit him in the knee very hard to get him to focus. They hit so hard that the trainee would often get bruises on his knees.

The Thrill of My First Solo Flight

The training area in the Randolph Air Base was divided into Areas A and B. One was mainly used for teaching take-off and landing. Once a trainee became good at these skills, the instructor decided whether or not he should advance to the next phase. If a trainee was determined to be good enough to try a solo flight, the instructor would tie a red ribbon to the end of an aircraft's wing. This was

U.S. Randolph Air Base In the first picture, I am second from the left, together with fellow trainees and our instructor. If not for my father's far-sighted admonition, I would have missed out on this opportunity. I wonder how my life would have evolved in that case.

meant not only to congratulate a trainee on his first solo flight but also to let other pilots know to yield to him as he was a novice solo pilot, just as automobile drivers these days place a "Student Driver" signs on their cars.

I had already completed a solo flight back in India. But new emotions surged through my entire body as I made my first solo flight in America. I could not suppress my joy and sang out loud during the flight. I felt as if the world were mine. I was so pleased not to see the head of an instructor in front of me. I was truly experiencing what people mean when they say "I'm walking on air."

What came up in my mind most during a solo flight was my family. I felt a lump in my throat when my grandmother and my parents crossed my mind. In my heart formed pride that was ineffable. But I couldn't fly solo all the time, as an instructor flew with me whenever I had to learn a new flight technique. The last course of the training was a long-distance solo flight. I had to fly my aircraft alone to a distant air base that my instructor picked.

The mission I was given was to fly eastwards from Randolph Air Base to a naval base in the Mexican Bay. When I reached the airspace above the bay, I saw several naval air bases below. I chose one of them and landed my aircraft. The landing method for a naval aircraft was different from that for an air force aircraft, as the former took off and landed from aircraft carriers. Naval trainees were trained to land by touching all four wheels down at the same time, while air force trainees were trained to land by touching the two front wheels first, then gradually slowing down the aircraft before finally touching the two rear wheels.

I moved my aircraft to refuel it after landing safely. An officer came to me in a jeep and started swearing at me. Not knowing what was going on, I told him that I had come from Randolph Air Force Base.

"Why the hell did you land like that?" said he angrily, ignoring my words.

He used strong language because by the Air Force's landing method I used my aircraft could have gone over the edge of an aircraft carrier and crashed into the sea. After getting an earful at the naval base, I was scolded again upon return to Randolph. The reason this time was different: I had landed my aircraft in the wrong air base. The naval base had several air bases. I made the mistake because they all looked similar. Though I got plenty of scolding, I successfully completed my first long-distance solo flight safely without an accident.

During my training at Randolph, I would go to downtown San Antonio on the weekends. At that time, racial discrimination was extremely prevalent in America. Almost all places including railway stations, schools, and offices were segregated into white only and black only areas. My colleagues and I were in an awkward position when going to public places like movie theaters because we were neither black nor white. When we would ask an attendant which area to go to, he would tell us to go to the white only area. Wherever we went, we had to ask cautiously.

Once completing our training at the Randolph base, we went to the Williams Base, fifty kilometers southeast of Phoenix, Arizona. We mostly flew the Mustang there, while American pilots flew the

15 OCT 46   CLASS 47-B-I (CC-36-P)   PRIMARY   RANDOLPH FIELD, TEXAS

Chinese Trainees and U.S. Instructors at Randolph

In the first picture, taken on October 15, 1946, I am fourth from the right in the front row. In the second picture, taken on February 17, 1947, I am sixth from the left in the rear row. It's apparent that many trainees dropped out in the meantime.

P-80 fighters nicknamed "Shooting Stars." It was very hot in Phoenix. The daytime temperature went up to about 38 degrees Celsius. The airframe of an aircraft would heat up so much by early afternoon that I nearly burned my hands whenever I touched it to board. As soon as I would got on wearing my flight suit and carrying a parachute on my back, my entire body was drenched in sweat.

During my training in the Williams Base, I used to go to downtown Phoenix on the weekends, too. An old Korean man lived there. He said that he used to live in Hawaii and LA before, but moved to Phoenix because he did not like seeing Koreans fight each other. When I visited him through some acquaintances, he welcomed me, telling me to drop by every Sunday. I do not remember his full name, but remember that his surname was Jeong.

One day, I went to a swimming pool in the city with my Chinese colleagues to seek respite from the heat. But the manager blocked us and said that we could not enter because we were colored.

"We are your allies who fought against Japan shoulder-to-shoulder risking our lives," said my Chinese colleagues, infuriated.

When the Chinese trainees protested fiercely, the manager made a call somewhere and afterwards let us in. While we were treated relatively well in San Antonio, where many foreigners visited, Phoenix was a tough place for people of color. Colored people had a difficult time entering restaurants and movie theaters and would have to wait for a train in a place segregated from white people. But the U.S. government treated us equally as American soldiers. We were given free room and board and got paid fifty dollars a month. We usually spent no more than half of our monthly pay, but were able to live sufficiently comfortably, as in those days a bottle of beer cost five cents and twenty cents were enough to fuel up a car.

My First Meeting with Syngman Rhee

A few days before Christmas in 1946, I received a letter from Dr. Syngman Rhee, asking me to come and see him in Washington, D.C. I was still at Randolph at the time. It seemed to me that many Americans took off about two weeks around this time and visited their family, but I had no place to go to. I assumed that my father had asked Dr. Rhee to see me if possible on his trip to the U.S.

The problem was how to get to Washington, D.C. Just in time, though, an instructor told me that he would be taking a bomber to New York and offered to take me and a Chinese colleague with him. It was a four-hour train ride from New York to Washington.

Since we, trainees who had taken off from India, had had no time to look around New York on our way to Randolph, my colleague and I spent some time in the downtown area sightseeing. We went to Times Square and Fifth Avenue. We stayed in a facility administered by the YMCA and paid one dollar per night. Several persons stayed together in one room, shared the bathroom and restroom. We also looked around Chinatown, which was not far from our lodging. On the night of New Year's Eve in 1947, we saw many soldiers following young ladies and unhesitatingly kissing them the moment the clock struck midnight. The whole scene was so surreal to us we gazed absentmindedly and bumped into a utility pole.

Capitol Hill, Washington, D.C.
In Washington, in January 1947, I met Syngman Rhee for the first time.

While wandering about New York, I happened to run into Ahn Jin-saeng, the second son of Ahn Jeong-geun, near the YMCA. He had studied shipbuilding at the College of Engineering at Genoa University during the war with the help of the Chinese archbishop Yu Bin. The archbishop had a close connection to Italy as he had studied at a Pontifical University as well as the University of Bologna. Mr. Ahn told me that he had taken part in the underground movement to overthrow the Mussolini regime. He later served as a diplomat in Italy, France, and Burma. He was on a short visit to the U.S., and we just happened to run into each other.

We roamed about the city and visited many sites with Ahn Jin-saeng. On the subway train none of us knew the difference between "local" and "express" trains. The "local" train stopped at every station, while the "express" train stopped at only some of them after passing through several stations. We happened to be on an "express" train and soon panicked when the train passed right through our stop. Seeing that we were at a loss, an American passenger told us where to transfer to a "local" train, and we finally got back on track.

After a few days of sightseeing in New York, I headed down to Washington, D.C. to meet with Dr. Syngman Rhee. At the time, a man named Im Byeong-jik was Dr. Rhee's personal secretary. Im naturally fell into his job while accompanying Rhee over a long period. Im would go on to become the Minister of Foreign Affairs and the Korean Ambassador to the United Nations. Dr. Rhee had asked the Korean Provisional Government to appoint Mr. Im as a Korean Liberation Army officer. Mr. Im chose to walk around in a Korean Liberation Army uniform in America before he was arrested by a military policeman. As it turned out, an Asian man donning such a conspicuous military uniform could not escape the policeman's eyes. Moreover, for an individual of a nation that had not even normalized diplomatic relations with the U.S. to walk around the U.S. capital in a military uniform was problematic. Dr. Rhee stepped in and was able to resolve the issue, but it could have become a diplomatic issue.

Dr. Rhee met me at the Carlton Hotel close to the White House. At the end of meeting, as I was about to leave, he asked me to come with him to a dinner meeting with Dr. Lin Yutang the next day. It seemed that he wanted to introduce me to him since I could speak Chinese. The next day, I went to Dr. Lin's house with Dr. Rhee.

"This is a Korean and Kim Koo's son. He is currently affiliated with the Chinese Air Force," Dr. Rhee introduced me to our host.

Dr. Lin gave me a warm welcome. Besides my meeting with Rhee, I had nothing else in particular to do in Washington. I left D.C. once I bade farewell to Dr. Rhee. I had taken a free plane ride to New York on my way to Washington, but there was no such free service on my way back to the Randolph Air Force Base. Since train fare was rather expensive in America, my Chinese colleague and I took the Greyhound long-distance bus. Stopping every four hours or so for rest, the bus took about two days to go from Washington to San Antonio.

Our bus was forced to come to a standstill due to heavy snow near Dallas. We stayed a night there waiting for the roads to be cleared, but we were out of money. We were able to come back to San Antonio only after we pawned our wrist watches for a few dozen dollars. I had a nose bleed as soon as I arrived due to fatigue from the long road trip. When we told our instructors that we had taken the Greyhound all the way from Washington, they were speechless.

That was my first meeting with Dr. Rhee. He was born in 1875, one year before my father. Ahn Chang-ho (born in 1878) was two years younger than my father, Ahn Jung-geun (born in 1879) was one year younger than Ahn Chang-ho. Thinking of their respective age, different men of the same generation, I was overcome with mixed emotions. I suddenly wondered how my liberated fatherland was faring. I longed to return to my fatherland.

Return to My Dear Country

Upon the completion of our training program in San Antonio and Phoenix, my colleagues and I took a train to Los Angeles. We stayed there one night before proceeding to San Francisco. LA had the second largest Korean population in the U.S. behind Hawaii. Walking around downtown, I happened to come across the office of the Great Korean Comrade Society, which was a Korean organization that supported Syngman Rhee. I went in. The people in the office were surprised at the sight of a man in a military uniform. Once I told them about myself and why I had come to America, they all welcomed me warmly.

But the expressions on their faces completely changed when I mentioned that I wanted to visit the Great Korean People Society, an organization that supported the Korean Provisional Government and Ahn Chang-ho. When I asked for its location, they grimaced and said it was located right across the street. They were hostile to the society. I grew indignant and said to them,

"Gentlemen, why are you still fighting each other in this distant land? What is this, when we should be standing united in one voice? Here, in America, people from all over the globe have come to build such an advanced country, while we, who hail from a small country, are divided into so many factions yet again and still fighting each other. Does this make any sense at all? Isn't this why we are still wandering around in distant lands and are derided as "nation-destroyers?"

After my fiery speech, I visited the Great Korean People Society.

People there gave me a very warm welcome once I told them who my father was. They did not seem to be as antagonistic to the Great Korean Comrade Society as the Comrade Society was to them. Even when I told them that I had went to Washington to see Dr. Rhee and spent Christmas and the last days of the year there, they showed no particular reaction. At the same time, I did not feel entirely at home there, either, as I had already gone through an unpleasant experience at the other Korean society.

We took another train to San Francisco. We stayed at a base there a little while before boarding a ship for China. When the ship passed under Golden Gate Bridge, I became emotional, thinking that "Oh, it's time to say goodbye to America! Will I ever come back?" The ship was scheduled stop first in Hawaii before heading out to Shanghai. However, it had to make a detour around Alaska because of the bad weather in the waters near Hawaii. It was summertime and we were all wearing summer clothes, anticipating our stopover in Hawaii. We ended up shivering in the bitter cold of Alaska. Each of us was assigned a certain task, since sitting still made seasickness worse. Most of us were tasked with cleaning the area around our own sleeping quarters.

Between training days, whenever I could I bought several things I wanted to bring to Korea. What remains most vividly in my mind is the Zenith radio I bought shortly before leaving the Williams Base. At the time, it was a cutting-edge radio that one could listen to anytime and anywhere by using batteries. I turned it on when our ship passed over the sea south of Japan, headed toward Shanghai. I could hear programs broadcast from Seoul. I have never been more thankful to have a radio before or since then.

I arrived in Shanghai at the end of August, 1947, and traveled to Nanjing for my discharge. However, I learned there was no apparent way for me to travel to Korea. I visited Ahn Jeong-geun. He was living near Hongkou Park (now Lu Xun Park) in Shanghai, and taking care of Koreans as the president of the General Association for Aiding Koreans. He was also raising my niece Kim Hyo-ja who was born to my brother and his wife, Ahn Mi-saeng. My sister-in-law had returned to Korea with my father and was in Seoul at the time. I told Mr. Ahn that I would come back for my niece once completing the discharge procedure in Nanjing.

In Nanjing, I met up with Min Pil-ho, who belonged to the Korean Mission to China. Park Chan-ik, the head of the mission, was staying in Manchuria at the time. Dispersed in various places throughout China, the mission worked hard to help Koreans under challenging circumstance in which Koreans were sometimes misunderstood to be collaborating with Japan.

Mr. Min, the head of the Nanjing mission, encouraged me to go and visit some Guomindang folks since I was there. He contacted Chen Guofu, who had helped my father in the past, and arranged for my visit. I met with Chen and extended my gratitude to him. I rode in the jeep that the mission owned to look around Nanjing, and saw no significant change since my youthful years. My discharge procedure progressed without a glitch, as my father had sought President Chiang Kai-Shek's good offices on it before leaving Chongqing.

"As a member of the Chinese Air Force, my son is studying in

America. Once he returns to China at the end of the war, I would appreciate it if you facilitate his return to me in Korea right away."

On returning to Shanghai, I met with Kim Dong-su, who had engaged in anti-Japanese underground activities together with Yi Ha-yu, Yi Jae-hyeon, and my brother when Shanghai was under Japan's control. They were been able to engage in such activities mainly because even the Japanese Army could infiltrate the British and French concessions at will. But once they came on the radar of the Japan's intelligence network, they left Shanghai for Chongqing. Kim had returned to Shanghai after Japan's surrender.

Kim was not at liberty to return to Korea together with the first Korean Provisional Government wave of returnees, as his mother lived in Shanghai. Once he returned to Korea, he joined the army, and eventually made the rank of general. In the aftermath of liberation, the Korean Provisional Government officials made their way back to Korea in several groups over a period of some years. Lim Hak-jun, who would become my father-in-law and at the time worked for a streetcar company in the British concession, did not return to Korea immediately, either. The same held true for Jang Du-cheol, a key figure in the Korean Provisional Government, who was in charge of financial management in a big company.

Kim Dong-su took me to visit both Lim and Jang and in their respective houses in Shanghai. I naturally exchanged greetings with their daughters, too. Kim had intended to introduce me to the two families so that I might be linked up with one of the daughters in the families for marriage. In view of my age, Mr. Kim thought I should settle down and look after my father as a married man. At the time, I was blithely ignorant of his intentions. I took a ship headed for Busan with my niece Kim Hyo-ja. It was a ship transporting wounded Japanese prisoners of war. Many Koreans living in Shanghai were on board, too. The U.S. soldiers kept the prisoners of war in a lower part of the ship, while assigning the relatively comfortable quarters to the Koreans.

Once the ship docked in Busan, the passengers were not allowed to leave the port right away. They could leave the port only after going through quarantine inspections. Cholera was rampant at the time. It was the beginning of September, and it was still hot. During the tedious inspection period, I could not withstand the heat and dove into the sea for a swim. After completing the quarantine inspection and immigration procedures, I took the train to Seoul with my niece.

The September 5, 1947 issue of the *Donga Ilbo* reported on my return to Korea as follows:

Kim Shin, Kim Koo's son, arrived in Busan aboard an American ship via Shanghai. He arrived at Seoul Station at 8:05 PM on September 2… Kim Shin said that he has returned to Korea after attending the Chinese Military Academy in Kunming, going to India and then to America where he graduated from an aviation training school in Texas. Kim expressed his feelings thus:

"I don't know how to express my joy and excitement at coming back to my country for the first time in thirteen years. It is difficult for me to say everything in detail all at once, as my Korean is a bit rusty after having lived abroad for so long. But I will be assisting my old father to work on building our nation. Since I am trained in aviation techniques, I will do my best to contribute to Korea's national air defense."

Chapter 6

Dark Clouds over Our Nation's Sky

Reunion with My Father and Talks of Marriage

We arrived in Seoul late at night and headed straight to my father's house, Gyeong Gyo Jang. Several key figures of the Korean Provisional Government including my father had stayed together in this house following liberation. By the time I arrived, former Korean Provisional Government figures had moved out and were staying at the Hanmi Hotel in Myeong-dong. Those who stayed in the hotel were people without family, while those who had families lived with them at home.

I found my father was with his secretary, bodyguard, and a lady serving as a maid. The next day, my father and I ate together at a two-person table face to face for the very first time in my life.

"Oh, I can't believe a day like this has finally come!"

I was infinitely happy. On the other hand, I was also sad. I was not able to spend much time with my father at home, as I was soon swamped with invitations to lunch and dinner from friends and associates once news of my return spread. Seeing that I was going to so many dinners and coming back home a bit drunk, my father lectured me on what I had to bear in mind when drinking in Korea.

"In China it is acceptable for your secretary or friend to drink your glass of alcohol on your behalf if you are unable to drink, but in Korea it is absolutely unacceptable. Indeed, there are many who, after living long in China, come back to Korea and indulge to excess, unfamiliar with the culture."

My father went on to say, "If you are confident that you can handle your liquor, you may drink. Otherwise, you should not drink at all."

From that moment on, I drank cautiously at all times and in all social settings that called for alcohol consumption. Fortunately, I never got in trouble or passed out even when I had had one too many. Apart from the drinking etiquette, there were many other things that were unfamiliar to me, after having lived abroad for more than ten years. For example, people used Japanese-style Chinese characters rather than the original Chinese ones when writing. Also, when a married couple was walking together, the husband always walked a few steps ahead of the wife, and the wife consciously followed him a few steps behind. I found these and several other cultural norms odd.

Every Sunday, my father took me to a church service inside a tent run by Reverend Han Gyeong-jik. It was a church where people from North Korea gathered to worship God. Many North Koreans had come down to the South under the Soviet occupation. Thanks to them, I could hear about developments in the North at church.

After some time had passed, my father told me I should get married as I was old enough to start a family of my own. It appeared that several people had asked him if they could introduce potential brides to me even before I had arrived in Korea.

At the time, the best age for Korean males to get married was considered twenty-four or twenty-five. At twenty-seven years old, I was considered slightly over the hill. When I told people my age, many assumed that I had already been married at least once. I told my father that I would not get married for the time being, as my grandmother, before passing away, had told me not to get married before the age of thirty. She thought that a man should get married when he had the ability to support his family and that a man would not be able to achieve such independence before the age of thirty.

"You would be in big trouble if you got married early without the ability to support your family. It is alright for men to wait until thirty years of age, so don't get married before you're thirty," my grandmother had advised me in earnest.

As a young man, I did not really understand my grandmother's words. But now, they made sense. At the same time, I thought now that Korea was liberated and I was back my native land, perhaps I was approaching the right time to get married. After much consideration, I told my father that I was open to getting married. Thereafter, folks close to me diligently tried to arrange for a meeting with a prospective bride marriage on my behalf. Kim Dae-eon, a friend of mine who had attended the same elementary school with me, was particularly enthusiastic.

"Hey, a nice family I know has invited you for dinner tonight. Why don't you give it a try," he told me, urging me to accept the invitation without any explanation.

"What family?" I asked, curious as I was.

"The family of a gentleman who has studied in the U.S. Just do it."

Kim did not give me any further detail. The invitation had already been sent, and I had no choice but to accept it. My hosts loaded the table with so much food I thought the table legs might break. I made conversation with the head of the household and drank with him. When the dinner was almost over, a young lady brought in a tray full of sliced fruits. She was dressed in a graceful traditional Korean costume. She entered the room with her eyes cast down at the floor and her face beet red. At the time I was unaware of the significance of that moment, but later learned she was being introduced, or rather, presented, to me as a prospective bride. My friend Dae-eon came to see me two days later.

"How did it go?"

"I was well treated with lots of food and I had a good time."

"No. I didn't mean that. Did you get a good look at her?"

"How could I when she was all red her head facing way down?"

Kim stubbornly insisted that I should get engaged with her. I thought it ridiculous. I thought that marriage should be preceded by lots of dating like going to the movies together, and getting engaged to someone whose face I barely got a look at made no sense at all. But Kim Dae-eon proceeded to explain to me why engagement should precede the dating.

"Dating a girl would be alright if you were eventually to marry her later, but if you were to date her and not marry her, she may end up unmarriageable."

I asked why, not understanding what he meant.

"If a girl ends up only dating a man without marrying him, there's bound to be a rumor that she only fooled around with a man and got rejected, thus damaging her marriage prospects."

As I still refused to get engaged to the woman I'd barely set my eyes on, Kim introduced me to several other families. Presumably, Kim told the ladies I would meet to raise their heads a bit when they entered the room. So, most of them did, while they all still kept their eyes to the ground. Kim nagged me with questions whenever I met someone.

"How did it go this time?"

"She is good looking, at least," I would candidly reply.

Encouraged by my words, he would not hesitate to tell me to get engaged. As much as I appreciated my friend's good intentions, I could not commit to marriage in this way.

Assisting My Father

Again, it was in September, 1947, when I was twenty-seven years old, that I returned to my country. I was overcome with so many feelings after having gone through so much in my youth. My joy was tinged with sorrow. Thirteen years had passed since my escape to China in 1934. Traversing through China, India, and America before returning to my homeland virtually meant I had traveled around the entire globe. Those were dangerous and tough times, but I also felt that I had gained a broad worldview thanks to my travails and extensive travels. At the time, very few Koreans of my generation had had a chance to see so many places as I.

The one thing I felt most bitingly traveling through different countries was the sorrow of being stateless. This hit me particularly hard when I had to face the citizenship issue before my trip from India to America. The Chinese government was able to guarantee my identity, allowing me the good fortune of going to America. But had it ignored my case, my dream of becoming a pilot in my liberated fatherland would have never come true.

When I went to China for the first time, I did not feel too strongly this sorrow of the stateless person, presumably because I was too young. I began to feel it more, however, as I attended school. Among my classmates there were many displaced Chinese students who had fled from their hometowns because of the Japanese invasion. Whether Korean or Chinese, they all shared a deep sorrow stemming from having their hometown taken away.

Those who had been forced to leave Korea for China had only good feelings for their country. Probably because they went to China once their fatherland was taken from them, they tended to think positively even of Korea's negative realities. Everything looked great to me as I stepped foot inside my country again for the first time in thirteen years. Seeing people going around dressed in traditional Korean clothes, I thought, "Oh, they are my compatriots." Everything was novel and delightful. But I could not find the beautiful scenery that the elders of the Korean Provisional Government had boasted of so much. Every single mountain lay bare, the outcome of deforestation, and the people also looked bare and hungry. It soon dawned on me that liberation was not an end but just the beginning.

My marriage issue fizzled out and time went by. By 1948, the political situation in Korea became very complicated. The foreign trusteeship issue had made the Korean left-right relationship only worse. Amidst the political chaos, I focused only on assisting my father—which is not to say I was his sole secretary. Mr. Seonu Jin was his main secretary.

Mr. Seonu came from Jeongju, South Pyeongan Province. He joined the Korean Liberation Army in the middle of attending Singyeong University in Manchuria, taking charge of propaganda and current events broadcasting at the Department of Troops Information and Education of the General Headquarters. He became an attending secretary to my father in January, 1945. My job was different from his. For a while, it was mainly to deliver the correspondences between my father and Syngman Rhee. At the time I returned to Korea, Dr. Rhee lived in a house called Do Nam Jang. As of November, 1947, he lived in a different house named Yi Hwa Jang. Whenever I went there to deliver my father's letters to Dr. Rhee, Mr. Gwak Yeong-ju received me at the gate.

"Dr. Rhee is waiting for you. Please come on in."

Mr. Gwak was in Dr. Rhee's good graces and was promoted to the Chief of the Blue House Police Department (now the Office of Presidential Security) in 1956. But he was executed after the May 16, 1961 military coup for protecting political gangsters and giving the command to fire on student demonstrators during the April 19, 1960 student uprising.

During the time I was assisting my father in Gyeong Gyo Jang, Chung In-bo paid frequent visits to the house. One day, Mr. Chung made a proposal to me, presumably because he felt bad to see me

With father and niece, Kim Hyo-ja, at Gyeong Gyo Jang
Father loved his grand-daughter. In exile he would also express his love for kids whenever he would come across them, although the little ones would run away shouting, "It's Tiger Grandpa!"

apparently engaged in no particular job.

"Why don't you teach Chinese in school since you are proficient in it?"

I declined in earnest. When he asked why, I was compelled to answer why.

"Although I am really fluent in Chinese, I am not very good at Korean."

He never again suggested that I teach Chinese after that. When I was once cleaning my house, I found a picture on which my father had written, "Widang Inhyeong Dongji" (Widang Brother Comrade). Until then, I had not known Chung In-bo's penname. One day when Chung Yang Mo, Chung In-bo's son, visited me, I asked him what was his father's penname, assuming it was Widang. The moment he affirmed my assumption, I handed the picture to him.

My Father Decides to Visit North Korea

On June 3, 1946, Syngman Rhee made remarks to the effect that South Koreans needed to establish a separate government with only in the South. My father was in a blaze of anger after hearing Rhee's remarks.

"What was the point of the Korean independence movements in the first place if we were just going to do something like this? Koreans absolutely must not establish a separate government in the South alone. Should the South and North be formally separated, then a fratricidal war between the two sides is inevitable."

My father took a different political stance from Dr. Rhee's, because his greatest concern was to avoid the tragedy of Korean compatriots pointing guns at each other. After the U.S. military government withdrew, Dr. Rhee co-opted pro-Japanese collaborators, as he did not have his own political support base at home. Since the Korean Resistance Party established by the Korean Provisional Government faction was powerful at the time, pro-Japanese collaborators were all the more desperate to align with and reinforce Rhee's political power. The relationship between my father and Dr. Rhee began to become frayed in this way. By then, North Korea itself had already completed the groundwork for a communist government.

Believing that the future of the Korean nation lay in peril, my father proposed to North Korea a joint South-North political leaders' conference. He announced that he would go to North Korea on April 19, 1948. Most of the Korean Provisional Government people supported his decision. But, on the day of my father's departure, he could not step out of his own house as rings of students opposing his visit had encircled it.

"You shall never go to North Korea," they said, lying down and blocking the front yard of our house.

My father tried to persuade them not to block him.

"I am trying to go to North Korea in order to save our nation. We did not persevere in the independence movement just to see our nation divided. Whether we succeed or not, we must at least try to establish a single government in our entire country. If we simply give up on establishing a single, united government because it is difficult, we can but go down in the annals of history as traitors to history."

The students did not clear the track, however. So, I thought of an alternate way out. Surveying the back side of Gyeong Gyo Jang, I determined that it would be possible to stack wooden apple crates at the bottom of the backyard wall and climb over it. My father's car was out of the house grounds for maintenance at the time. After making all the necessary preparations for a trip, I came down to the basement with my father. I then made a phone call to the driver, Jeong Tae-hun, and asked him to bring get the car to the back of the house. I then called Mr. Seonu Jin down to the basement, and the three of us went through the basement passage to the backyard and climbed over the wall. My father and I took the back seats of the car, while Mr. Seonu sat in the front passenger seat. Thus did we depart for Pyongyang.

The Journey to Pyongyang

My father had already foreseen the possible adverse effects of not achieving liberation on our own. Shortly before the liberation on August 15, 1945, Commander Zhu Shaozhou in Xian had hosted a dinner party for the Korean Liberation Army, which was prepared to advance into Korea. In the middle of the party, he announced the news of Japan's surrender. Far from being happy to hear the news, my father drew a deep sigh.

"Alas, the Japanese invaders have surrendered! Instead of being good news it's as if the sky is falling. We went through hell and high water to prepare to participate in the war, and now it's all in vain.

Since our troops have yet to advance into Korea, it's all but inevitable that the voice of the foreign powers will be louder than our own in the post-liberation years."

As my father had expected, our nation's future was subject to the power maneuverings between the United States and the Soviet Union, and we were fighting among ourselves sharply divided into rightist and leftist camps. It was under such circumstances that my father decided to visit North Korea in an attempt to prevent the worst case scenario—our nation breaking into two.

After managing to get out of our house, we drove quite a while and took a break in Geumcheon before heading to the Imjin River. We could not cross the river by car, as there was only a railroad bridge across the river. Thus, we crossed the river in a large wooden boat, stowing our car onboard. After crossing the river, we kept driving until we encountered Soviet soldiers standing guard at the 38th parallel at a spot shy of Yeohyeon. They signaled us to stop. They approached us and asked who we were. When we answered their question, they cleared the track immediately. They apparently had already been informed of us.

Beyond the 38th parallel, we went northward a little and arrived in Yeohyeon. As the sun had set, we decided to stay there for the night. North Korean agents approached us, asking questions and inspecting our belongings. I had concealed a golden ring in my belongings so that I could sell it in the event we came to be in urgent need of cash in North Korea. I put the ring at the bottom of a cigarette box and placed a few cut cigarettes on top of it. Thus hidden well, the ring passed the inspection easily. As the North Korean agents kept asking too invasive and useless questions, my father yelled at them in indignation.

"What are you doing when I am on my way to Pyongyang to take part in the South-North Political Consultative Conference to address the grave issue of the future of our nation!"

They then stood down, and apologized that they had been instructed to ask those questions. The next morning, as we were about to depart for Pyongyang, Kim Jong-hang, the chief secretary for Kim Il Sung, showed up to escort my father to Pyongyang. As a graduate of Waseda University, he had an elite educational background. Later, during the Korean War, Seonu Jin would have a meeting with him in Seoul.

The chief secretary had arrived in Yeohyeon the prior day and had waited for us. However, as we had arrived too late in the day, he had gone off to Sariwon thinking that we would not be coming at all. He had come back to us early that morning after being informed we were there. My father and I took a Russian car that the chief secretary had brought, as North Koreans took our car aboard a train to Pyongyang for some unspecified reason. Mr. Seonu Jin and our driver Jeong Tae-hun also got on the train to Pyongyang.

On our way, we saw signs with the slogan "Down with Kim Koo and Syngman Rhee" placed on utility poles and walls. It seemed that the North Korean party had thought that we would not be able to make it to North Korea. As we had shown up unexpectedly, however, they had not had enough time to get rid of the slogans. Instead, they had painted over them with black ink. But as the ink had dried up, the letters had become visible once again.

歴 史 的 刹 那

Historical moment
My father (middle), Mr. Seonu Jin (left), and I crossed the 38th
parallel on April 19, 1948.

"Hey, you must really hate me!" said my father to the chief secretary, looking at these slogans.

Sweating profusely, the chief secretary apologized.

Before we arrived in Pyongyang, many people had already arrived in groups to participate in the South-North Political Consultative Conference. They had all submitted a visitors list to the North Korean authorities in advance. Those who had not been included in the list were not able to attend. Mr. Kim U-jeon, who was originally from Pyongyang and had returned to Korea after taking part in the Korean Liberation Army, was one of those people who, despite wanting to attend the conference, had been omitted from the list. Before we had set out, Kim visited me and asked me to take him to Pyongyang with us. He said,

"My father-in-law lives in Pyongyang, but I cannot go there as I am not included in the visitors list. Can you help me out?"

Mr. Kim persuaded me by arguing that he could be of great help, as Pyongyang was his hometown. I thought it made sense to put him on our visitors list. However, in his memoir, *Following Kim Koo's Life: The Story of the Last Korean Liberation Army Soldier*, published in 1998, Mr. Kim describes what had happened around the time of the visit differently. According to his description, I had not wanted to go to Pyongyang and it had been he who had scolded me, saying, "How could you not want to go when your own father is going?" which is far from the truth. Later, I called him in and demanded a thorough explanation for this distorted description.

At the time of my father's announcement to visit Pyongyang, many people around him objected to the visit. During the years in

Shanghai, Yi Dong-hui, suggesting that my father adopt a communist line of resistance against Japan, said to him, "If we just adopted communism, then we would not need to carry out a separate and arduous independence movement." My father responded strongly, "What on earth are you talking about? We must struggle on behalf of our nation above all in the spirit of nationalism!" Those who knew my father's opposition to communism through this kind of episode were concerned that my father, should he go to Pyongyang, could be held against his will.

But my father remained stubbornly undeterred by such risks and was resolved to go. This is why I had stepped forward and volunteered to escort him to North Korea. My father strongly objected, but in the end, I managed to persuade him. This is the truth.

Father Objects to a Separate North Korean Government

We stayed at a regular civilian house in Sangsu-ri, in the central part of Pyongyang. Though the house was not big, it was a well-built cozy two-storied structure. The owner of the house was a man who had made a fortune by running a gold mine. My father and I stayed with a few key figures in the Korean Provisional Government, including Eom Hangseop. Kim Kyu-sik stayed elsewhere. When we woke up the next day, Kim Du-bong visited us and proposed to accompany my father.

I had known Kim Du-bong since I was in Shanghai. He was a

linguist, a scholar of the Korean language. When my mother passed away, he used the Korean phonetics to indicate the date of her death on her tombstone. He had returned to Pyongyang after the liberation. He had become the vice president of the North Korean Provisional People's Committee before establishing the Korean New People Party with communist activists with whom he had worked together in Yanan and assuming its leadership. But his party was eventually subsumed by Kim Il Sung's Korean Communist Party under pressure from the Soviet Army.

We went to the conference hall with Kim Du-bong. The conference was held in the Moranbong Theater. As our car approached the venue, I saw out of the window a man dressed in a Mao jacket pacing back and forth in front of the theater. As we got off, he approached and welcomed us. It was Kim Il Sung. My father was seventy-three years old at the time, whereas Kim Il Sung was just thirty-seven years of age. Informed of our imminent arrival, Kim had been waiting outside to welcome us. When all of us got off the car, Kim Du-bong introduced my father to Kim Il Sung, and then my father to the North Korean leader. Kim Il Sung's first words were:

"It is my great honor to meet Mr. Kim Koo, our great elder in our anti-Japanese independence movement."

Kim then made politely apologized for the interrogative questions and the intrusive inspection of our belongings that we had dealt with on our trip. To his polite welcome and apology, my father reciprocated with a polite greeting of his own:

"In Chongqing, I heard a lot about your armed struggles in Manchuria. It's too bad the great distance between us made it

My father at the South-North Joint Meeting My father delivered a congratulatory speech at Moranbong Theater in Pyongyang on April 22, 1948.

difficult to get in touch with you."

After my father's greetings, Kim turned to me standing next to my father, and sized me up and down.

"This is my son," my father said.

"Comrade, thank you for your efforts in bringing your father here," he said, extending his hand to shake mine.

During the August 15 Liberation Day Celebration in 2005, a North Korean delegation headed by Kim Ki Nam visited Seoul. When I met the delegation and told the story of shaking hands with Kim Il Sung, the North Korean visitors all clapped their hands. In North Korea, having shaken hands with Kim Il Sung is a big deal, indeed.

After briefly exchanging greetings, my father and Kim Il Sung entered the conference hall. In fact, the North Korean party, after having waited for South Korean delegates' arrival for a while, had already held the opening ceremony upon hearing that my father would not be able to visit due to the human wall of students that surrounded our house. But as we finally had arrived, they went through the opening ceremony once again.

The opening ceremony was flooded with excessive exaltations of Kim Il Sung. A performance group read out shamelessly sycophantic poems and songs in tribute to Kim. It was hard not to blush at the excesses. The group even had the temerity to deliver a speech that glorified Kim Il Sung's exploits as heroic independence fighter in the presence of numerous senior leaders of the independence movement. I thought to myself, "What on earth is this absurd ceremony?"

Finally, it was my father's turn to give a speech. In his speech, father talked about the harsh tribulations of the Korean people before liberation, and how our entire nation of thirty million people, in the south and north alike, had been invaded by Japanese. He also expressed his wish that the entire Korean nation would unite so as to establish a new country now that it had been liberated.

My father also spoke of the reason for his visit, which was spurred by his opposition to the plan to establish a separate government in the South. The audience in the conference hall applauded vigorously in unison. However, upon hearing that my father was also opposed to the establishment of a separate government in the North, the audience fell into dead silence. When I saw there was no applause whatsoever at my father's remark that Korean unification must be achieved by our own efforts instead of those by the Soviet Union or the United States, I thought that the prospects for establishing a unified government would be exceedingly bleak.

Years later, when I looked into the newspapers issued at the time of the conference at the Library of Congress in Washington, D.C., I could not find a single line about my father's opposition to a separate government in North Korea. All the newspapers mentioned only that Kim Koo had opposed a separate government in the South. It was apparent that the North Korean authorities had omitted father's opposition to a separate government in the North in their press release to foreign newspapers.

The conference did not proceed smoothly, as there were simply too many people in attendance. Therefore, my father proposed having a four-way conference, a "Four Kims Conference" among Kim Koo, Kim Kyu-sik, Kim Du-bong, and Kim Il Sung. The North Korean party itself also proposed a similar conference almost at the same time. The four Kims then met every day and also went sightseeing around Pyongyang occasionally between meetings. The occasional tour of Pyongyang was intended to allow for sufficient time for comprehensive talks without rushing through. For this reason, we stayed in Pyongyang longer than we had anticipated, returning to Seoul only on May 6, after having departed Seoul on April 19.

During the four Kims conference, I would wait for my father in the secretarial office near the conference room. Among those who had come up from South Korea, those whose native places were in the North visited their hometowns or met with their old friends. The North Korean authorities kept constant watch on where South Korean visitors went and what they did. Since the North Koreans in power had yet to consolidate their rule, they must have suspected that South Korean visitors might be staging some sorts of plot to sabotage them.

One day when I was waiting in the secretarial office, a North Korean surveillance agent came to report to the chief secretary, speaking in Chinese. They spoke in Chinese in order to keep to themselves what they were saying in the presence of South Koreans. Apparently, they did not know that I was fluent in Chinese. I listened in on their conversation pretending not to understand anything they were saying. The agent reported to the chief that, although they had two agents follow the South Koreans, they had lost track of them, as there were four South Koreans who went in separate directions. The chief scolded him, telling him that they should have followed them to the end even if it meant disguising themselves as local merchants in order to keep track of whom they contacted and where they visited.

May Day Celebration in North Korea

We also attended the May Day Celebration during the four Kims conference. The celebration was carried out at both civilian and military levels. My father was assigned the seat to Kim Il Sung's right on the reviewing stand. To my father's right stood other South Korean visitors. To Kim Il Sung's left stood North Korean officers. I stood behind my father, and assisted him when necessary.

Performing in the celebrations, ordinary citizens marched in unison in an extremely organized manner, the result of intense practice. While marching, the mobilized citizens shouted things about national unification and imperialism before suddenly declaiming, "Down with Kim Koo and Syngman Rhee!" "Down with them, down with them, down with them!" Kim Il Sung's face turned beet red. I don't think they did so intentionally to offend us with knowledge of our attendance. Instead, it was a spontaneous outburst, the result of hours of practice and indoctrination.

I diligently took pictures of such events and landscapes in Pyongyang. I had sold the aforementioned golden ring in Pyongyang and had purchased a German-made camera with the money. I received help with the transaction from Kim U-jeon's father-in-law. Once, as I was about to change the film in the middle of taking pictures of a People's Army march, someone approached me and snatched my camera away. He pulled out the roll of film from the camera. Fortunately, he could not lay his hands on the rolls of film I had already used to take photos, as I had left them with our driver. The driver had hidden them in the spare tire compartment of our car.

When I returned to Seoul, I developed the rolls of film and took a close look at the pictures. I saw once again that the People's Army was trained extremely well. Since I had been in the Chinese and American militaries, a few pictures were sufficient for me to assess the army's level of training. The People's Army was in another league altogether compared to South Korea's National Defense Guard. It was armed with the Russian submachine gun PPSH-41, which Koreans had nicknamed "multi-bullet gun," and had a very powerful arsenal of artillery as well.

Key officers in the People's Army had abundant combat

At Mt. Jeongbang, en route to Seoul from Pyongyang, May 4, 1948

experience, because they had been part of the Chinese Communist forces when China had been at war against Japan. In contrast, South Korea did not have comparable military power. In the name of disarming the Japanese Air Force, South Koreans had even gone so far as to take off propellers from Japanese aircraft to make rice cookers or window frames. But North Koreans actually used Japanese aircraft for their military purposes. I watched a few Japanese aircraft flying during the May Day Celebration. Inexplicable fear and a sense of imminent crisis swelled up in a corner of my mind.

People I Met in Pyongyang

I was able to meet Madam Ahn Shin-ho, the sister of Ahn Chang-ho. She was once engaged to my father. The North Korean party invited my father to a place that looked like a temple. A table for ancestral worship had been set. The setting was intended for my father to pay respects to his mother in an ancestral memorial rite. Our hosts had gone out of the way to be considerate, but they had gotten the date of grandmother's death wrong. It was not the anniversary of her death. At any rate, they had also invited Madam Ahn to this place. Afterward, we looked around the vicinities of Pyongyang with her.

Young visitors like me would be entertained by young folks from the secretarial office. When some of us visitors asked if there were bars we could visit, they replied that Pyongyang no longer featured bars modeled on the American imperialists. We were insistent, however, and asked to be taken to a place where we could unwind

With Ahn Chang-ho's family

and have a drink. Then they took us to laborers' lounge. There we saw North Korean women all dressed in white gowns pouring beer for the guests.

I also noticed a woman who was watching over the female attendants. Once she had left the room, we asked the attendants where to find old-style bars. We ended up visiting a place one of the attendants had mentioned and found that the bar was closed off from the outside with all windows and doors tightly shut and featuring female attendants. One of them said Communist Party officials visited every day.

I also met with Kim Sang-yeop in Pyongyang. She had been a close friend of mine in Chongqing. As Kim Du-bong's oldest daughter, she had a strong character like a hero's. She was dressed in a People's Army uniform. She recognized me right away and said to me,

"I've heard that you were trained in America. Quit what you're doing right away and move up here. Following America around won't open up any doors for you."

In actuality, those who really had no future were people of the Yanan faction who had returned to North Korea. They were all purged later on. This led Chinese leaders to grow frustrated with Kim Il Sung. When Mao Zedong had fought against Chiang Kai-Shek, Mao, in consultation with Peng Dehuai, pushed down all the way south to Hainandao, taking two Manchuria-based Korean brigades in the vanguard. Later, Mao expanded the two brigades to four divisions and left them under the control of Kim Mu-jeong who would lead them to participate in the Korean War. Despite this shared history,

Kim Il Sung had all of them purged, which greatly irritated Mao.

When my father was about to return to South Korea after the conference, Kim Il Sung tried to persuade him not to go. He argued that my father may be in danger upon return home. Kim Il Sung suggested that he visit Gidong (aka Teotgol) near Haeju, Hwanghae Province, which was my father's hometown. Gidong was where our family gravesite was. I had visited it with my grandmother during a school break when I had lived in An-ak. Kim Il Sung told my father to visit there since he had mobilized people to pave the road leading to our family gravesite.

My father replied that he would visit Gidong next time and that he would just go straight back home. He explained that people would begin to think that he had been won over by the communist party, if he did not return right away. We hurried back to South Korea. When we crossed the 38th parallel, many people including journalists rushed toward us. Unlike on our journey to Pyongyang, we crossed the 38th parallel by foot.

I am well aware that there have been many commentaries and debates surrounding my father's visit to North Korea. Some argue that his visit was the result of excessively idealistic views, far removed from the political situation of the time. Others claim that it was a naive idea which did not take into account the possibility that he could have been politically exploited by Kim Il Sung. Still others put forward other opinions regarding his visit. As a person who escorted my father to North Korea, I do not want to comment on every single one of the many opinions. I just remind myself of a line from *The Analects* of Confucius:

"Zhi qi bu ke wei er wei zhi."

This translates to "One must try to the very end even if he knows that it is not feasible." The line refers to Confucius who strove to create a world based on benevolence and propriety, even though he knew that such a world would be almost impossible to achieve.

My father was far removed from the kind of person who weighs the probability of success and failure, calculates relative advantages and disadvantages, and only then determines whether to advance or retreat. He never took a step back on the great task of national reconciliation and unification, in the imperative of avoiding permanent division and war. He understood the state of affairs and the contours of the conditions and circumstances as fully as anybody else. Still, he left no room for even the smallest retreat. He just willed himself and did everything he could in his powers.

I do not think that people can measure the depth of sincerity of my father's mind with temporary standards of the day that vanish before long like ripples. A deep river runs long. He thought that the great and deep stream of history from conflict to harmony and from division to unification would flow on and that all of us should strive to ensure that the current lives on. As he had been at death's door several times in the course of dedicating himself to Korea's independence and had closely worked with patriotic martyrs who made the ultimate sacrifice, he was determined to "try to the very end" all the more because he "knew that it was not feasible."

My father and the many martyrs of the Korean Provisional Government did not struggle against Japan in the expectation that their struggle would prevail. In this great cause, they just had to go forward without looking to left or right because they had no choice but to struggle at the risk of death. They did not expect that their way would lead them to a certain result. For the Korean Provisional Government to stand up against the huge and mighty Imperial Japan was nothing less than revolutionary.

What is the original meaning of revolution? It is to transform the mandate of heaven altogether and upturn the great currents of the time by the roots. That is why it is difficult for a revolution to succeed even if we devote ourselves to it with our lives. We have no choice but to strive to make the impossible possible. Revolution is like striking a rock with eggs and trying to pierce a rock with raindrops. It can only succeed with time and sacrifice. With a determination to carry out that original sense of revolution, and with a will to pave the road to the survival of the entire Korean nation my father embarked on his trip to North Korea.

My father felt despondent to see dark clouds cast over liberated Korea by an impending internecine war in spite of not only the rightists and leftists but even the anarchists all having fought against Japan in unison under the flag of the Korean Provisional Government. "For what did I devote my life to the independence movement, risking my life? How can I hold my head up before the souls of so many patriotic martyrs who died on foreign soil?" If those critical of my father could understand even one ten-thousandth of his feelings, they would be ashamed of their lame words regarding what was right or wrong, or the successes and failure of his actions. He embarked on a path from which he could not step off.

Part 3

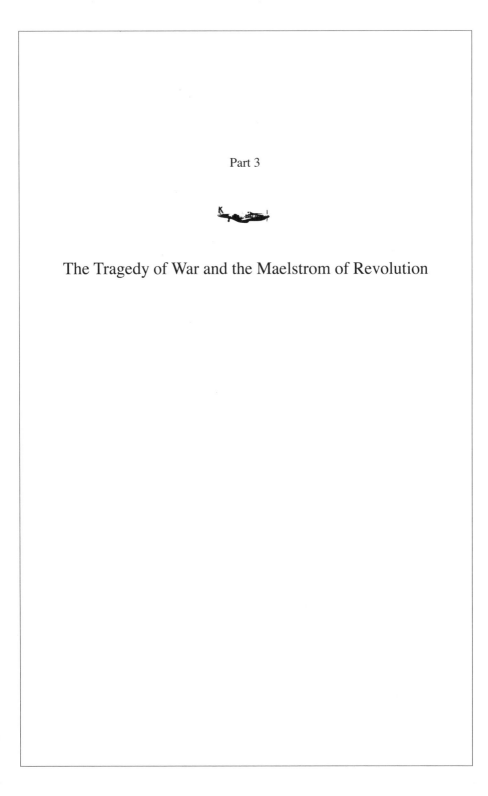

The Tragedy of War and the Maelstrom of Revolution

Chapter 7

Entering the National Defense Guard and Serving in the Army Air Force

Bringing Back from China the Souls of Deceased Koreans

A short while after the trip to Pyongyang, in June 1948 I went to China to honor my grandmother's dying wish. At the time, the Chinese Communist army was mauling over the Guomindang army through much of China. My father told me to bring back the remains of our family and other deceased Koreans as the situation in China was becoming more and more serious by the day. One of many obstacles lying in the way was that there was no direct route to enter China. I ended up boarding a ship at Busan for Hong Kong, then onto Shanghai. From Shanghai, I flew to Chongqing.

On my visit to Chongqing I was accompanied by Min Yeong-su, who was Shin Gyu-sik's maternal grandson and the son of Min Pil-ho. Min Yeong-su had been an agent of the Headquarters of the Advance Operations Troops of the Korean Liberation Army. Since the air fare was very expensive, Min and I each carried two sacks of cash with which to buy our tickets. The sales clerk counted the bills one by one to check for counterfeit bills, as counterfeits were not uncommon in wartime China. Even as the clerk was counting our money, the official exchange rate was fluctuating by the minute. On a typical day, the difference in the exchange rate between the morning and afternoon would be more than double.

Fortunately, we ran into Jimmy Gwak, a Korean who worked for a Chinese airline as an engineer. When we asked him for help, he took us to a bank to change our dollars into bank notes. Thus we managed to buy our airplane tickets in Shanghai. When we returned to Shanghai two weeks later upon the completion of our job, the exchange rate had depreciated to a fourth of its value before. That was how much the economy in Shanghai had broken down. Food shortage was the biggest problem. Grain dealers closed their shops and hoarded food as grain prices would only go up each day. As a result, hungry people started rioting and looted shops for food.

At the time, one would see ten thousand *yuan* bills flying around in the streets of major cities. They were worth no more than scraps of paper. A small piece of bread cost thirty thousand *yuan*, while a pair of German-made leather shoes cost as much as 350 million *yuan*. As money had become so worthless, people used gold or U.S. dollars for any big transactions. Distrust of money led to distrust of the government. And the Communist party took advantage of such a situation. It propagandized and agitated that Chinese people should not fight each other but band together and drive out the corrupt Guomindang government. I sensed the Communist party's victory in the civil war was only a matter of time.

The main reason I went to Chongqing with Min Yeong-su was that the collection of the remains of deceased people required government permission. Since soldiers raiding ancient tombs for treasure was a common occurrence at the time, even the relocation of ordinary graves required permission by the local government. Mr. Min's father, Min Pil-ho, was working in the Korean Mission to China in Nanjing at the time. He had his son assist me because Yeong-su, who was similar in age to me and was quite familiar with the locality, whereas I would have had a hard time finding the gravesites by myself.

Fortunately, the Guomindang government issued an official document instructing the local government to extend to us cooperation. After submitting it to the government of Qijiang, Chongqing, I was able to gather the remains of Yi Dong-nyeong. This document is still kept in the Qijiang local government. It was my first visit to Chongqing in some four years, and I saw that the city had changed a lot. By then, the Guomindang government had relocated in Nanjing. Without much expectation, I reached out to a man who had purified the water from the river and supplied it to my family when we had lived in Chongqing. To my surprise, he responded and came to help us out. I also reached out to a Korean who had run a stationery store named "*Gangbi dawang*" (strong pen great king), whose name now escapes me.

In this way, with help from many folks, I was able to gather the remains of my grandmother, my brother, and Cha Ri-seok all buried in Mt. Heshang. Afterwards, I went back to Shanghai to collect my mother's remains. In sum, I collected the remains of five people, including those of Yi Dong-nyeong's. This was all I could manage at the time. If I had had more people to work with, I could have collected the remains of many more Koreans, regardless of their political orientation as leftists or rightists. It was not difficult to find my mother's grave in the French concession, as I had visited it in 1947 on my return trip from the U.S. Lim Hak-jun's daughter accompanied me to my mother's grave. My mother's tombstone featuring the inscription by Kim Du-bong still stood there.

As we were collecting the remains in Mt. Heshang, we found both small and big streams of groundwater passing beneath the graves. This was almost inevitable as the gravesites had been randomly selected without close examination. But Yi Dong-nyeong's remains, as well as the earth around his grave, were in a better condition probably because the location of Yi's gravesite was far better suited as burial grounds.

Carrying the cremated remains, I left Chongqing for Shanghai, from where I took an airplane to Hong Kong. There, I took a Philippine ship to Incheon. When I came on board the ship, I carried the remains as if they were just regular luggage without declaring them to the officials, as transporting human remains required elaborate boarding procedures. As the ship passed the coast off Shamen, China, I heard on the radio the news on the impending establishment of the government of the Republic of Korea.

When I arrived in Incheon at three o'clock in the afternoon on August 8, 1948, my father stood waiting at the dock to greet me in person. Yi Dong-nyeong's son was also there. Yi Dong-nyeong's remains were taken to his son Yi Ui-sik's house in Hoihyeon-dong, Seoul, while Cha Ri-seok's remains were taken to Gyeong Gyo Jang. Their remains were again transported to Huimun Middle School for a public funeral on September 22, and then permanently enshrined in

Hyochang Park.

After holding a funeral for my grandmother, mother, and brother, my father and I took their remains to Jeongneung, where we would find them their gravesites. Kim Hong-ryang, who had come to Seoul at the right time, helped my father in this task. He chose a propitious site on a hill that overlooked a mountain in the front and a brook below. There, we buried the remains. All this took place between June and September 1948.

Many years later, on April 9, 1999, the remains of my grandmother and brother were relocated to the Second Graveyard for Patriots at the Daejeon National Cemetery. Three days later, on April 12, I buried the remains of my father and mother in the same grave in Hyochang Park. It was all the more significant because the year 1999 was the 50th anniversary of my father's death and the 80th anniversary of the establishment of the Korean Provisional Government. After the remains of my mother had been buried in Jeongneung, Seoul in 1948, as mentioned above, they had been relocated again to a graveyard in Songjeong-ri, Namyangju, Gyeonggi Province. The remains of my grandmother and brother had also been relocated to this graveyard sometime later.

Thus my mother was reunited with my father seventy-five years after she passed away in 1924. Oh, my dear mother! She experienced none of the quietness and happiness of an ordinary family but had to endure so much hardship taking care of her husband who was in prison and supporting the Korean Provisional Government all before dying from an illness in a distant foreign land. Now that she was put to rest, although belatedly, in eternal peace together with her husband, I felt relieved of some of the heavy burdens of filial duty that I had carried for so long.

It was also moving to enshrine the remains of my grandmother and brother who had passed away before our nation's liberation in the Graveyard for Patriots of the National Cemetery. I prayed again and again that they would rest in peace overlooking an independent and prosperous Korea from heaven. I put silver spoon and chopsticks wrapped in a red cloth in my grandmother's mortuary urn, as I had done in the case of her previous graves. I did it because I had always regretted that my grandmother had never really had a good meal free of troubles, and I felt sorry for not taking good care of her while she was living.

Marrying the Second Daughter of Sir Lim Hak-jun

When I went to Shanghai to collect the remains of deceased Koreans, I met with Lim Hak-jun. He asked me what business had brought me to China. When I answered, Mr. Lim suggested that I, on my way back to Korea via Shanghai after collecting the remains in Chongqing, stay at his house before leaving for Hong Kong. Checking into a hotel with the remains of the deceased would not have been well received by the hotel management.

Before setting out from Mr. Lim's house after a few days of stay, Mr. and Mrs. Lim suggested having one last dinner together. During the mean, Mr. Lim asked me,

"You would make such a good husband, you must be surrounded

In front of the statue of my grandmother with my wife
The statue was erected on the front yard of Gyeong Gyo Jang
after my father's death.

by legions of women suitors. Yet, why are you still single?"

I answered honestly, "Unlike in China, the circumstances in Korea do not allow men and women to date freely. Korea's social constraints do not comport with my views."

"What do you think of our second daughter?" the Lims asked simultaneously.

She and I knew each other well because she had accompanied me when I had gone to my mother's tomb and because we had often gone to see movies together. Though we had never expressed our hearts to each other, we had, in a word, dated. Well aware of this, Mr. and Mrs. Lim wanted to see whether I was willing to marry her.

"I would certainly, but first, I need my father's permission," I answered, without much hesitation.

After taking care of all the funeral services in Korea, I told my father that I had received help from Mr. Lim and had stayed at his house. My father said he knew Lim Hak-jun's family well. I thought that this was a good opportunity to talk to bring it up.

"With your permission, I would like to marry Mr. Lim's second daughter, with whom I have much in common. She went to school in Shanghai, thereby speaks Chinese, and even English, fluently," I said.

"His is a good family. You may marry her," my father said.

Preparations for the wedding proceeded smoothly. As the civil war between the Communist party and the Guomindang had spread to Shanghai, Lim Hak-jun moved back to Korea with his family. In December 1948, I married Lim Yoon Yeon, Lim Hak-jun's second daughter, in Namdaemun Church. My father stressed time and again for a modest wedding. Hence, the wedding dress for the bride was

Wedding In December 1948, I married Lim Yoon Yeon, the second daughter of Lim Hak-jun. To my bride's right are her father and mother, and in front of her stands Kim Hyo-ja, my niece. My father-in-law played an important role in the growth of the Korean protestant church in Shanghai.

made of cotton cloth instead of silk. He also told me to donate all the cash gift to a camp where people who had moved to the South from North Korea were put up. Dr. Syngman Rhee gave me a blanket as a wedding gift.

After the wedding, we went to the Yuseong hot springs for our honeymoon. Following our honeymoon, we spent Christmas in Gyeong Gyo Jang. When church members gathered outside our house and sang Christmas carols, my father insisted on having them come inside and treated each person to a bowl of hot rice-cake soup.

What happened to the 200,000 Dollars Chiang Kai-Shek Gave My Father?

When I went to the Korean Mission to China in Nanjing to discuss how to collect the remains, I saw a picture of Dr. Syngman Rhee on the office wall. They had hung the picture upon hearing that Dr. Rhee would stop by Shanghai and Nanjing on his way back to Korea in April 1947 upon his return journey from America, which he had visited in December 1946. Prior to that time, it had been my father's picture hanging on the wall.

There was a good reason why Dr. Rhee, instead of flying to Tokyo and then flying on an American military aircraft back to Korea, chose to stop over in Shanghai and Nanjing. When the Korean Provisional Government was about to return to Korea in the weeks following liberation in 1945, Chiang Kai-Shek had given my father 200,000 U.S. dollars. Since my father did not have a real political base in the power vacuum that was liberated Korea, Chiang had intended the gift a contingency fund for my father to be used as he deemed fit. But father left the money behind in China when he returned to Korea. By and by, Syngman Rhee came to hear about it and asked a favor of my father.

"I need some of the money for diplomatic activities. May I use some of it?"

"Yes, you may," father agreed without hesitation.

That was why Dr. Rhee stopped by Nanjing on his way back from America. But the Chinese government refused to give the money to him on the ground that they could not dispense the money on a mere verbal agreement with my father as told by Rhee. The authorities demanded a written document attesting to it in my father's own writing.

A portion of the money had previously been spent. In the aftermath of Korea's independence, when Park Chan-ik and Park Yeong-jun were helping Koreans in Manchuria, the Communist troops swept over Manchuria and had some Koreans forcibly repatriated to Tianjin, Shanghai, and other cities. The two then contacted my father and told him that they were trying to help Koreans make their way back to Korea but were having a hard time, as money had run out.

At the time, Mr. Liu Yuwan was the Chinese Consul General in Korea. Mr. Liu had already been very helpful to my father in the period leading up to the establishment of the Republic of Korea. My father invited him to Gyeong Gyo Jang and politely asked him for a favor. I interpreted their conversation.

"President Chiang gave me 200,000 dollars in 1945. I need to use some of that money. Could you help me to make this possible?"

Mr. Liu immediately contacted Foreign Minister Wang Shijie. Before long, Liu received a reply in the affirmative. But there was one condition. My father needed to write a letter in his own handwriting and also stamp it with the same seal that he had used in China. My father did so, and then sent the letter asking the Chinese government to dispense $100,000 to Park Chan-ik. That was how so many of our compatriots in China were able to make their way back to Korea.

When the Korean Provisional Government people returned to Korea and were put up in both Gyeong Gyo Jang and the Hanmi Hotel, they were all under economic duress. Many people went without a proper meal. Under such circumstances, an individual visited Gyeong Gyo Jang one day and offered to help out. However, he turned out to be a pro-Japanese collaborator. People like Jo Wan-gu adamantly refused to take any money from a pro-Japanese collaborator. As the days of hunger and economic duress continued, however, the Korean Provisional Government folks made a suggestion to father.

"Unam (Syngman Rhee's pen name) seems to be doing much better than us. Why don't you borrow some money from him and resolve our hunger problem?"

My father was the kind of person who never talked about money. As his comrades kept talking about borrowing money, however, he visited Dr. Rhee. But Dr. Rhee flat out rejected my father's request, telling him that he did not have any money to give. I suspect his cold refusal had something to do with lingering resentment over his

Welcoming the Chinese Consul Liu Yuwan at Gyeong Gyo Jang   I am in the far right in the second row, while Mr. Liu is in the first row, second from the left.

failure to his hands on the 200,000 dollars. All this took place at a time when Mr. Seonu Jin was my father's secretary. I heard about it from Mr. Seonu sometime after all this had taken place.

There were several people who lent help to the Provisional Government people when they were going through tough times. These folks helped out not because they wanted some reward in return, but simply because they came from the same hometown as some of the Provisional Government people. Mr. Gang Ik-ha was one among such helpful people. He came from Jaeryeong, and ran a big business. He established the Korean Life Insurance Corporation, Inc. in 1946.

When my father was making a tour of the southern regions upon his return to Korea, the city of Gwangju, in South Jeolla Province, was undergoing a severe flood. When father arrived in the city, people came and gathered around him, and donated gold rings, golden hairpins, etc. in spite of the difficult circumstances. It was a gesture in support of my father's leadership and work. My father thankfully accepted the gifts and promptly gave all of them to local officials to be used for helping flood victims. My father had never spent even a single penny for his own well-being.

Joining the National Army

I entered the National Army on August 23, 1948. Before the establishment of the Republic of Korea on August 15, 1948, there was only the South Korean National Constabulary. With the formal establishment of the South Korean state, the Republic of Korea Armed Forces consisting of an army and a navy was established. But Korea had a long way to go in terms of establishing the foundations of a real national military. Although I was a pilot, I could not join the air force because there was no separate, independent air force at the time. The air wing of the armed forces belonged to the army or navy in the forms of an army air force and a naval air force. It was not until October 1, 1949 when an independent air force was established. When I first joined the armed forces, I was assigned to the Army Air Force. Most of those who applied for the Army Air Force were those Koreans who had worked for the Japanese Air Force. Only a few of us had a Chinese background like me.

Before I went to China to collect the remains of deceased Koreans, I used to frequent Mr. Jang Deok-chang at his house in the Gwanghwamun crossroads together with some folks who had been in the Japanese Air Force. Mr. Jang had flown civilian airplanes, and his aviation skills were so excellent that the president of a Japanese airliner had his daughter married to him. He came back to Korea with his Japanese wife when the war was over. Since he had nothing particular to do in Korea, however, he earned a living by selling cigarettes and other small items from his house.

We occasionally gathered in Mr. Jang's house for overnight meetings during which we talked about what we might do together when the national armed forces would finally be established. It was in the middle of those days when I went to China to find the remains of deceased Koreans. When I returned from my trip, the people whom I met with before were receiving military training in Susaek, Seoul. When I, too, went to Susaek to receive training, Captain James Hausman, U.S. Military Advisor to the Commander of the National Constabulary, asked me if I had a certificate to prove that I had received pilot training in America. I, of course, answered in the affirmative and presented credentials. I was duly commissioned to the rank of second lieutenant.

The air base used by the Army Air Force at the time was located in Yoido. It had an aircraft hangar used by the Japanese Air Force, buildings for repairing aircraft, and a sports ground. When the U.S. Air Force withdrew from Kimpo Air Base, the Americans handed over the residence buildings where families of the U.S. servicemen had lived. Thereafter, the Korean service men of the Army Air Force could invite their families to live in these facilities.

Flying under the Han River Bridge

When the U.S. Air Force left Korea, it left us their aircrafts. They were the L-4 model, which could be disassembled into three parts: the engine, the body, and the wings. Thus, it could be stored in a big box. In short, it was a self-assembly aircraft. Its maximum speed was about as fast as that of a car speeding down a highway. The L-5, which we were to receive later, was only slightly faster than the L-4. The L-4 was no different from a glider with an engine.

The L-4 aircraft had the roundels of the U.S. Air Force on their wings and bodies. We began to change them into our own roundels featuring the Taegeuk (Yin-yang) insignia of the Korean national flag. Taking a close look at the U.S. roundel, we realized that it would take a lot of work to rub them out completely and replace them with the Korean insignia. So, we decided to modify the U.S. roundel into Korean ones. The U.S. roundel was a white star in a circular field flanked by a red stripe on each side. We left the stripes intact and just changed the white star into the Taegeuk mark.

One started the engine of the L-4 by spinning the propeller by hand. Still, it was special feeling to fly an aircraft featuring the Taegeuk mark. I think I might not have been so happy if I had grown up in Korea. It was my lifelong dream to be a soldier of the Republic of Korea and to wear the military uniform of the Republic of Korea and fly an aircraft with the insignia of the Republic of Korea. As it had remained my dream since the day I visited the Mirim Air Base in Pyongyang on my school trip that was made possible by my classmate's parents, the emotion that swept over me as I flew an aircraft with the Taegeuk insignia was beyond expression.

I flew my aircraft over Seoul and its vicinity every day. One day, I was flying low over the sand beach of the Han River. The Han River Bridge came into sight, and I flew my aircraft under the bridge. I did it in heightened emotional state, I was so overwhelmed by flying an aircraft featuring the Taegeuk mark. I did it two or three more times. But some people saw it and told what they saw to other people. My "feat," which never came out in the press, was to be known not only in Korea but even abroad.

General Kim Jeong-ryeol, too, saw me passing underneath the bridge while on his way to work in his Jeep that morning. He had been a captain in the Japanese Air Force and had participated in the war in the Southeast Asia theater as a fighter pilot. When I returned to the Yoido base, there he was waiting for me. He asked me where I learned to fly and told me that he saw me fly under the bridge. He then reprimanded me, saying that I should not fly an aircraft under a bridge ever again.

Strictly speaking, flying an aircraft under a bridge was a violation of the military code liable to criminal prosecution. General Kim pointed out that a pilot should never engage in such an act because it was dangerous not only to the pilot but to others a well. As my punishment, I was barred from flying for a month. This story had never been made public or conveyed to the press. But when I attended a Children's *Paikbum IlJi: Kim Koo's Autobiography* essay contest for children a few years ago, however, a child came up to me and asked,

"Grandfather, did you really fly an airplane under the Han River Bridge long ago?"

When I answered yes, he became overjoyed and asked me to take a picture with him. Another time, when President Roh Moo Hyun visited the Kim Koo Museum and Library, he asked me,

"General Kim. Is it really true that you flew a plane under the Han River Bridge as a young pilot?"

I had not flown under the bridge in order to brag about my flying skills. I myself knew very well that flying in such a way was dangerous. Far be it for me to show off by pulling dangerous stunts. I did it only because I could not suppress the joy that came over me as I flew an aircraft with the mark of the Republic of Korea over the skies of the Republic of Korea.

My Activities in the Army Air Force

The Army Air Force was first based in the Yoido Air Base, but moved to the Kimpo Air Base before returning to Yoido again. It had three squadrons at the time. Although at the time we did not have enough aircraft to create three full squadrons, the planners did so in preparation for an increase in the number of aircraft. I was assigned the third squadron commander position. Kim Yeong-hwan, General Kim Jeong-ryeol's younger brother, was the first squadron commander. I remember that he had not had a lot of flight experience before then. The second squadron commander was Jang

Seong-hwan, who graduated from Waseda University and had mainly flown transport planes rather than fighter planes.

While the Army Air Force was getting itself into order, the April 3 Incident broke out in Jeju Island. We flew L-5's from Yoido to the island for reconnaissance and scattering leaflets. We were also sent for the Yeosu-Suncheon Incident and carried out the same tasks. Occasionally, we transported important persons, too. Since we did not have any armed aircraft, we could not carry out anything beyond transportation and non-lethal operations. Later, we took part in the Ongjin battles. Since Korea was divided into South and North, both of which had its own government, in those days small skirmishes and larger battles broke out frequently. We also scattered anti-Communist leaflets over Haeju flying by night.

President Chiang Kai-Shek visited Jinhae in August 1949. In name, the purpose of his visit was to promote the establishment of the Asian Nations' Anti-Communist League, but his real agenda was something else. I met with him in lieu of my father, as Chiang's visit took place soon after my father's assassination. The real purpose of his visit was to borrow Korean troops. At the time, the Guomindang army was on the verge of defeat by the Communist forces. Since the Communists had pushed the Guomindang forces down south by deploying ethnic Koreans troops in Manchuria at the forefront, Chiang tried to follow suit and counter with ROK troops at the frontlines.

Had my father, who was close to President Chiang, been living at the time, I wonder what kind of judgment he would have made and how he would have responded. The truth is, South Korea could not afford to lend its troops to Chiang because it itself was in a standoff with North Korea across the 38th parallel. One year later, North Korea invaded the South, bringing about the tragedy of an internecine war.

Chapter 8

What's There to Say Now That You Are Gone?

A Preventable Assassination

As the 38ᵗʰ parallel became consolidated as a de facto border, my father and his former colleagues of the Korean Provisional Government made every effort to unite the two Koreas divided into South and North.

"Paikbum was used by the Communist party," some said, however.

"Paikbum must harbor a personal desire to be the president of the South."

When my father took part in a memorial service for the patriotic martyr Yun Bong-Gil upon returning to Korea, he suggested that we should repeat the phrase "Let us love our country in pain or pleasure" from the fourth verse of the national anthem.

"Father, why are you suggesting that we sing the line one more time?" I asked.

"You must love your country not only when you feel happy, comfortable or well but also when you feel pain, hurt or bad. I was able to persevere in fighting abroad on behalf of Korea's freedom and endure all hardship in prison or any other circumstance because I believed that one's love of my country must never waiver. It is not true love of your country to love it only when you are well and to betray it and sell it down the river when you are sad, tired, hungry or cold," my father said.

That was how my father felt about his beloved nation at all times. Who are these people who say that my father betrayed the Korean nation for his own personal ambitions following Korea's liberation? Do they know anything about him? Do they know that he had devoted himself to the Korean independence movements with a single-minded devotion to his nation? He knew very well the intentions of the North's Communist party. But he had witnessed the Chinese tragedy of internecine warfare between the Nationalists and the Communists. All he could do was employ any means to try to prevent such an internecine war from breaking out in liberated Korea.

My father went to Pyongyang to prevent at least the establishment of a separate government in the South. He knew this would be a formidable task, as various factions of the independence movement were converging in Pyongyang. Kim Du-bong and Kim Yak-san, who had been active in Chongqing, but also political forces from Yanan were now also in North Korea. Today, some historians argue that my father tried to do what was "impossible," that he was "insufficiently prepared," or that he "did not understand" the international situation. But I believe that the most pressing task of the day was to prevent the establishment of a separate government in the South alone, which could only seal the division. The precarious situation did not allow for weighing this and that.

To speak frankly, Syngman Rhee played a role in shaping the negative public opinion on my father. At the time Rhee returned to Korea, he did not have a firm political base. In contrast, the Korean Resistance Party, of which my father was a member, enjoyed considerable support in Seoul and many other regions. Dr. Rhee knew very well that he had no choice but to cooperate with the party. As my father made every effort to establish a single government over the entire Korean peninsula, Rhee came forward and strongly argued for the establishment of a separate government in South Korea, criticizing my father for going down an impossible path.

The Special Committee for the Investigation of Anti-National Activities was created by the demand of the majority of the people. The committee arrested one pro-Japanese collaborator after another. But the pro-Japanese policeman No Deok-sul, who was notorious for having arrested and tortured Korean patriots as a high-level detective under the Japanese colonial rule, visited Dr. Rhee and asked him to stop the activities of the committee in return for support from him and his cronies. Rhee took this up and disbanded and disarmed the committee. Eventually, the nationwide effort to punish pro-Japanese collaborators fizzled out.

As events unfolded in this manner, the pro-Japanese forces became more and more arrogant. Ahn Du-hui, who shot my father, was only a pawn. The assassination of my father was the result of an elaborate conspiracy by pro-Japanese forces in political circles, the military, and the national police. In fact, my father's assassination was wholly preventable. As the political situation turned serious, people began to talk a lot about the growing political circumstances that were unfavorable to my father.

One day, a young man in the Northwest Youth Association informed Park Dong-yeop, the provost of Daegwang Middle School, of a plot to assassinate my father. Mr. Park in turn informed Kim Seung-hak of this plot. Mr. Kim had played various roles in the Korean independence movement by creating a liaison organization for the Korean Provisional Government, raising war funds, and recruiting hundreds of patriotic young men into the Korean Liberation Army. He met with my father the day before the assassination.

"Paikbum, you are in danger. People say that wicked bastards have planned to assassinate you. You should go abroad for a while."

"Don't say such things that are unnecessary. How can I leave my fatherland now after having longed for its freedom for so long?" said my father, rejecting Kim Seung-hak's advice.

Mr. Kim came to see me after he failed to persuade my father. He said,

"It seems that something serious is about to happen before long." He told me that I should try to persuade my father to be voluntarily hospitalized, which would provide him some security. He also said that my father should refrain from going out to places where big crowds gathered.

"Father, you'd better go to a hospital for the time being as things don't look good," I implored him, greatly concerned.

He was adamant. "I have never been afraid of such things my entire life. I will do what I have to do even if my neck breaks tomorrow."

Nobody could break his stubbornness.

The next day, I escorted the UN Temporary Commission on Korea. The commission was dispatched by the UN to investigate the escalating stand off between the South and North, including the serious skirmishes in the Ongjin area. I escorted the commission on an airplane to go on a field investigation. Not long after we arrived at our destination, our interpreter Yi Su-yeong hurried over to me. He told me to go back to Seoul immediately because something urgent seemed to have transpired. I said to myself as soon as I heard it.

"Oh, no! It's finally happened."

My Father's Funeral

From Ongjin I piloted a plane myself to return to Seoul. My original plan was to go directly to the Yoido Air Base. But it occurred to me that I should first fly over Gyeong Gyo Jang first. Looking down from the sky, the road leading up to our house and the front yard were dotted with people in funeral white. I realized there and then that something really serious had transpired. I grew emotional, on the verge of tears.

The time it took for me to get from the Yoido Air Base to Gyeong Gyo Jang was the longest time I had to endure in my whole life, although the time it took to travel the distance by car was not all that long. I arrived at last and ran upstairs where my father's body had been placed. Mourners flowed in an endless stream. As there were simply too many mourners filing in, we decided to move my father's

My father's funeral
Members of the Women's Patriotic Association are mourning on June 27, 1949,
the day after my father's assassination.

body to a more spacious room down in the basement. But before moving his body, we held a coffin ritual in the reception room on the first floor.

Catholic priests, Buddhist monks, and Protestant pastors performed rituals one by one. The chief of Saint Mary's Hospital, Dr. Park Byeong-rae, together with other priests and nuns, first performed a Catholic ritual before other religious figures arrived. Monks then performed a Buddhist ritual in the front yard, followed by a Christian ritual by Protestant ministers. After watching the Catholic ritual over my father's coffin, I moved my father down to the basement.

Regarding plans for my father's funeral, people from the Korean Resistance Party and key figures of the Korean Provisional Government discussed the procedures. In the middle of the discussion, Minister of Finance Kim Do-yeon and Minister of Commerce and Industry Im Yeong-sin showed up as representatives of the government. They told us that it had been decided at the cabinet meeting that my father would be given a state funeral and that the government would pay for the funeral expenses. I remember that the funeral expenses were approximately nine million won, and that about two-thirds of the costs were defrayed by the government. Upon hearing their words, Jo Wan-gu exploded in anger.

"You bastards! You murdered him, and now you offer him a state funeral? Just go to hell!"

The meeting place turned into bedlam. I was choked up again. What Mr. Jo had said was precisely in line with the public's view on my father's assassination. After people calmed Mr. Jo down, we

My father's coffin borne out on July 5, 1949

resumed discussing the procedures for the funeral. While some argued for a state funeral, others made a case for an "ethnonational" funeral. The final conclusion reached was a state-ethnonational funeral in consideration of both views.

Syngman Rhee came with his wife, Madam Francesca Donner, to pay his respects, too. It was around 9:50 AM on July 4, one day before the send-off ceremony of the deceased upon the completion of the ten-day funerary period. Dr. Rhee briefly bowed to the portrait of my deceased father and shook hands with me and then left. Later I learned that a false rumor had gone around at the time, that Dr. Rhee was the first to come to Gyeong Gyo Jang upon hearing the news of my father's assassination and had told me that he would heretofore look after me as his adopted father. The truth was that he came only at the last day of the funerary period and only perfunctorily shook hands with me before leaving.

When my father was shot to death, my wife was six months pregnant. Father had taken his daughter-in-law to an obstetrical clinic near the Bank of Korea to ascertain whether the baby was a boy or girl. An obstetrician told him that it was a boy. He was very pleased to have a grandson who would carry on the family line. He was concerned that his pregnant daughter-in-law may overexert herself somehow and endure a difficult pregnancy. He repeatedly asked her to stay home and rest.

"My dear, try not to do much work around the house and get plenty of rest."

My father, who loved his daughter-in-law and his grandson inside her womb, was killed before he was able to meet his first grandson. I was overcome with a regret and grief which tore my heart apart. After the public funeral, people shouldered the bier and walked to the Dongdaemun Stadium. A huge crowd gathered along the roads. There had not been a bigger funeral since the establishment of the Republic of Korea. When the bier left, my pregnant wife tried to followed it from behind. But friends and family members managed to persuade her to rest at home.

I stood in front of the bier, while distant relatives followed it next to me. Students marched along the flanks of the bier, while a military band marched at the head of the procession. My father's car followed slowly at the back of the bier. The Dongdaemun Stadium was filled to capacity. Several people gave funeral addresses. The address that touched people's hearts the most was Eom Hangseop's:

Oh, teacher! Our teacher! What's there to say now that you are gone? All we can do is wail. We weep and weep and we have nothing to say but to speak with our tears. Heaven sent you to this land with the mandate to deliver this nation. Hence, you knew only suffering and persecution throughout the seventy-four years of life on earth. You gave up your youth, fame, prosperity, and comfort and lived only for the liberation of the fatherland with a single-minded devotion while wandering in remote foreign lands.

What's there to say now that you are gone? All we can do is wail. We weep and weep and we have nothing to say but to speak with our tears.

Here, for a moment, we think of the phrase, "The moon rises high in the sky and shines over a thousand rivers." Come to think of it, you are certainly not gone. You live in every heart of thirty million compatriots. Though your fleeting body has returned to earth and your soul has gone up to Heaven's paradise, your will and spirit will forever live with this nation and its history.

Oh, teacher! Before your great spirit, we solemnly pledge to fulfill our beautiful and noble duty as believers in you by honoring your will, following your footsteps, and living for the nation to the very last moment of our lives.

The government supplied pistols to the policemen guarding the bier at the day of the funeral procession for fear of possible riots. It also placed an armored vehicle at every strategic corner in the vicinity. Around the Seoul Train Station armored vehicles equipped with loaded machine guns were placed. It might as well have been martial law. Although so many people came from provincial areas to take part in the funeral, the government went so far as to block them halfway.

After my father's death, I was persistently checked and pressured by invisible forces. One day, when I went to clean my father's grave, I found detectives checking the identities of everyone on their way to the grave. They even tried to check mine.

"You bastards! Don't you have your own father and mother? How dare you harass me when I am visiting my own father's grave? Who ordered you to do this?" I yelled at them in indignation.

"We are just doing as we were told by our boss," they mumbled, taking a step back.

The pro-Japanese forces began to harass the members of the Korean Resistance Party as soon as my father was gone. They built a database on all party members, including even those residing in the countryside. They then branded the party as a pro-communist on the grounds that it had led the South-North talks.

There was a lot of important information kept in Gyeong Gyo Jang. The organization charts and member lists of the local branches of the party, oaths written in blood by party members, and even severed fingers preserved in bottles filled with alcohol sent by members were kept in the basement.

The most important pieces of information were the ones related to the party organization. I thought that all party members would be arrested if I had kept the entire organization charts and member list intact. So, I incinerated all the data related to the party in the boiler room in the basement. If I had not done this, more people might have suffered persecution. Although Kim Hak-gyu, the director of the organization bureau of the party, is commonly known to have burned the data, it was, in fact, I.

When people were being rounded up and forcibly enrolled in the National Guidance Alliance, which was created to reeducate leftists, many members of the Korean Resistance Party were targeted, as they were considered not different from the communists. One of them was Shin Hyeon-sang, who paid frequent visits to Gyeong Gyo Jang. Shin was an anarchist. The real reason why he was forcibly thrown into the alliance and later killed was that he knew exactly who the pro-Japanese collaborators were. When many members of the alliance were massacred in Daejeon Prison during the Korean War, all the imprisoned Korean Resistance Party members forcibly enrolled in the alliance were also killed. Mr. Shin was one of them.

After the funeral, I sorted through my father's belongings. I gave away his clean clothes to those in need of them. When I opened his briefcase, I found it was empty. When he was still living, many a time his briefcase was filled with cash. But before long, it would invariably be all gone. Occasionally, there was gold inside. That would also disappear before too long. When I asked why, father answered that he had given it all away to his comrades who were worse off than he.

My father had no desire for wealth or power. I think that was why he could lead the Korean Provisional Government. While numerous factions fought one another to seize the leadership of the independent movement, they—even the communists—eventually came to appreciate my father's sincerity and came together to unite under father's leadership in the common cause of anti-Japanese resistance.

As my father had, I, too, lived under poor conditions since my childhood. I took it as my destiny. What is the point of living rich to someone who has been deprived of his state? It is a great blessing for one to have one's own country, whether it is big or small, rich or poor.

From Gyeong Gyo Jang to Geum Hwa Jang

Gyeong Gyo Jang, where my father and key figures of the Korean Provisional Government had put up upon their return to Korea, was a house under the ownership of Choi Chang-hak, who had run a big business during Japanese colonial rule. He lent his house to the incoming former Korean Provisional Government officials for free. But now that my father had passed away, it was time to return the house to its rightful owner. Although Mr. Choi did not ask me to leave, I felt like a fish out of water, living in the big house without my father's presence. As I was contemplating where my wife and I should move to, the Chinese Consul General in Korea, Mr. Liu Yuwan, offered timely help.

During the U.S. occupation of southern Korea, the U.S. Military Government in Korea had managed the properties left behind by the Japanese, that is, "enemy properties." When the U.S. withdrew in 1948, it vested them in the newly-established Republic of Korea government. U.S. Military leaders had occupied the relatively better-preserved buildings and left them in good condition. Returning exiles like Dr. Kim Kyu-sik were also provided with "enemy property" as they did not have any place to live in. Consul General Liu Yuwan, too, had asked the U.S. military government to provide him a suitable building for the Chinese Consulate General and had received a house called Geum Hwa Jang, which was located around the Seodaemun crossroads. It used to be a house owned by a Japanese person who had run a construction company. In its immediate vicinity were houses that had belonged to the employees of the construction company.

When my father needed to get in touch with someone in China, he usually did through Consul General Liu in his Consulate General, Geum Hwa Jang. On many occasions he spoke on the telephone with influential Chinese persons including President Chiang Kai-Shek at Geum Hwa Jang. Mr. Liu enthusiastically helped my father since he well knew of the special friendship between my father and Chiang Kai-Shek. But there came a time when Mr. Liu had to leave Korea, as his new assignment was announced, which was the United Nations headquarters in New York. Well aware that I was about to move out of Gyeong Gyo Jang, Mr. Liu told me that I could stay at Geum Hwa Jang once he left. I was thankful and moved in. But I did not know that the house was government property.

Neither did I know that someone had had her eyes on the property even before Mr. Liu's Consulate General had moved into it. It was none other than Syngman Rhee's wife, First Lady Francesca. She had visited the house the first time when Americans had lived there and had wished to move in herself after they had left. But she had not been able to act upon her wish for various reasons. However, it seemed that she had rekindled her wish now that the Consul General of China had left Korea and I had moved in.

One day, as my wife and I were living at Geum Hwa Jang with our newborn child, Minister of National Defense Shin Seong-mo dispatched his secretary to me. He recommended that I leave Geum Hwa Jang and move to a new house in Noryangjin which Minister Shin had arranged for me. The house recommended by Mr. Shin, which was on the hill, had been inhabited by a Japanese doctor who had used it as a clinic. I told the minister's secretary that I would not move. Later, even though Minister Shin came to me in person and asked me to leave, I adamantly refused.

I had good reason not to be pushed out of Geum Hwa Jang. First of all, I had legal rights. The Korean government routinely sold enemy properties to civilians through auction. Should there be an occupant living in the property at the time of the auction, the occupant had the first priority. Legally, therefore, I had priority rights to Geum Hwa Jang, should there be an auction for it. It was unreasonable to evict an occupant of a property over which he had priority rights. Second, I did not want to be pushed out by government forces as my father had been shot and killed to a great extent due to the government's connivance and willful neglect.

Since First Lady Francesca had her eyes on Geum Hwa Jang, the government continued to press me to leave the house. But I stood my ground to the end, until 1962. By then Rhee had been thrown out of power and I was able to go through the legal process and purchase the house from the government, and finally register the house under my name.

Besides First Lady Francesca, there was another person who had his eyes set on Geum Hwa Jang. It was Kim Yong-u, who served as the Minister of National Defense for two years under Rhee, from 1956 to 1958. Mr. Kim, who lived in Ahyeon-dong, Seodaemun, was looking for a house where he could host parties for foreign generals. He liked Geum Hwa Jang so much that he tried to register it as the official residence of the Minister of National Defense. The Director of General Affairs of the Defense Ministry visited me virtually every day and tried to bluff me into letting go of the house, I was absolutely determined to say no. After all, I had not yielded even to pressure from the president. I was not about to fold under pressure from a Defense Minister.

However, there was a time when I had no choice but to leave Geum Hwa Jang. It was during the Korean War. When the North Korean Army occupied Seoul, the Soviet military advisory group occupied my house. Until then, I had arranged all of my father's tables and chairs and placed his writing brushes in the same he had when he was living. I learned later that North Korean soldiers put seals on all the articles left by my father. When I returned after the war, I found Geum Hwa Jang in a severely damaged state. The First Lady only gave up on it after hearing about the extent of the damage.

Conversation with President Syngman Rhee

As First Lady Francesca was pressuring me to leave my house through Defense Minister Shin, I thought I should go and visit President Rhee. It took a long while for me to hear back once I submitted a request for a meeting with President Rhee. I finally got an appointment. When I went to the Blue House, Kim Jang-heung and Gwak Yeong-ju, who were President Rhee's longtime bodyguards, received me. They had me searched from my head to my toes. They suspected that I might be carrying a weapon.

"What are you guys doing?" I asked, clearly showing I was offended.

"We can't help it but abide by official regulations. Things are now different as he is now the head of the state," they answered unapologetically.

The first topic I brought up when I met President Rhee was the inspection I had been subjected to on my way to visit my father's grave.

"It is already so infuriating that my father had to die so tragically. And now, this? Every single person who is on his way to pay respects at my father's grave has to be inspected one by one? Even I was checked."

When I finished, President Rhee called in his chief secretary and asked him if what I had just said was true. He answered that he would look into it. Then I raised the Geum Hwa Jang issue.

"Uncle, do I not deserve to live there?"

I called President Rhee uncle rather than "Mr. President." I chose to, as he had treated me like a nephew in the past, and I thought addressing him "Mr. President" might create some distance between him and me. Rhee did not make an issue of my calling him uncle. He called in the chief secretary again and exchanged a few words with him. I saw his cheeks twitch as he talked to the chief secretary. Rhee had a habit of doing that when he was in a bad mood.

"People are saying a lot of things about you. I think you would benefit from going overseas. Why don't you go to the United Kingdom and study air force strategy some more. The UK now is a small country, but it has tradition. You may learn much by studying there. I will take care of your family while you study in the United Kingdom."

But I said in no uncertain terms that I would not go.

"Since I am the only person in the Korean Air Force who has received official pilot training in America, I should be training others who have not enjoyed such a privilege rather than going off overseas, don't you think? Moreover, I have already lived abroad too long. I feel infinitely honored to serve my country as a Korean serviceman."

Our conversation ended awkwardly in this way.

At that time, the director of the Seoul Police Department was Park Byeong-bae, who had served in the Japanese Army. The director of the Seoul Police was such a powerful position that he was on the friendly terms with people like Gwak Yeong-ju and Kim Jang-heung in the presidential mansion. When the government of the Democratic Party was established in the wake of the April 19, 1960 Uprising, Park became the Vice Minister of National Defense for political affairs, presumably because he had some connections to key members of the party. Since I became the Air Force Chief of Staff following the April righteous uprising, I had numerous occasions to visit the Ministry of National Defense. One day, I ran into Park. When he saw me, he recalled the days of the Rhee presidency and told me something I could not immediately comprehend.

"My heart beats faster whenever I see you, General Kim."

Not knowing what he meant, I asked him why.

He then confessed that as the director of the Seoul Police Department, he had secretly investigated who had planned and directed the annual "Air Force Day" celebrations. October 1 is currently celebrated as "Armed Forces Day." But in the 1950s, it was known as "Air Force Day." Each "Air Force Day," Air Force pilots made a formation flight over the sand beach of the Han River near the Han River Bridge. The planes also strafed and bombed model North Korean tanks. The ROK president attended the "Air Force Day" event each year without fail. Foreign diplomats and important officials were also in attendance, as were invitees from all walks of life, including students and soldiers.

Since it was I who planned and directed each year's "Air Force Day" event in those times, people in the presidential office were said to have been deeply concerned about possible accidents: they feared I might go berserk and drop napalm bombs on the riverbank. Park Byeong-bae told me that's why his heart beat faster each time he saw me even after so many years. I imagine that for Rhee, as he was constantly fed information of this sort about me, it made sense to wish I would be out of the country.

On the other hand, I don't necessarily want to jump to conclusion that he encouraged me to study in the United Kingdom just to be safe from an imagined attack from me. There is also the possibility that he was watching out for me, that he wanted to save the sole surviving son of Paikbum. He may have thought given the political mood of the day that had I remained in Korea, people would have been wary of me and may even try one day to get rid of me. His suggestion for me to go overseas was probably triggered by a combination of these considerations.

The "Plot" to Assassinate President Rhee

In the aftermath of my father's assassination, the agents of the intelligence bureau watched my every move. They checked who I contacted and who visited my house. When I went out, a jeep would always follow me. As much as they tried to conceal their identity, rotating agents and frequently showing up in different clothing, I could easily tell that I was being followed because their car was always a military vehicle.

To them, I was a major thorn in the side. They even made up an absurd report that I may be planning to fly an aircraft into North Korea. After that report was filed, I was barred from flying. I was literally grounded. After a while, I was sent off to the Army Infantry School in Siheung. I was pushed out of the Air Force not only because the intelligence bureau's machinations but also because there was a clique opposed to me inside the Air Force.

After I was driven out of the Air Force, I passed each day being extra cautious. Once I was home from work, I did not go out or meet anyone lest the authorities grow even more suspicious. One day, a young man of about thirty years in age who was quite shabbily dressed visited me. When I asked who he was, he answered that he had something to tell me in confidence in a quiet room. I took him inside.

"I was secretly sent to you by General Kim Il Sung. I came here with an important task," he said, looking around the room.

I found him a strange character. But I asked him to go on just to hear what he had to say.

Wearing a serious look, he said, "I am here to assassinate Syngman Rhee."

I was quite dumbfounded, but asked, "And how do you plan on doing this?"

"When his car passes through Gwanghwamun, I will block it with a truck and shoot him," he replied.

Clearly, his so-called plan was ridiculous. He went on,

"Since I crossed the 38th parallel on foot, I have hardly eaten or slept. I am sorry to visit you like this, as shabby as I look. I will return in three or four days. In the meantime, please prepare a little bit of money and a pistol for me."

He left in haste as soon as he was finished. I felt that something serious was about to take place. The next day, I requested a meeting with Defense Minister Shin Seong-mo and went to his official residence in Mapo. I told him about what had happened and asked him to provide me protection as I felt threatened. From that night onward, two agents of the intelligence bureau in plain clothes were stationed around the clock right next to my house.

During my visit with Defense Minister Shin, there was another guest in the living room. I could hear what he was saying, as there was only a thin partition between us. He was telling Mr. Shin to completely clean house and wipe out those who had participated in the independence movement under the Korean Provisional

Government. He even brought me up.

"We should completely root them out. If you leave Kim Shin alone, there may come one day unthinkable danger."

As Minister Shin knew I was there close to them, he told the other guest to keep quiet as somebody might hear him. The man who was speaking with Minister Shin was Choi Dal-ha. In China, Choi had purchased a state tobacco enterprise in Qingdao. He had tried to lead the activities of the Korean Mission to China in Nanjing in vain in the wake of the Korean Provisional Government's return to Korea, as came into conflict with Min Pil-ho, the deputy head of the mission. For this reason, he held a grudge against those who had engaged in the Korean independence movement abroad and was trying to persuade Minister Shin to repress independence fighters who had returned from abroad.

Defense Minister Shin Seong-mo himself had also spent much time living abroad. He had lived in Vladivostok and Shanghai and studied in the UK before acquiring the mate certificate of competency and traveling to many places around the world. Since Shin and I shared the common experience of individuals who had returned to Korea after much time abroad, there was a natural bond between us, although we would grow apart from each other in subsequent years due to various reasons.

The suspicious young man indeed came back to see me after a few days. This time, he was neatly dressed. As soon as he entered my house, the intelligence agents pounced on him, handcuffed him, and took him away. As Defense Minister Shin had hinted to me that all this may be a conspiracy against me, I watched closely over the wall the young man being led away. The agents and the young man were all giggling as they walked away. All this was indeed a conspiracy that the intelligence bureau had plotted to set me up. If the young man really had come from North Korea, his arrest would have made headlines in the newspapers. But there was not a single report of his arrest.

As I found out later, the mastermind of this plot was Kim Chang-ryong. He is also a key suspect behind the assassination of my father. A day after Kim was shot to death on January 30, 1956, President Rhee removed all the documents in Kim's office. I wondered just what was in those documents that the president had to dispose of them himself.

Given that the intelligence bureau had to set me up and that President Rhee had encouraged me to go abroad, I sensed that they would keep trying to get rid of me. I visited Dr. George Fitch, a former American missionary in China, who was in Korea at the time. Fitch had played an essential role in providing shelter for my father in the immediate aftermath of the patriotic deed by Yun Bong-Gil in Shanghai, 1932.

I asked him whether he could help me and arrange for me to go to America. Dr. Fitch asked me what was up. When I told him about my predicament, he became deeply concerned and expressed his deep sympathy and regrets. At the same time, he advised me to be patient and toughen it out, as I was still young and the political wind will in time blow over. He also pointed out that going abroad after being ostracized by my own government would only work against my long term interests. As much as I had misgivings about the safety of my family, I took Dr. Fitch's advice to heart and decided to stay in Korea.

Chapter 9

The Tragedy of Internecine War

The Korean War Breaks Out

On June 25, 1950, I was driving my father-in-law, my wife, and our son to Incheon to buy food in preparation for the first-anniversary memorial service for my father, which was the next day. As the anniversary drew nearer and nearer with each day, my heart felt heavier and heavier.

But Kim Si-yeol, who was my driving assistant, drove out to Incheon to find me and deliver the urgent news that a war had broken out. He told me that the Air Force headquarters had issued an order summoning everyone. After sending off my family to Geum Hwa Jang, I immediately went to the Yoido Air Base. Two North Korean Yaks were attacking the hangar and runway. Shells ricocheted off the ground and flew toward civilian houses. Soon, nearby residents came out to protest. Mistaking the situation as a training exercise, they complained that we were shooting in such a way that shells were flying to their houses. I told them that a war had broken out and that the bullets were being fired from communist fighters.

Soon, Air Force Chief of Staff Kim Jeong-ryeol arrived on the scene. General Kim told me that he had received an urgent message from General Douglas MacArthur's Supreme Allied Command asking how many pilots in the Korean Air Force could fly the F-51 Mustang. I reported to him that I had learned how to fly the Mustang in the U.S. Kim reported back to MacArthur's command that there was one pilot who could fly the Mustang and told me to go with him to the Suwon Air Base.

After briefly explaining what was going on to my family, I headed for the Suwon Air Base on June 26. A transport plane was waiting for me with the engine running. Ten pilots including me took the plane to the U.S. Air Base in Itazuke, Fukuoka, where we would receive training and then fly ten Mustangs back to Korea. The ten pilots were: Colonel Lee Geun-seok, Lieutenant Colonel Jang Seong-hwan, Lieutenant Colonel Kim Yeong-hwan, Lieutenant Colonel Kim Shin, Captain Gang Ho-ryun, Captain Park Hui-dong, First Lieutenant Kim Seong-ryong, First Lieutenant Jeong Yeong-jin, First Lieutenant Lee Sang-su, and First Lieutenant Jang Dong-chul.

When we arrived at the Itazuke Air Base, it was raining hard. We were very worried as poor weather was a big impediment to learning how to fly an unfamiliar warplane. Moreover, since most of us had flown only a Japanese aircraft, it remained to be seen whether we could learn how to fly an American aircraft within such a short period. Unaware of the situation, our compatriots back home had great expectations of us and wanted us to fly American fighters back to Korea as soon as possible.

To make matters worse, the last time that our American instructor had received flight training was more than ten years ago back in the U.S. He had not flown an aircraft recently. Hence, it was not surprising that he did not know the proper training methods and procedures. Fortunately, I had brought along the aviation training manual I had used during my training in America just in case. I gave our instructor a F-51 Mustang manual. He was very happy to get his hands on it and asked me to interpret what he said to the trainees and to give them a basic explanation on the aircraft.

Since beginners could not handle the Mustang right away, they flew on the training plane AT-6 with the instructor. They were supposed to grow accustomed to flying the training plane before actually flying a fighter, but there was no time for that. We received aviation training for fighters immediately after practicing just a few times take-off and landing with the AT-6. We had in mind flying the Mustangs back to Suwon or Kimpo following our truncated training, but Seoul fell to the North Korean invaders during our training. So, we flew to Daegu. It was July 2, 1950, a full week after the Korean War had broken out. It took at least a few months to properly learn to fly an American fighter, but we were put in actual combat missions after only a week, or, rather, four days, of training.

The next day after we arrived at the Daegu Air Base, I flew a fighter over the Chu-pung-ryeong valley and then toward the downtown Daejeon area in low-altitude flight. At the time, the government and the headquarters of the armed forces had relocated to Daejeon. General Kim Jeong-ryeol watched me flying the fighter and was excited to see that the long-awaited fighters had finally arrived. I flew my jet to the Yuseong Air Base. Although the runway was short and not even paved, I attempted a landing.

Flight training in War We were trained by a U.S. instructor in Japan before being provided with F-51s. I am third from the left in the back row. I took notes and served as the interpreter. If not for war, the prohibition on my flying may never have been lifted. At the time, the government viewed me in the cockpit of a jet as a potential threat.

Flying over Hyeonhae (Genkai) Sea   I took this picture of the ten of us flying F-51s back to Korea soon after take-off from a base in Japan.

Soldiers of the Air Force and an American military advisor, who had watched me land, gathered to see who had flown back the fighter. Shortly, General Kim came in a jeep, too. As soon as he saw me, he grew angry and yelled,

"How dare you attempt a landing on this poor runway?"

I replied calmly, "I took a chance as I am used to this model and also I thought that my landing here would help boost the troops' morale."

The Korean Air Force in War

A few days after we had arrived in Daegu, General Lee Eung-jun and the Governor of North Gyeongsang Province Jo Jae-cheon visited the air base and informed us that the North Korean Army was launching a river crossing operation in Chungju. They asked us to deter the operation as the North Korean Army otherwise would imminently cross the Mun-gyeong-sae-jae pass to enter North Gyeongsang Province. We replied that we were not tactically prepared for it. They nonetheless asked us to do it by all means as time was of the essence. After briefly conferring among ourselves, we decided first to go on a reconnaissance flight. It was decided that Jang Seong-hwan, Gang Ho-ryun, Jeong Yeong-jin, and I would go.

When the four of us flew out, we found the road down from Janghowon covered by a cloud of dust. It meant that there was big traffic down south. We looked down flying over the road in low altitude to ascertain whether the troops were ours or enemy troops.

Upon closer inspection, we saw North Korean soldiers jump down from trucks to escape into nearby fields and paddies. They then started firing machine guns at us. We fired back and destroyed several of their vehicles.

After a few sorties, an American advisory group came from the Itazuke Air Base to give advice on general aircraft management including arming, maintenance, refueling, loading and so on. In fact, Colonel Lee Geun-seok had been killed in action on July 4 while attacking North Korean tank troops in Suwon. His death was at least in part due to the fact that we had to fly unfamiliar aircraft after only a very short training. Thinking that at this rate, every single pilot would be killed before long, the Korean Air Force decided to withdraw fighters from the frontline and move them to Jeju Island. There, we all received supplemental training, while new pilots were trained.

Later, we also received additional training from time to time throughout the war because we had not received training on models other than the Mustang. Our supplemental training took place at the Yokota Air Base in Japan. There, we also received "link" training. A link referred to a sealed room made out to the shape of a cockpit with the same dashboard as in a real cockpit. Looking at the dash board, we practiced how to prepare for all the different situations that could happen in a real situation.

We were also trained to exactly observe the instructor's directions on lowering and elevating the altitude of the aircraft. We lowered or elevated the altitude by specified height every one or five minutes, doing exactly as we were told. This training is important because

Pyongyang Bombing ROK fighter planes were about to take off for the third raid on Pyongyang, on August 29, 1952. It involved 1080 aircraft, including 36 ROK F-51s.

lowering or elevating the altitude abruptly causes the aircraft to lose speed. It is like the engine of a car stopping when one does not shift gear properly when climbing up a hill.

We also went to Japan several times to fly back the aircraft offered by the U.S. Air Force. We picked them up from the Kisarazu Naval Base in the Tokyo Bay. The U.S. Navy would dismantle the aircraft into its components–propeller, wings, and body–and transport them to Japan on an aircraft carrier, as carrying the whole aircraft on the deck of an aircraft carrier might cause it to be corroded by sea salt. We would wait in a hotel for American soldiers in downtown Tokyo before being informed that the assembling work was finished for us to pick up the planes. We then flew them back to Korea to the Sacheon Air Base.

The U.S. Army called the Sacheon Air Base K-4. Since it was difficult for Americans to pronounce and remember Korean names and geographical locations, they called Korean air bases by adding numbers to the letter K. K-1 was the Kimhae Air Base; K-2 the Daegu Air Base; K-3 the Pohang Air Base; K-4 the Sacheon Air Base, and so on. Suwon Air Base was called K-13, while the Osan Air Base, which was used by the U.S. forces, was called K-55. K-16 was the Yoido Air Base, while K-18 was the Gangneung Air Base, which was used as a base when we advanced into North Korea.

Going to Gyeongju with the Army

By the time we were ready to fly sorties in full force, the war had turned against us. The North Korean Army had advanced down to Daegu, Yeongcheon, and Pohang. I was assigned to Gyeongju to assist the army, and carried out reconnaissance missions. I flew a reconnaissance aircraft along the east coast up to Yeongdeok and Gangneung. When the republic of Korea troops pushed up to the north, I flew up to Wonsan and Hamheung.

In Hamheung, I happened to meet Park Eun-sik's son, Park Si-chang, a colonel at the time. Colonel Park was part of the civic action staff at the First Corps at the time and later played a major role in the Heungnam evacuation. As can be seen in the case of Park Si-chang, former soldiers of the Korean Liberation Army were likely to be excluded from the combat branch, while former soldiers of the Japanese Army made up its mainstream.

I was dispatched to the army because of an incident in Daegu Air Base. When I worked at the base, I frequently saw local Daegu officers use military jeeps to drive around their families. This made me angry because while troops from other regions were desperate to know if their families were dead or alive, the local officers were using military vehicles for personal use. So, together with some colleagues, we beat up a few of those Daegu officers to teach them a lesson.

But Defense Minister Shin Seong-mo and the Chief of Staff happened to see the Daegu officers' faces all bruised and swollen. Among those beaten there was the younger brother of the Chief of Staff. In the end, we were imprisoned in a military police jail and demoted by one rank. Those imprisoned with me were the first company commander Kim Yeong-hwan and the second company commander Jang Seong-hwan. Due to this incident, I was dispatched to the First Corps of the army and was relegated to flying not a fighter but a light aircraft to carry out transport and reconnaissance.

While I was in Gyeongju, the war situation turned urgent. North Korean troops were getting close to the city. South Korean troops took station on the peaks surrounding Gyeongju for defense. However, there was constant fluctuation in the fortune on the battlefield. The peaks would be occupied by South Korean troops during the day and by North Korean troops at night. Thus, the army frequently requested support from the air force. Since the front line was in such chaos, however, unintended bombings on our own forces occasionally took place. Moreover, American pilots were frequently confused about the names of places such as Jeonju, Cheongju, Chungju, Jinju, and so forth. To them, these names all but sounded the same and their similar spellings did not help, either. So, South Korean troops marked their areas by placing red signs on the ground.

However, once the North Korean troops took notice of this, they followed suit.

To counter this move by the north, the South Korean troops began air-ground joint operation exercises. These were exercises where the army and air force carried out an operation together, communicating with each other by radio. For example, artillery units would shoot white or red smoke bombs to an area to be air-raided and contact the air force by radio. But, once again, the North Korean troops came to be aware of this, and started monitoring our radio. They would shoot smoke bombs to our locations as our aircraft approached. U.S. bombers then would mistake our troops for the enemy and drop napalm on our troops. A napalm bomb caused such enormous flames and rapid rise in temperature that even tanks could not stand the heat. In these circumstances, there were more than a few cases in which the army and the air force were not in synch.

The worst was friendly fire involving civilians. To the west of Angang leading up to Yeongcheon was the Hagok Reservoir. Refugees usually traveled along the roads in between fields and paddies and avoid big roads traversed by vehicles. As I flew a light aircraft over it on a reconnaissance mission, I saw refugees gathered near the reservoir. I also saw two U.S. Mustangs fly by behind my aircraft.

Amid the mayhem I could not see at first what had just happened. Later I learned that they had taken off to bomb napalm on throngs of what turned out to be refugees. Innocent refugees were bombed out of the blue. U.S. pilots, who were all of a sudden thrust into war and wholly new to Korea, were unfamiliar with the terrain and faced difficulty in identifying enemy combatants. In the end, missions that relied solely on coordinates begot innocent victims due to the inability to distinguish between friend and foe. Witnessing such problems first-hand, I advocated the implementation of mobile Airborne Forward Air Controller system in order to minimize civilian collateral damage.

In 2009, the Truth and Reconciliation Committee confirmed based on the U.S. Army Air Force Mission Reports that the 39th bombing squad of the 18th fighter-bomber squadron of the U.S. Air Force strafed the refugees gathering on the banks of the Gigye River in Angye-ri, Gandong-myeon, Gyeongju, on August 14, 1950. Unfortunately, this could not have been the sole unintended tragedy and misery of this war.

When I was in Gyeongju, I stayed in the house of a section chief of the tax bureau with a few other air force officers. He had fled south and left the house vacant. Actually, all civilians in Gyeongju had been displaced by then. What they found when they returned were badly damaged houses in which virtually nothing was left intact. But the house of the section chief where I stayed sustained little damage because we protected and maintained it until he came back. All we did was eat a few chickens in the backyard.

Retrieving My Father's Car

When the First Corps advanced north and occupied Gangneung, aircraft could not take off from or land at the Gangneung Air Base, because its runway had been damaged by gunfire from U.S. Navy

My Father's Car My niece, Kim Hyo-Ja, standing in front of my father's car.

ships. Since I piloted a light aircraft, however, I could use a temporary air base near the city and continue my reconnaissance missions.

Upon recapturing Gangneung, the Republic of Korea forces continued to advance north up to Haegeumgang, Wonsan, and Hamheung. I flew into North Korean territory as well, but was soon told to return to Seoul. When I first reported to Wonsan Air Base, I spotted a C-54 U.S. transport plane that was about to head back to Seoul after having transported tank fuel to Wonsan. I walked up to it, wanting to ask the pilot if he could haul my Jeep back to Seoul.

A U.S. officer then approached me and asked if he could check out my handgun. It was a Soviet handgun that I had found on the battlefield. The officer asked for how much would I sell him the gun. I asked if he would be willing to transport my Jeep in exchange for the handgun, which he agreed to. I flew my aircraft back to Yoido and found my driver and my Jeep waiting for me, as the transport plane had arrived first.

At my house in Seoul I found that my family had come back after fleeing Seoul. My wife recounted what the family had gone through and asked me why I had been demoted. I was surprised she knew of it. It turned out that she had tenaciously asked after me to all the families of the troops that were on the front lines who had returned to Seoul. As the war situation had become critical, I had not been able to stay in close touch with my family. Other than the fact that they had fled Seoul, I had not known anything about how they were faring, nor had I tried to find out. In a sense, I had been a heartless husband and father.

A short time after I returned to Seoul, my troops were called to advance into to Pyongyang. I took command of an air force ground troops unit in Yoido and led it to Pyongyang by land. On the way, I saw an army officer towing a car which was connected to another car by cable. The car being towed looked like my father's. It had the numbers 2331 on its license plate, which add up to nine, or *gu* (a homonym of my father's first name). It was indeed my father's car. I talked to the army officer.

"This car belongs to my family. How come you are in possession of it?"

"This is a car that General Choi Yeong-hui took from the enemy."

After verifying to the officer that the car was my father's, I got the car back from him and took it with me to Pyongyang. In Pyongyang, I brought the car into an airplane hangar and did some repairs.

But the car would not start no matter what I tried. I just had to leave it sitting in Pyongyang. Later, when our troops retreated from Pyongyang, I had the car towed back south.

When I returned to Seoul, I met with my father's former driver, Jeong Tae-hun and told him what had happened. He smiled and explained that he had fitted a device that prevented the car from starting so that no one else could take it. Finding my father's car in North Korea was close to a miracle. I was very grateful to Mr. Jeong. After I took back the car, I felt my father's presence in it. It felt almost as if I had been reunited with him.

China's Entry in the War and Parachute Letters

Once the Korean Army advanced into the North occupied Pyongyang, the ROK Air Force troops occupied the Mirim Air Base. Never in my wildest dreams did I think at this point in time that we would be retreating from the city very shortly thereafter. Even General MacArthur had believed that the war would soon be over and all U.S. troops would be home by Christmas. The Korean forces pushed all the way up to the Amnok (Yalu) River, while the U.S. forces all the way up to the Duman (Tumen) River. However, the unexpected involvement of the Chinese communist forces forced us to retreat.

Many of the Chinese soldiers who participated in the Korean War were those who had formerly served in the Chinese Nationalist (Guomindang) forces and had defected to the Chinese Communist Party. There was an internal Chinese reason for this. During the

Chinese Civil War, the Chinese Communist Party waged against the Guomindang both a hardline and appeasement policies, inducing the defection of many troops. As the number of defectors grew, however, it became increasingly difficult for the communist party to give them the same treatment as it did to the original members of the People's Liberation Army. Furthermore, the defectors could not be completely trusted. Hence, the view grew within the Chinese Communist Party leadership that the hundreds of thousands of defectors needed to be somehow gotten rid of.

One solution that the party came up with was to dispatch them to Korea. Only one rifle was issued to every ten soldiers, because, if everyone was issued a rifle, party leaders, the muzzle may come to be pointed at them. Out of the ten soldiers, the soldier in the front carried the rifle, while the nine others followed him in a line. If the soldier carrying the rifle got killed, the next person in line picked it up and continued to press on. That was one way Beijing dealt with the Guomindang defectors.

There were many Guomindang defectors among the Chinese prisoners in the main Prisoners of War camp in Geoje Island, South Korea. Thus, many of the defectors in the camp wished to be repatriated to Taiwan at the end of the war. As much as China insisted that the Guomindang defectors had volunteered to participate in the war to assist North Korea, those who eventually were repatriated to Taiwan proved, through testimonials about their experiences in communist China, this claim to be false.

Through the Korean War, China was not only able to resolve the Guomindang defector issue, but also benefited from receiving the

Soviet Union's newest weapons. Beijing armed the People's Liberation Army with these Soviet weapons, while leaving the defectors with the outdated weapons used in China's anti-Japanese war and civil war.

While I stayed at Pyongyang Air Base, I flew to An-ak where I had lived as a boy. I looked down over the town, and saw that much of the old still remained. The Ansin School that I had attended was still standing exactly where it had been, and Sim Sang Elementary School, which many Japanese children had attended, was still there as well. Later, I took a Jeep to visit An-ak.

In An-ak, I met up with my former teachers and friends as well as some of my grandmother's old friends. I then crossed the river, either from Sincheon or Jaeryeong—I do not remember which it was— to look around a bit more. That's when I saw many corpses along the riverside. It was said that they were the bodies of North Korean communists. Once the Republic of Korea troops pushed north and approached the area, seeing that the status quo had changed, many of the villagers who had suffered under communist rule went after the local communists and killed them, even their families. According to Professor Shin Yong-ha, Professor Emeritus of Seoul National University, North Korea claims that these mass killings were carried out by U.S. troops. But as the U.S. Army used only main roads, they were never even near there.

During this time of back and forth on the battlefield, the South Korean Air Force took station at Gangneung and was charged with the mission of cutting off enemy supply lines and bridges as well as bombing key enemy facilities. But the army wanted the air force more to participate in its own operations in their battle fronts. The army considered the air force as artillery brigades, which was misguided. In strategic terms, it was much more important for the air force to cut enemy supply lines.

At that time, the army held the initiative when it came to military operations. It wanted all the other forces to unconditionally meet its demands. Strategically speaking, however, the quickest way of ending a war is to destroy the enemy's supplies base. It was due to this reason that the U.S. came up with the concepts of strategic and tactical air forces at the end of the Second World War. While the tactical air force mainly supports the army, the strategic air force flies far behind enemy lines to destroy its facilities for military supplies.

The efficacy of destroying facilities for military supplies behind enemy lines was proven by the U.S. during the Second World War. The U.S. government, upon consultation with business leaders, targeted oil production facilities and ball bearing factories. Without fuel no heavy armor could move, and ball bearings were an essential component in all machines. The U.S. government acted on this advice and proceeded to destroy Germany's major supply factories and bases to great effect.

When our forces retreated from Pyongyang in the wake of the Chinese army's advance, I took a T-6 to An-ak one last time. Before boarding my T-6, I roped letters onto a small parachute and brought them into the aircraft. My letters said that since both the South Korean and UN forces were retreating, the local people should flee to the south, too. I dropped the parachute with the letters as I flew over An-ak, thinking that the local people, as removed from the main roads as they were, would not hear about the South Korean and UN forces in retreat. This makeshift plan actually worked better than I thought it would. Once I returned to Seoul, I found that quite a few people had gotten the message and fled south.

Chapter 10

Making the Korean Air Force Proud

Tent Life at the Gangneung Air Base

After China's entry in the war, our forces and enemy forces continued to engage in fierce battles across the 38th parallel. My subordinates and I flew eleven F-51 fighters to Gangneung. At the base were U.S. Marine Corps fighters as well. The Marine Corps aircraft were mostly jets that took off from and landed on aircraft carriers. The Marine Corps was a part of the U.S. Navy, but it had a separate air force to supplement its land operations. As the best spots on the Air Base had already been taken up by the U.S. forces, we had to flatten the sandy field in the northern part of the base to tent over it during the frigid winter.

We awoke one morning to the sight of massive piles of snow on the top of our tent. Snow had covered the entire airstrip, leaving only the tops of the propeller blades of our planes in sight. As it continued to snow all through the winter, our supply lines would often be interrupted. At such times, we had to go into the city and get food ourselves. We even hunted pigeons and crows.

At the time, U.S. soldiers raised dogs that were very docile. One day, a dog wandered toward our tents. Somebody suggested eating it. While others spoke out against it, for fear of getting caught, in the end we ate it. When the Americans realized that the dog had gone missing, they looked everywhere for it. When they asked us if we had seen the dog, we flat out said no.

The hardest part about living in the tents was pulling the beds out of the tent. Whenever a pilot was killed in action, we needed to remove his bed from the tent. Our morale would sink whenever this happened. Thus, I, as the commanding leader, would frequently sortie with my troops the day after a comrade fell.

While it was rarely the case in the army for the commanding leader to go out and fight in the frontlines, the air force was different. All the combatants were officers. Enlisted personnel were on the ground, taking care of repairs, fueling, or loading guns and bombs.

Since pilots had to learn all sorts of complicated information, many of them were highly educated. The training period for a pilot took at least two to three years. Even after being appointed as a second lieutenant, a pilot could not simply start flying aircraft. Only after spending much time watching seniors fly and advancing to the rank of first lieutenant could a pilot finally start flying in actual operations. Once a pilot reached the rank of colonel, he would start planning the operations rather than directly participating in them. Thus the relationship between pilots was that of a teacher and an apprentice as well as that between two comrades. This was the unique culture of the air force.

While staying in Gangneung, the pilot's routine consisted of going on sorties and drinking. On the days the pilots did not sortie, they

As an Air Force Officer
In the cockpit, it was hard to smile even posing for a picture on the ground.

mostly spent their time getting drunk. I grew tired of this scene and one day asked an interpreter to teach my subordinates English from a basic level. Attendance, however, was poor. In an attempt to increase attendance, I started to attend class myself. After all, they could not simply skip a class that their commander was attending. But their complaints were still loud. They asked what the point of learning English was, when they could very well die the very next day. I urged them, however, to learn English in order to expand their horizons, sharing with them my experiences traveling to foreign countries when I was young.

Toward the end of the war, the UN Command selected one outstanding officer from each of the participant nations and gave him the opportunity to visit major cities in Europe and the U.S. Kim Seong-ryong, one of my subordinates, was chosen to represent Korea. Later on, he would become the Air Force Chief of Staff. The selected officers visited Washington D.C., New York, San Francisco, London,

Paris and other cities. Upon returning from the trip, Kim gave a public lecture on his experiences overseas in a large theater in Daegu.

"What did you feel in those foreign countries?" I asked him after the lecture.

"I felt the world was really big. I only wished you had forced us harder to study English....I regret I didn't try hard," Kim said.

"Why do you regret that?" I asked.

"There were many beautiful ladies who approached me to dance with them, but I was irritated that I could not communicate with them, with my poor English."

"Ha ha ha. It's still not too late to learn English, now that you know its importance!" I joked.

While Kim and I were joking, I was on one hand happy to hear his comment but on the other regretted not having pushed them harder.

Making the Korean Air Force Proud

The air forces of the U.S., Australian, Great Britain, and other countries participated in the Korean War. Operation orders came down from the combined headquarters, and most of the orders were about attacking railroad bridges, ammunition storehouses, and harbors. Before carrying out an operation, reconnaissance aircraft would fly to the location of the operation and take pictures of the surroundings. After that, the headquarters would analyze the pictures, determine several targets for attack, and assign targets to each of the participating nations' air forces. A sortie order would then be issued, along with the pictures and coordinates of the targets, as well as the exact time of sortie.

Usually, the Korean Air Force was sent to the vicinities of the Yalu River and to the north of the Cheongchen River. When the Korean Air Force approached these target areas, Soviet MIG-15 aircraft would begin to fly in from Manchuria. The MIG was a very powerful aircraft, able to climb up to thirty thousand feet in altitude. The most our planes were capable of doing was twelve to fifteen thousand feet. Thus, when we set out to bomb our targets, U.S. jets would fly over at a predetermined time to provide cover.

Hence, timing was the most important factor in any bombing operation. Being too early and being too late were both bad, as we found out the hard way. Occasionally, poor execution in terms of time coordination would lead to our bombers being shot down by the MIGs. When I was the squadron commander at the Gangneung Base, many times when of my men were killed in action I would head the bombing formation myself and fly out in order to boost morale, regardless of my rank as a colonel.

To evade UN bombardments, which were usually carried out during the day, the North Korean forces moved mainly at night. Mostly, the U.S. forces took charge of nighttime bombings. In one operation, U.S. bombers destroyed a railroad bridge in Seungho-ri over the Nam River, a tributary to the Daedong River in eastern Pyongyang. It was a strategic point of the supply route that ran from Pyongyang to the central eastern frontlines. But enemy supplies kept on making it southward, even after this important supply route had been destroyed. The U.S. forces then sent reconnaissance aircraft to the bridge area at night to drop flares and take pictures. It turned out that the enemy forces had built a new bridge near the old one.

After this discovery, the U.S. tried to bomb the new bridge, but encountered heavy resistance by numerous anti-air craft shells. Unable to get close to the target, U.S. bombers simply resorted to dropping bombs inaccurately from up high. U.S. pilots were sent back home after completing about a hundred sorties. What mattered more to them was reaching that number, regardless of whether the operations were successful or not. Thus, many of them simply erred on the side of caution and refrained from conducting high-risk bombings.

That was why the UN Combined Forces Command decided to charge the Korean Air Force with the mission of bombing the newly constructed bridge. We made sorties for the mission on the morning and afternoon of January 12, 1952, but failed to destroy it. It was a useless strategy to descend from an altitude of 8,000 feet and drop bombs from 3,000 feet as the U.S. forces had done previously. Eventually, I decided to use a risky tactic of descending from 4,000 feet and dropping bombs at 1,500 feet. On the frigid morning of January 15, we deployed two fleets consisting of six F-51s and were able to destroy not only the bridge but also the anti-aircraft gun positions, bunkers, and buildings around it.

Since we flew lower and bombed from a closer distance, the dropped bombs exploded even before our bombers had flown up to a higher altitude. One of our bombers was hit in the rear part by a bomb's shrapnel. Although a significant part of the body had been blown away, the pilot was fortunate enough to return the plane to the base safely. If not for the tremendous courage and audacity on the part of my pilots to attempt the low-altitude bombings, the mission would have been impossible to pull off.

Shortly after this successful operation, the UN Combined Forces Command held a meeting among all commanders in Seoul. As I entered the meeting room, everyone in the room went quiet and looked at me. One U.S. officer then said to me, "Congratulations, the Republic of Korea Air Force."

It was a compliment for the Korean Air Force for accomplishing something that the U.S. Air Force could not after numerous attempts. I learned later on that this officer had placed a bet on whether or not the Korean Air Force would succeed in the operation. He had won.

From the Frontlines to Air Force Headquarters

One time, I made a sortie with my pilots to bomb an ammunition storehouse located to the north of Panmunjeom. Since the target was heavily defended with multiple anti-aircraft guns, the operation was rather challenging. However, we succeeded in getting past the enemy's gunfire and destroyed the storehouse. As we flew back after completing the operation, one of my pilots told me by radio that there was smoke was coming out of the wings of my aircraft.

While it was standard procedure for a pilot to eject from a damaged aircraft, I was not at liberty to eject myself and give up my aircraft quite at that point, as I was still deep within enemy territory.

As an Air Force officer I led my men in many sorties, although as the commanding officer, I was not bound to. But raising troop morale was imperative, and I've no regrets.

I decreased the speed of my aircraft as much as I could and kept flying, steadily descending. With each minute, my pilots flying next to me urged me to eject as the smoke was getting bigger and bigger.

I ordered my pilots to fly on without me and somehow continued to press on in my damaged aircraft. After a while, I was finally approaching the Yoido Air Base. I radioed to the air-traffic controllers at the base that I needed to make an emergency landing and told them to clear all aircraft on the runway. The moment I landed, the engine shut down. Had I landed even a minute or two later, I could have crashed.

As every aircraft on my fleet, except for mine, had made it back to the Gangneung base, the personnel there reported the situation back to the Air Force Headquarters in Daegu. As soon as I arrived at the Yoido Air Base, I myself informed the Daegu headquarters through the U.S. forces on the base that I was safe. However, as the report from Gangneung had already reached the Korean Air Force Chief of Staff in Daegu, the issue became bigger than necessary and I was summoned to the headquarters. When I reported to Daegu, the chief of staff was fuming.

"Why the heck were you in a cockpit yourself when you are the commanding officer in charge of the base?"

"I needed to do something to raise the morale of the troops, as the number of men killed in action kept rising."

I tried to justify my actions to the chief of staff, but he did not buy it. He reassigned me to the Daegu headquarters. But, first, I was ordered to enroll in a command leadership course at the Air Force Academy in the U.S. Although we were in the middle of the war, I was sent to the U.S. with three other officers. At the academy I met officers from all over the world studying there, from South America, Europe, the Middle East, etc.

Upon returning to Korea, I was no longer fighting in the frontlines but sitting behind a desk at the Daegu headquarters. At the headquarters, besides the chief of staff and myself, there was not a single person with pilot experience. Among my colleagues were highly educated men who spoke good English, like Park Chung-hun, who would become Minister of the Economic Planning Board and acting Prime Minister, and Yun Cheon-ju, who would become Minister of Culture and Education, among others. But they did not know a thing about war strategy, for they were civil administrators and academics. In any case, I got along well with them at Daegu.

Although the Republic of Korea Air Force was newly established, it underwent rapid growth over the course of the Korean War. Of course, there were times of loss as well. One day, after I had returned from completing my leadership strategy course at the U.S. Air Force Academy, I was to attend a ceremony celebrating the founding of the combat wing of the Air Force in Gangneung. Those invited to the ceremony included General Kim Yeong-hwan, the younger brother of General Kim Jeong-ryeol.

General Kim Yeong-hwan was then the head of the Sacheon Air Base. He told me that he would send over an F-51 to Daegu where I was staying, and asked me to fly to the ceremony together. When I replied that I was unable to go take off soon due to other commitments, he left for Gangneung ahead of me with Lieutenant Colonel Kim Du-man. General Kim Yeong-hwan told me by radio that he was about to head for Gangneung after flying in circles over the Daegu headquarters, where I was. However, not after even an hour had passed when one of the aircraft that had flown out with General Kim returned by itself. It was Lieutenant Colonel Kim Du-man. He reported that General Kim and he had run into a stretch of heavy sea fog nearby Pohang.

Flying through sea fog is much more dangerous than flying through clouds. With clouds, since there is significant air space beneath them, a pilot can fly without too much risk of hitting the ground. With sea fog it's an entirely different story. As sea fog and the sea converge, a pilot runs a high risk of hitting the sea. Both

Lieutenant Colonel Kim and General Kim had entered a big patch of sea fog, and General Kim did not reemerge. An extensive search for his body yielded no result. Thus, we placed his clothing inside his casket in lieu of his body and held his funeral at the National Cemetery. To lose a man of talent like him was a sad chapter in the history of the Korean Air Force.

Piloting an air force aircraft always carries a risk. When we were dispatched on a mission to destroy a railroad bridge, we would usually encounter enemy anti-aircraft fire from the hills next to it. As the enemy forces normally positioned their anti-aircraft guns in tunnels built into the hills, neutralizing enemy fire and destroying its railroad bridge was a very challenging task. There were many pilots who lost their lives on these missions from being shot down while trying to maneuver their aircraft close to the target. To counter these enemy tactics, the U.S. developed a new bomb with a special fuse called VT (variable time).

The bomb had a propeller placed in front of its fuse. When the bomb was dropped, it went down with the propeller spinning and exploded in an umbrella shape approximately 50-100 meters above ground. The fuse had an electronic device that would detonate the bomb when it reached a certain height above ground. This explosive was highly effective against the machine guns and anti-aircraft guns that guarded railroad bridges and cleared the way for us to complete our mission.

This explosive had a safety pin–a metal wire–that prevented the propeller from spinning before it was dropped. Once, however, repair men had fastened the metal wire on one of these bombs the wrong way, and the bomb went off inside an aircraft, annihilating both the pilot and the aircraft. An egregious maintenance error had led to a massive tragedy.

American aircraft were heavier than Japanese aircraft partly because the area surrounding the cockpit was plated with steel to provide extra protection for the pilot. After dropping bombs or strafing targets while flying at low altitude, an aircraft must quickly return back to a higher altitude. However, pilots who had been in the Japanese Air Force and were used to flying lighter Japanese aircraft had a hard time executing this while flying U.S. aircraft and occasionally crashed. It was as if they were trying to ride an unfamiliar, heavy motorcycle after only having ridden a bicycle.

Mishaps regarding shooting weapons were not uncommon. During the ceasefire negotiation, I often flew out with my pilots on a reconnaissance mission to the regions near Haeju. During the reconnaissance flight, we would often see famers with oxen-pulled carts and also North Korean vehicles traveling from Gaeseong to the ceasefire talks at Panmunjeom. I gave out strict orders not to attack any of them.

One day, however, one of my pilots, Captain Ok Man-ho, after seeing dust kicked up by ten odd vehicles coming down southward, proceeded to strafe them. But they turned out to be North Korean vehicles on their way to the ceasefire talk. The North immediately protested to the UN forces. They made the specific claim that an F-51 Mustang had shot at their vehicles. When I asked my pilots if anyone had fired at the vehicles, all of them replied no.

During the Korean War, pilots returning from combat missions would report how many enemy aircraft they had shot down in battle. Initially, the pilots' oral reports were taken without verification. Thus, pilots would report even the slightest damage they had inflicted on the enemy aircraft as an aircraft downed. By and by, the U.S. forces fitted a device that took pictures automatically each time a pilot fired. Thereafter, how an aircraft engaged in battle could be verified by analyzing the pictures taken by the camera device.

After the film from Captain Ok's aircraft was processed, it was verified that he had indeed fire on the North Korean vehicles. While we were all severely reprimanded for this incident, Captain Ok was still able to smoothly advance up the ranks over time, eventually becoming the Chief of Staff of the Air Force. In a social meeting held many years later in which former Air Force chiefs of staff gathered together and were recounting tales of times past, Captain Ok still denied any culpability in the incident. Let bygones be bygones, I suppose. Captain Ok, or rather General Ok, is a proud veteran of our air force who distinguished himself in war. I humbly pray for General Ok, who passed away in May 2011.

Among the many sorrowful things I experienced during the war, nothing was more heart-wrenching than the internecine war itself. Since I took part in the many missions I was tasked with as a pilot, I would at times be overcome with the bitter question, "Did I make such efforts to learn how to fly an aircraft only to fight against my own compatriots?" Of course, defeating the invading enemy and winning is the fundamental duty of any soldier, prerogative, and I am proud that I always stayed true to my calling.

When I first received flight training, nay, even earlier, when I first experienced the indiscriminate bombing by Japanese planes over Nanjing and Chongqing, I've dreamed of flying a warplane featuring the Taegeuk insignia and defeating the Japanese fleet—targeting the heart of Imperial Japan. When I entered the air force unit of the Korean armed forces after liberation, my heart would beat faster just thinking about defending our nation's skies with our nation's warplanes.

However, history has not allowed me to realize those visions, dreams, and resolutions. Yes, I did fulfill the duty of defending the skies of our free nation, but my enemy, our enemy had now become our fellow Koreans. It is futile to have regrets over history. What is more important is self-appraisal and the resolve never again to repeat the tragedy of the past. The resolve to prevent another internecine war, the effort to move forward from conflict and tension to reconciliation and cooperation—that's what's far more important.

Slanders against Me Resume

The war was over, and we moved from Gangneung Air Base to Suwon Air Base. The Korean Air Force received fighter jets from the U.S. forces, and they were better suited for use in Suwon than Gangneung.

With the end of the war, I once again became the victim of widespread slander. What was now different from before the war was that now slanders came also from my rivals in the Air Force as well as political circles. During the war, there were very few people at the Air Force Headquarters who had anything to do with actual fighting.

With no one with first-hand experience in battle and knowledgeable about military matters to oversee them, the folks at the headquarters dealt with accounting and personnel matters at will. As people who actually knew about these matters as I joined the headquarters, they began to hold me in check.

I had in mind going on to attend the National Defense University for post-graduate education and then serving as the Superintendent of the Air Force Academy before retiring from the military. Few welcomed being assigned to the graduate program, because although it was a brief one-year assignment, one would invariably grow distant from active-duty men who were more plugged into the locus of power. But I did not harbor untoward aspirations to further advance my career in the military, and was pleased to be assigned to the university. In the meantime, slandering against me only grew. A rumor even went around that I had defected to the North on an aircraft. My wife went so far as to tell me not go out at all and just stay at home.

At that time, it was quite common for a chief of staff nearing the end of his term to try to resort to ways to extend it. One common method was to send off his vice chief of staff, the most likely candidate for the next chief of staff, to the National Defense University. Since I had no desire to be the chief of staff and planned to retire before long, I volunteered to go to the school in place of the vice chief of staff. But when I was back a year later, I was assigned to the post of the vice chief of staff, while the incumbent vice chief of staff was sent to the National Defense University. I was so assigned because they knew that I would never be able to become the chief of staff under the rule of the Liberal Party headed by Syngman Rhee.

However, as events would unfold, the chief of staff was forced to resign before serving out his term due to the outbreak of the April 1960 Student uprising, and General Lee Jong-chan became the Minister of National Defense under the interim government. Defense Minister Lee appointed me as the sixth Air Force Chief of Staff. General Lee had resigned from the post of the Army Chief of Staff due to his objection against President Rhee during the political crisis caused by the rigged presidential election on March 15, 1960. For this reason, he empathized with my predicament.

When the April Revolution broke out, Han Gap-su, who was the chief secretary for Yi Gi-bung, Chairman of the National Assembly, and a scholar of Korean language, gave me an urgent call. I had worked with Han in the secretarial office of the Air Force Headquarters. He asked me whether there might be an effective way to deal with the developing situation. It appeared that Yi had put Han up to call me. Although he did not specify what he wanted from me, I could gauge that they were seeking my support for striking the student demonstrators with greater force. I sternly told him it was out of the question. Within days, the Liberal Party collapsed, and with it, all surveillance and slander against me came to a stop.

Chapter 11

My Service as the Air Force Chief of Staff and the May 16th Military Coup

The Backstage of the May 16th Coup

In the aftermath of the April 19 Student Uprising, the Syngman Rhee government was replaced by the Heo Jeong interim government, and General Lee Jong-chan was appointed Minister of National Defense. Earlier in the year, General Lee had been fired from his position as the Army Chief of Staff by the Rhee government for voicing opposition to the March 15 rigged presidential election. It had not been long since I had been appointed Vice Chief of Staff of the Air Force upon returning from the National Defense University when General Lee offered me the post of Air Force Chief of Staff.

I declined his offer on the grounds that I had only recently become the vice chief of staff and that I was not fully prepared to take on the new job. But he insisted I accept the offer as there was much work to do and many flawed practices to address in the military. Thus, I accepted his order and was appointed the sixth Air Force Chief of Staff. My new duties were not drastically different from what I had been doing all along, so the transition was quite smooth, at

As Chief of Staff of the ROK Air Force
On an inspection tour of the radar base on Baekryeong Island. The strategic importance of this northernmost island in the West Sea cannot be overstated. It's close to An-ak, Hwanghae Province, where I spent my boyhood years.

least at first.

Meanwhile, the interim government was replaced by the government of the Democratic Party through an election. Yun Bo-seon became the titular president, and Chang Myon became the prime minister, who was the de facto new leader. But, alas, the new government of the Democratic Party from the start was embroiled in factionalism, with the party divided into new and old factions bitterly contending with each other for power. Within a short period, Defense Ministers changed all too frequently, as did the Army Chief of Staff, who was the center of the Korean Armed Forces: from General Choi Yeong-hui to General Choi Gyeong-rok to General Jang Do-yeong.

The political chaos triggered thoughts of launching a military coup in the minds of some. General Park Chung Hee was one. In fact, General Park had planned for some time a coup during the Liberal Party years under Rhee, but folded once Rhee resigned from the presidency in the wake of the outbreak of the April 1960 Uprising. But he finally resolved to carry out his plan once the government of the Democratic Party, which was in drift, only deepened the political chaos and aggravated the economy.

As the Air Force Chief of Staff, I was frequently briefed on such backstage activities and chatter inside the military. At the time of Park Chung Hee's coup, not all the top brass within the army was behind Park. General Jang Do-yeong, who was of higher rank than General Park and senior to Park in terms of the time in the service, initially stood at the forefront in support of Park, but turned against the coup later due to disagreements with Park. In the aftermath of the coup's success, Jang received a death sentence, which was commuted little by little to his release. Jang eventually went off to the U.S. for studies, which was akin to a political exile.

I was summoned to the Army Headquarters in the immediate wake of the coup. When I arrived there, the revolutionary army was creating an atmosphere of terror by occasionally firing guns. General Jang Do-yeong as well as many other senior officers from all quarters had gathered. There, I met General Park Chung Hee for the first time. He was short, skinny, dark-skinned, and wore a serious look on his face. Seeing me, Park greeted me,

"General Kim, we've not met before, and you may not know me. But I know of you well, as I've read *Paikbum Ilji* several times and was deeply impressed."

Park also said that he, in planning the coup, had thought me not someone who would oppose the coup. Rather, he thought that I would help him and his revolutionary army as I had been unduly victimized under the Liberal government. He also told me that he was sorry for not reaching out to me and enlisting my assistance prior to launching the coup, and went on to explain that he had not kept me in the loop out of concern that in the case of failure, I would come under even greater persecution. All the while, Park spoke calmly and to the point.

It is certainly true that I was under constant surveillance and became the victim of numerous slander campaigns under the Rhee government. Park had already ascertained the general stance of the Air Force through General Jeon Myeong-seop before enacting the coup. At the same time, Park was not overly concerned about the Air Force blocking him, as he thought, even in the worst-case scenario, he could control the landing and taking-off of aircraft just by strategically placing tanks on runways.

After speaking with various people from the Air Force, Navy, and Marine Corps, General Park asked General Jang Do-yeong to stand at the forefront together with him. In the immediate aftermath of the coup, Park lacked widespread recognition and legitimacy. When General Jang declined this request, the attitude of low-ranked officers of the junta turned all of a sudden threatening. General Jang called me in to a bedroom attached to the office of the Army Chief of Staff and sought my advice.

"Young majors and lieutenant colonels of the army are threatening me with their guns. What do you think I should do?"

"Rank is irrelevant to them. They have put their own lives on the line. They will not listen to anybody who opposes them. Should you try to put them down by force, Seoul will turn into a battle field. Shouldn't we avoid it at all cost?" I said.

General Jang also brought up our delicate relationship with the U.S., that is, that the coup will complicate it. I advised that in the end, this is a domestic matter, and that we would be able to address our relations with the U.S. in time. What he had actually wanted to hear from me, however, was a pledge to join hands and put down the young officers by force. At any rate, in the middle of our conversation, General Lee Han-rim somehow found out that I was at the Army Headquarters and called me there.

"Hey, why are you in the Army Headquarters when you are supposed to be at the Air Force Headquarters?"

"Something serious has taken place, and we are gathered here to discuss how best to address the situation."

Once the coup broke out, General Lee, under signals from the U.S., contemplated carrying out an operation to quell the coup leaders. In order to do so, he first needed to ascertain the intentions of the Air Force, for if he were to mobilize his troops from Wonju and encounter an attack by the Air Force while attempting to advance into Seoul, he would find himself without recourse. That was why he had to call me to assess the Air Force's stance on the coup. Upon hearing my answer, he assessed that the Air Force was now in the same boat as the revolutionary army. In the middle of such uncertainty, the U.S. also changed its stance on the coup and came to accept it as fait accompli, which made it impossible for General Lee even to attempt to quell the coup leaders.

Once a common understanding was reached within the military, General Park Chung Hee went to see President Yun Bo-seon with the Chiefs of Staff of the Army, Navy, and Air Force, the Commandant of the Marine Corps, and Colonel Ryu Won-sik. President Yun took a passive stance and told the military leaders to proceed as they deemed fit. But General Park wanted President Yun to take care of foreign affairs, while he would deal with domestic affairs. General Park and Colonel Ryu did their best to persuade the president to stay on.

I left after a while, when I thought that I did not need to be there any longer. Thereafter, those who stood in the way of the military junta were forced to resign or were arrested. General Jang was put on military trial, too. To my surprise, he selected me as a witness. He did so because he wanted me to testify on his behalf and address the

As Chief of Staff of the Air Force I served as the sixth Chief of Staff of the Air Force, 1960-1962.

allegation that he had been against the coup from the very start.

I appeared in court and testified. I was asked what General Jang and I had talked about in the Chief of Staff's room. I answered, "General Jang asked me how I viewed the situation, I told him that what just happened has very serious implications for the future of our nation. Our first order of business is to prevent at all cost Seoul becoming a sea of fire and bloodshed." I will not deny that my testimony did help to an extent General Jang's defense.

Air Force Reforms following the Coup

When I entered the air force after liberation, I, together with Yi Yeong-mu and Choi Yong-deok, were the only persons in the force who had served in the Chinese military. Most others had come from the Japanese Army. Yi later defected to the North due to false accusation of being in collusion with people inside North Korea whom he had been acquainted with in China. Choi would serve as vice Minister of National Defense and the Air Force Chief of Staff. The bias against those with China background and for those with Japan background was lot worse in the army. Those who were former officers of the Japanese Army took all the key positions with command rights, whereas those who had come from the Chinese Army were thoroughly excluded.

In the Air Force, those with pilot background should exercise command rights. It was a big problem that those who had never flown an aircraft held real power in the Air Force. Upon becoming the Air Force Chief of Staff, I made up my mind to address this problem. The coup was timely in that it provided me a better condition for carrying out this. First of all, I removed all the people who were not directly related to Air Force affairs from the Air Force Headquarters. Once I did this, a junior officer who had served in the Japanese military came to me, speaking in a slightly threatening tone.

"Sir, you must have some nerve and good reason to dare to clean house like this when your term will be over before you know it. You never know what kind of retaliation may be coming," he said.

I smiled and shot back, "I will use all my power until the very last five minutes of my term. I don't care one bit about repercussions once my term comes to an end."

The very day my term ended, I sent my guard soldier, driver, car, military hotline, etc. all back to headquarters. Previous chiefs of staff used to hold on to their cars and keep using their guards and drivers even after their terms had ended. During my term as the chief of staff, I put an end to such practices and had all of them return what they were no longer entitled to. Former chiefs of staff were displeased, but I believed that it was the patriotic duty of the soldier not only to fight courageously in war but also not to waste tax-payers' money. That's why I gave up on all those perks the moment my term came to an end.

During my term, I also uprooted the inveterate practice of officers submitting fake receipts for reimbursement and using the money for personal gratification. I thought the practice a criminal act that did great harm to our country.

Although more than a few bore resentment against me, many more younger officers supported me. That is why, when I visit military camps even today, young officers who have never met me often come up to me to salute me. It is gratifying to know that I did the right thing.

The Inside Story of America's Acceptance of the May 16th Coup

When Major General Park Chung Hee led the coup, most of his followers were not of high rank. Most were lieutenant colonels who were graduates of the eighth class of the Korea Military Academy. When the coup broke out, the U.S. tried to co-opt Army Chief of Staff General Jang Do-yeong and General Lee Han-rim, a field army commander, who were higher in rank than Park, in order to hold him in check. The key figure in this plan was General Carter Magruder,

Commander in Chief of the UN Command and Commander of the U.S. Forces in Korea.

General Magruder had an added incentive to put down the coup in addition to his official orders from the U.S. government. With retirement from the service just around the corner, Park Chung Hee's coup on his watch would certainly be a blemish on his career. Together with Vice Commander and Air Force Lieutenant General Emery Wetzel, General Magruder mobilized all the Korean generals who had good relationships with the U.S. to put pressure on Park from all corners.

"Force him or persuade him, but he has to go. Let him know that he won't be punished if he lays down his arms and goes back to where he was."

But General Magruder and the U.S. government were mistaken when they thought that Park Chung Hee would be fazed by this. They thought Park's coup was the result of a personal desire for power, much like coups in Latin America. But this was not a coup that broke out all of a sudden out of a personal urge for power, but the culmination of long and careful planning since the days of Rhee's Liberal Party. Therefore, neither threat nor conciliation could make Park stand down. In the end, General Magruder met with General Park and his close aide, Kim Jong-pil, in person.

"The U.S. will not just stand and watch. As the supreme commander, I order you to lay down your arms and give yourselves up," Magruder told Park.

Park smiled and calmly replied, "We've put our lives on the line, and are not afraid of anything. If we were simply going to give up here, we would not have started this in the first place. We initiated the coup in order to save our nation and make it right. We know this is not the right way, but it's the only way."

To Park's hardline stance, Magruder also took a hardline.

"I will mobilize soldiers like General Lee Han-rim who are not on your side, and suppress you by force."

But Park and Kim remained impervious to such a threat.

"Should you try, we could not guarantee the safety of the U.S. soldiers and civilians in Seoul. We will resist."

Only then did General Magruder realize that this kind of threat could hardly undo the coup. However, he still could not accept it. He tried to resolve the problem through a different route. He had General Emery Wetzel try to persuade me. He invited me to his home and said,

"General Magruder and I will soon retire from military service. Please help us save our faces. I would appreciate if you could gather people in the Air Force and take care of the junta."

But I could not accept his request.

"You are wrong to think that. These people started the coup willingly putting their lives on the line. They are not about to relent in the face of threats. Even if many people are opposed to their coup, they will fight back."

As I was meeting with General Wetzel, U.S. Admiral George Pressey was meeting with the Navy Chief of Staff Lee Seong-ho and the Commandant of the Marine Corps Kim Seong-eun. He tried to persuade them using the same logic that General Wetzel had with me. Pressey called me in to the Naval Headquarters as well.

When I got there, Admiral Pressey had told the Korean generals that "Park Chung Hee's true colors are ambiguous. I am not sure if he is on the left or right, but seems closer to the left. You should be wary of him for the sake of your own future." In a nutshell, he was telling us that we should rein Park in if we wanted to live.

In the immediate aftermath of the coup, the U.S. conducted an investigation on who among the high-ranking Korean generals had studied in the U.S. I was the only one. At that time, someone told me to stop meeting with Americans, saying that there was a rumor going around that the Americans were trying to make me their front man. He told me that the rumor was already being circulated among the revolutionary committee. In fact, I maintained quite a close relationship with the American generals. Since both my wife and I spoke English, we were frequently invited to parties hosted by American generals, and we would invite them to our house as well.

Americans put pressure on Park and his men from all sides, but could not turn back the tide. Eventually, they changed their stance and came to support the coup leaders. They figured that to continue down the path of standoff might prompt North Korea to launch an invasion of the South. When the dust finally settled, Lieutenant General Wetzel, who had been in charge of intelligence, put down his uniform and flew back to the U.S. aboard a civilian airliner. Commander Magruder, too, made an unhappy trip back to the U.S. without a proper celebration of his retirement from military service.

Part 4

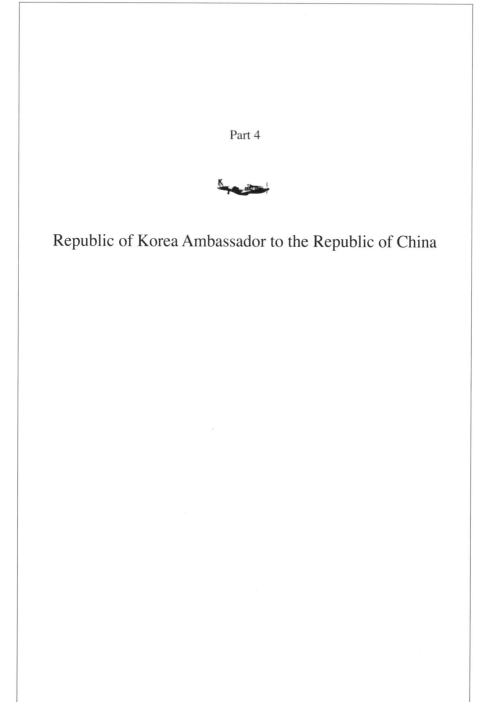

Republic of Korea Ambassador to the Republic of China

Chapter 12

On both the Diplomatic Backstage and Frontstage

Appointed the Korean Ambassador to Taiwan

In 1961 when I was working as the Air Force Chief of Staff, the May 16th Military Coup broke out. The next year, in September, I was appointed Korean Ambassador to the Republic of China. Among the generals who had not opposed the coup, those who were ranked higher than Major General Park Chung Hee were all appointed ambassador to foreign countries. It would have been uncomfortable for Park to work with those who were higher in rank in the military as his subordinates. Generals Lee Jong-chan, Lee Hyeong-geun, Chung Il-kwon, Paik Sun Yup, and Ryu Jae-heung were all appointed ambassador in the aftermath of the coup.

I was also selected for an assignment abroad. Kim Hyeong-uk, whom I knew personally, tipped me off.

"My older brother, you will be assigned ambassador to Taiwan when you are done with your tenure as the chief of staff."

I was rather happy to hear the news.

"That's good because I can speak Chinese and I have acquaintances there."

But when I came home upon the completion of my term as the chief of staff, General Park Byeong-gwon, who was the Defense Minister at the time, came over to my house and told me something unexpected.

"General Park Chung Hee tells me that he feels bad about sending you abroad again after your long travails in China. I was told to come over and make sure that your feelings were not hurt and to discourage you from going abroad."

Park Chung Hee was the kind of man who was hard-hearted when he had to be but could also be soft when he felt it was necessary. Minister Park continued to convey to me General Park's feelings.

"General Park wants to work with you together. 'Tell him I wish to work with him. Since the position of the Minister of Communication is vacant, tell him to take it following a brief period of rest, General Park told me to tell you."

Minister Park tried to discourage me from taking up the post of ambassador to Taiwan as he conveyed General Park's message. But my mind had already been made up.

"I have already made up my mind. I think I need a different sort of challenge after so many years in uniform. Why should I stay when all others are going abroad? What's more, since I have an affinity for Taiwan in terms of lifestyle, language, and personal relations, I would be a good choice for the job."

Even as I was firm on serving as ambassador to Taiwan, I was worried about one thing. I did not have any knowledge of or experience in diplomacy. I was now to transition from a military man to a diplomat, but did not even know the basics of diplomacy. The government did not have any programs for addressing this common problem, either. It unconditionally sent people abroad as diplomats immediately upon appointment without any diplomatic training.

At least, one advantage of serving as a senior military person was having far more opportunities to interact with American generals in both formal and social settings than senior civilian officials and, thereby, being familiar with the basic rules of protocol, including seating arrangement. When American generals invited us, they would follow international norms of protocol. The seating order was determined based on the guests' rank and relative seniority. Men and women were seated according to a certain rule. In the case of a long, rectangular table, the host and hostess were seated in the middle of the table across from each other. Then, the highest ranked person among the guests was seated to the right of the hostess, while his wife was seated to the right of the host.

When I went to Taiwan as ambassador, I found that diplomatic events were not so different. For example, when President Chiang Kai-Shek invited the diplomatic corps in Taiwan, the doyen of the corps was seated to the right of President Chiang, who would be the individual having served the longest as chief of mission in Taiwan. There was no discrimination in terms of national power. For example, if the American ambassador had been in Taiwan for a year, while the Pakistani ambassador three, the latter was recognized as the doyen.

But there were exceptions to the rule. When the event featured couples, to the right of President Chiang was not the doyen of the corps but Chiang's wife. The doyen would take his seat next to Madam Chiang, and the vice doyen's wife would take the next seat, with her husband sitting next to her. Men and women were seated in alternating fashion this way.

The experience of closely interacting with American generals in Korea proved very useful when I assumed my post in Taiwan. Nonetheless, I took up my post without training on how best to deal with diplomatic issues and tasks such as making statements on behalf of my government at official meetings or about addressing pending issues between nations. Those ambassadors who could not speak the native language of the country to which they had been appointed or English had a very hard time effectively carrying out their diplomatic mission. Although they would communicate with the native people through an interpreter, there was certainly a big difference between speaking through an interpreter and speaking directly on his own. Fortunately, I did not have such a language problem as I could speak Chinese very well and was also proficient in English.

President Chiang Kai-Shek's Good Will

I had already visited to Taiwan several times before I took up my post as ambassador there. I once accompanied Army Chief of Staff Lee Hyeong-geun on a visit to Taiwan when General Kim Hong-il was the ambassador there. The Army wanted an Air Force general to be on the delegation as General Lee would be flying to Taiwan on an Air Force aircraft. I was selected because I could speak Chinese well. As a brigadier general, I was the lowest ranking officer in our party. At the end of the visit, we took commemorative group picture with President Chiang Kai-Shek in his office. Afterwards, as we were about to leave the room, Chiang called me,

"Hey, Kim Shin! Come back here. Let's take a picture, just the two of us."

I felt it would be out of place for me to pose with Chiang alone, but ended up taking the picture with him. Later, when I visited the presidential office of Taiwan after becoming the Air Force Chief of Staff, President Chiang was very happy for me. I gather he was happy for me not only because of his special friendship with my father but also because I, who had first earned my wings in the Chinese Army, had now ascended to the highest position of the Korean Air Force.

Now that I had been appointed Republic of Korea Ambassador to the Republic of China after retiring from the military, I felt quite excited. I arrived in Taiwan on September 20, 1962, and waited for the ceremony of presenting my credentials to President Chiang. But I received no word from the presidential office for more than ten days. I became anxious because the Double Tenth, Taiwan's national foundation day, was now fast approaching. For the Double Tenth, the Taiwanese government invited all the chiefs of missions for a diplomatic ceremony. Until presenting one's credentials, an ambassador-designate could not engage in official diplomatic activities nor take part in the Double Tenth ceremony.

The Foreign Minister informed me of why the presentation of my credentials was being delayed. President Chiang was ill. He told me to wait a little longer. Fortunately, the presentation was scheduled

Presenting my credentials as Republic of Korea Ambassador to Taiwan
On October 9, 1962, I presented my credentials to President Chiang Kai-Shek, and my ambassadorship officially began.

for October 9, 1962. On October 9, a high official in the Protocol Department of the Foreign Office came to the Korean embassy in accordance with diplomatic procedures and escorted me and the senior staff of the embassy to the presidential office.

I was moved beyond words as I rode in a luxurious car flying the Korean national flag up in the front, headed toward the presidential office escorted by Taiwanese policemen on motorcycles in their full-dress uniform. Tears came to my eyes when I thought that I, the son of the leader of the independence movement, was now receiving this honor thanks to all those elders who had fought for Korean independence with their blood and tears in China. I tried to stop the tears as we were approaching the presidential office, but the tears only kept running as so many events of the past flashed through my mind.

A conversation with President Chiang was arranged following the relatively brief ceremony. Since I did not need an interpreter, I entered the VIP room alone. President Chiang entered the room with his Foreign Minister and Chief Presidential Secretary. He began with warm words.

"I don't want to treat you as a foreign ambassador. We are family. Paikbum and I fought together in the anti-Japanese war as comrades over decades. He devoted his life himself to that cause."

After closing his eyes and catching his breath for a moment, Chiang said to me,

"Come and see me directly if ever you have a problem."

"Since Ching-kuo and you are like brothers, be sure to talk to him when you have a problem," Chiang continued.

Ching-kuo was President Chiang's son. During our conversation, I noticed that Chiang's lips were all chapped. He looked as if he had a fever. Though he was ill, he held the ceremony taking into account my need to present my credentials before the Double Tenth. At that moment, my father's face flashed through and I choked up.

President Chiang frequently asked for my opinion on Taiwan's domestic affairs. That was because his own men tended to shy away from reporting bad news to him. Chiang Ching-kuo actually implored his father's advisers,

"Please report to me first. I will talk to him on your behalf."

I do not attribute such tendencies on the part of the son to his desire for power. President Chiang was a micro-manager, the kind of leader who tended to every detail himself. Even when the most trivial problem arose, he did not sleep until he came up with a solution. Thus, his health was always at risk. Worried about his father's declining health, Chiang Ching-kuo tried to check all reports and convey mostly good news to his father.

President Chiang was well aware of this and was concerned about it. He used to point out "*bao xi bu bao you*" as one of the reasons why he had lost mainland China. It meant to "report good news but not report worrisome news." He wanted to have a close relationship with me because he believed that, as a third party, I could assess Taiwan's domestic affairs more objectively. He asked for my opinion on even his family affairs as well as state affairs. Whenever he asked for my opinion, I revealed my uneasiness to him.

"I don't know about that. For me to comment on it would be interference in domestic affairs…"

When I mumbled the end of my words, he spoke to me with a serious look,

"No, No. Since you and I are family, there would be no interference in internal affairs. Do give me your honest opinion."

Soon, a rumor went around among Taiwanese government officials that Ambassador Kim Shin was the one most trusted by President Chiang. Some people even went so far as to ask me to help them get a promotion.

"If you speak well of me to him, I will be promoted this time."

I said to such persons firmly,

"Please, don't say such things to me. However close I may be to President Chiang, it would be interference in internal affairs for me."

I told them most sternly that I could not help in any way when it came to internal affairs—nor would I wish to.

President Chiang feels out America's Intentions

Even though the U.S. had misgivings about Park Chung Hee at first, the Korea-U.S. bilateral relationship took a major step forward in the wake of South Korea's support in the Vietnam War. In accepting America's request to dispatch ROK troops to Vietnam, President Park made several demands of his own. First, since deploying South Korean troops to fight in the Vietnam War may compromise security at home, the U.S. should guarantee South Korea's security. Second, America should replace South Korea's outmoded military equipment and arms with the latest assets. At the time, the standard issue arms used by the Korean armed forces was the M-1 rifle. The U.S. supplied M-16s to Korean troops fighting in the Vietnam War.

Presidents Park and Nixon agreed to have a summit in San Francisco in August 1968. Upon hearing the news, President Chiang summoned me to his official residence. By standard procedures, an invitation by the head of state would be made through the official channels of the Ministry of Foreign Affairs, but this time he summoned me directly. Once I arrived at his office, Chiang ordered his secretary, note-taker, and bodyguard to leave the room. Once everyone left, Chiang turned to me and said,

"You know what? I have a favor to ask of you."

"What is it, sir? Please tell me," I said.

"I've heard that President Park will hold a summit meeting with President Nixon in San Francisco. Could you ask President Park to ask President Nixon how the U.S. views Taiwan?" Chiang asked.

He was growing more and more worried about Taiwan's future, as the People's Republic of China grew stronger day by day, while Taiwan's influence was relatively receding. Should the U.S. ever abandon Taiwan, its fate would be precarious. Well aware of Chiang's concerns, I answered enthusiastically,

"I see. I will contact my government."

Chiang leaned forward toward me and said, "For this, you should either go to your country in person or write a letter and have it delivered through a reliable person. Make sure not to use telecommunications."

Chiang was concerned about the PRC eavesdropping. Just in time, a graduate of the second class of the Korea Military Academy, was passing through Taiwan on his way back to Seoul. I invited him to a meal, and asked if he could directly deliver a top secret document to President Park. He answered yes. In this way, I was able to have a document containing President Chiang's request to President Park.

On August 22, President Park held his summit meeting with President Nixon in San Francisco. While discussing several issues related to security in East Asia with President Nixon, including the Vietnam War, President Park brought up Taiwan.

"How does the U.S. government view President Chiang of Taiwan?"

"We consider President Chiang the beacon of hope to the Chinese people surrounded by a sea of Communism."

President Nixon most likely gave this answer on the assumption that there may have been some kind of communication between Presidents Park and Chiang. Afterwards, I contacted President Chiang's office to give him a report on the Park-Nixon summit meeting. He told me to meet Chiang Ching-kuo first. I then met President Chiang's son and informed him of the summit meeting, mentioning that I had President Park's signed letter to Chiang on the results of his meeting with Nixon. Very pleased to hear my words, he told me that he would be in touch soon.

A few days later, I went to the point of rendezvous Mt. Yangming to see President Chiang and his son. After discussing various other issues, I brought up with President Chiang President Park's letter. In the letter were the following words by President Nixon, "President Chiang is the beacon of hope to the Republic of China and the people of Taiwan as well as the entire Chinese people in the communist territory." Chiang's eyes welled up.

Taiwan's Bid to Participate in the Vietnam War

The Taiwanese government had a great interest in the political changes taking place in Korea following the May 16th coup. Taiwan was relieved when President Park proclaimed anti-communism as the overarching state policy. Taiwan felt it now had a staunch comrade in the struggle against Communism. In the event South Korea were to grow soft in its anti-communist stance, Taiwan would likely have found itself isolated and alone.

In fact, the Taiwanese government had considered participating in the Korean War. President Chiang conveyed to the U.S. his intention to dispatch troops to Korea several times. But the U.S. did not accepted Taiwan's offer out of concern that Taiwan's involvement would likely lead to China's involvement. Of course, China entered the Korean War regardless of Taiwan's non-participation. But Taiwan did contribute in non-combat roles. For example, Taiwanese interpreters were brought in to interrogate Chinese prisoners of war for gathering intelligence.

Taiwan also wished to take part in the Vietnam War. One Sunday, as I was resting at home, I was suddenly summoned to the president's residence. A seven-country summit led by U.S. President Lyndon Johnson was scheduled for October 24, 1966 in Manila, the Philippines. The seven countries were all participants in the Vietnam War: The U.S., Australia, New Zealand, Thailand, the Philippines, Vietnam, and South Korea.

"Isn't it for the sake of anti-communist struggle that President Park is fighting in Vietnam? Likewise, Taiwan, as an anti-communist country, must take responsibility. If we participate in the Vietnam War, we will be big asset since we are geographically close to Vietnam. So, I'd be grateful if President Park could inform President Johnson of my wish to participate in the war," Chiang said to me.

I reported this to President Park. Soon after the seven-nation summit, President Park sent me a long, personally signed letter. When important matters were concerned, Park would write in his own handwriting and sign it at the bottom. In this letter, Park described in detail Johnson's response to Chiang's offer to send Taiwanese troops to Vietnam.

In the end, President Chiang's wish was not fulfilled. President Johnson suggested that Taiwan should not participate in the Vietnam War because if Taiwan did, China likely would as well. Regardless of Taiwan's participation or lack thereof, however, China was secretly aiding North Vietnam. Although China did not officially declare its participation in the war, it sent engineer troops and howitzer artillery troops to the rear front of North Vietnam. The Soviet Union, too, supplied weapons to the Vietnamese communist forces through China, although officially it was not a belligerent, either.

Chiang's intentions for Taiwan's involvement in the Vietnam War was more than just engage in underground operations in select areas in support of the U.S. troops. Chiang had in mind dispatching a few divisions to Vietnam, which would then force their way into Yunnan Province in mainland China. Taiwan intended to reclaim parts of the mainland, should American support be forthcoming. Taiwan had even laid out a detailed strategic plan before testing the U.S. The Taiwanese embassy in Saigon had closely observed how the Korean troops were being treated by the U.S. in Vietnam and how they were faring in Vietnam. President Chiang was greatly disappointed that the U.S. rejected his offer, especially after having developed a strategic plan for Taiwan's role in the war.

Treaty of Friendship between Korea and Taiwan

During the Vietnam War, Korean National Assemblymen and high-ranking generals on their way to Vietnam to visit Korean troops invariably stopped by Taiwan. They did so in order to expand their personal network and because Taiwan was a friendly fellow anti-Communist nation. The Taiwanese side did not mind the continual flow of Korean politicians and generals, since feeling were mutual.

Unfortunately, this meant that the staff of the Korean embassy, including myself, was overwhelmed with taking care of an unending stream of important visitors. Koreans of influence visited Taiwan almost every day, and it was exhausting for us to have to take care of them, from greeting them at the airport to taking them around town. It became so exhausting that I eventually protested to my home government. I complained that the government should establish a branch of the Korea Tourist Service in Taiwan if it still wanted me to stay on as ambassador.

Most of the National Assemblymen who visited Taiwan asked me to arrange for a meeting with President Chiang. One time, some fifteen assemblymen visited Taiwan following a visit with the Korean troops in Vietnam. They asked me to arrange for a meeting with President Chiang, which I did. Chiang usually went out of his way to accommodate such requests as he wanted to maintain a good relationship with Korea.

At the end of the meeting, the time came for the assemblymen to take a picture with President Chiang. All at once, they made a big fuss, pushing and shoving, vying for the spot right next to Chiang.

His bodyguards turned pale at the sight. The Korean assemblymen likely wanted to show off their close relationship with Chiang to their colleagues and constituencies at home by posing for the picture right next to him.

Such were the poor manners and narrow-mindedness of members of the National Assembly at the time. The generals were at least better-mannered and more disciplined. When President Chiang met with Korean generals, he would confer on them medals as a friendly gesture.

Once I was summoned for a brief visit due to a certain internal issue within Korea. When President Chiang heard of my impending trip to Korea, he called me in. When I visited him, Chiang brought up the topic of a treaty of friendship between Korea and Taiwan.

"When a man and a woman get married, they register their marriage to become a legal couple. Korea and Taiwan are on friendly terms but have never made a formal contract. So, why don't we conclude a treaty of friendship between us even if it is only symbolic?"

In fact, only after I heard his words did I realize that the two countries had never concluded a treaty of friendship. There had been some talk of such a treaty of friendship during the Syngman Rhee years, but Rhee himself was apathetic to the idea, saying, "Why do we need such a thing when all that each side needs to do is be friendly?" Yet, as more and more key Korean figures including the prime minister, chairman of the National Assembly, assemblymen, and others came to visit Taiwan due to the Vietnam War during the Park administration, President Chiang wanted to take advantage

The treaty of friendship between Korea and Taiwan signed on October 11, 1964

The leftmost person is President Chiang's chief secretary Zhang Qun, and the fifth person from the left is Korean Prime Minister Chung Il-kwon.

of the increasingly friendly ties and conclude a treaty of friendship between Korea and Taiwan.

President Chiang explained the details of the treaty to us through his chief secretary Zhang Qun. Zhang and Chiang had attended the Japanese Military Academy as classmates. Chief Secretary Zhang had assisted Chiang for a long time. In fact, it was Zhang who had brought up the idea of the treaty with President Chiang.

In Korea I reported the matter of the treaty to President Park. At that time, he was busily going around all over the country to implement the First Five-Year Economic Development Plan. I briefed President Park in his car on his way to Seoul Train Station. Park cheerfully instructed me to work on the treaty. On October 11, 1964, the treaty of friendship between Korea and Taiwan was initialed by me on behalf of the Republic of Korea and the Minister of Foreign Affairs Shen Changhuan on behalf of the Republic of China in the presence of Korea's Prime Minister Chung Il-kwon who was visiting Taiwan. The two countries exchanged the instruments of ratification of the treaty of friendship in December 1965.

Chapter 13

Park Chung Hee and Chiang Kai-Shek

President Chiang Helps President Park

At first, many were suspicious of the nature of the Park Chung Hee junta. The U.S. kept an eye on it out of concerns that it may be leftist, because the Chairman of the Supreme Council National Reconstruction, Park Chung Hee, had been arrested in the Yeosu-Suncheon rebellion in 1948. Park had to declare anti-Communism the overarching state policy right away if for no other reason than to dispel others' suspicion.

President Chiang was quite pleased when Park firmly declared the anti-Communist stance, as he now had a comrade in the South Korean leader. But no matter how Park tried to enhance his image at home and abroad, questions of legitimacy lingered due to the fact that he had seized power by force. The U.S. was uneasy with the junta, and wished for the military rule to end as soon as possible. In the end, Park played the political card of promising to transfer power to a civilian government at the earliest possible date.

When Park Chung Hee declared that he would transfer power back to a civilian government, the U.S. and the Korean opposition parties kept pressuring him, "When?" They wanted the transfer of power to take place as soon as possible. When President Chiang heard of this issue, he called me in to his office and offered his frank opinion on the matter.

"I've tried to complete the revolution and rectify China for the past fifty years, but I haven't yet to complete the task. Korea is only now setting out on such a course, and Park is about to throw it all away by stepping down. This cannot be. Park must carry on and sustain the spirit of the revolution to the end. If he stops halfway, nothing will have been accomplished."

Chiang stopped for a brief moment, then went on in a slightly agitated tone,

"If Park transfers power to someone else, doesn't it mean that we'll simply all go back to where we were? For what then did he launch the military revolution in the first place? Once he has stepped out onto the stage, he must aim high, carry out reforms, and set the country straight. It doesn't make sense for him to yield to political pressure. It is exceedingly difficult for a civilian leader to purify muddy waters. My long experience tells me that General Park must will himself to carry on until the end."

President Chiang stressed his point once more before concluding with the following words.

"If he has the support of the people, then couldn't he carry on and lead through elections? To unconditionally transfer power to a civilian government and put an end to the military revolution is worse than not having started it in the first place."

By diplomatic convention, for even a head of a state to have such a conversation with a foreign diplomat would be unacceptable, as it undoubtedly is interference in the internal affairs of a foreign government. Yet, I knew his words came from his heart. I conveyed Chiang's opinion to Park Chung Hee the next time I had an opportunity to do so.

In the end, Park Chung Hee discarded the notion of unconditional transfer of power to a civilian government. Clearly, Park did not come to this decision solely on President Chiang's advice. He also decided to retire from the military and run in the next presidential election as a civilian, partly in consideration of the U.S. The U.S. provided aid to foreign countries with the view toward preventing the expansion of Communism. But a country could not expect to receive U.S. aid if it maintained a military dictatorship over a substantial period. Should the Korean people elect Park Chung Hee president, then the U.S. would have no legitimate reason to object to him.

At the time Chairman Park made up his mind to run for the presidency, Korea was beset by a rapidly growing problem in terms of food supply due to severe drought. The government tried very hard to address the serious problem. However, importing rice from the U.S. would take too long due to the distance, and importing rice from Vietnam would present a different problem, namely, that Vietnamese variety was the long-grain rice, which was different from the short-grain rice overwhelmingly favored by Koreans. The government then looked to Taiwan. Taiwan not only produced the kind of rice that appealed to Koreans' taste but also was close geographically. The problem was that Taiwan's grain reserves could not be tapped into under normal circumstances, as it was stored for use only in the case of an emergency. But the Korean government faced great pressure to come up with an appropriate measure. What's more, the situation of unstable food supply would certainly hurt Park Chung Hee's chances in the upcoming election. In the end, Park entrusted in me the task of importing rice from Taiwan.

"I know you enjoy a special relationship with President Chiang. Although one must distinguish between private and public matters, this issue concerns both private and public interest, no?"

I understood the gravity of the problem. I was successful in arranging for the purchase of Taiwan's rice reserves and having the entire quantity of the purchased rice transported to Korea by July 10, 1963. The upcoming presidential election was to take place on October 15, 1963. And how to transport the rice expeditiously became a big problem. The chief of the food bureau in the Taiwanese government Li Lianchun told me that he could sell the rice but could not take responsibility for transporting it. However, the Taiwanese army then stepped forward, mobilizing hundreds of military vehicles under adverse weather conditions to transport the rice to Gaoxiong Port and Jilong Ports. I was very sorry to President Chiang for all the troubles, but it was he who apologized to me.

"I am very sorry. If I were in mainland China, I would give the mere few hundred thousand tons of rice to Korea for free instead of accepting money for it."

On Park Chung Hee's future visit to Taiwan, Park thanked Chiang.

"Thank you very much for your words of encouragement during difficult times and for all your help."

Park thanked Chiang for his advice against the blind transfer of power to a civilian government and for his help during the food shortage crisis. In response, Chiang made a request.

"I would like you to assume the leadership of the anti-Communist struggle in Asia in the future."

After his return home from visiting Southeast Asian countries including Taiwan, President Park held a meeting with his top aides in his party, the legislature, and the military. Park remarked,

"Nothing really stood out in Thailand or Malaysia. But President Chiang's words to me touched my heart. He asked me to be the leader of the anti-Communist struggle in Asia."

Establishing a School for Koreans in Taiwan

During my term in Taiwan, there were not too many Koreans living there. Most of the Korean-Taiwanese who lived in Taiwan were those who had been forcibly repatriated there during Japan's colonial rule over Korea and had settled down by marrying Taiwanese. They lived mainly around Gaoxiong and Jilong, which were major port cities. Gaoxiong was like Busan in Korea and Jilong like Incheon. In Jilong, there lived some Korean-Taiwanese people who had lived in Shanghai and had come to Taiwan when the Guomindang government had retreated from mainland China. I remember Madam Jeong Seong-won, who had come to Taiwan by herself and opened a small church to engage in missionary activities.

Korean-Taiwanese lived in Taipei, too, but were few in number.

Additionally, there were traders, sailors, and students among the Korean community. There were actually more students than one might think. Upon coming to Taiwan as ambassador, I had my children attend an elementary school for Koreans in Taipei. There were elementary schools for Koreans in Gaoxiong and Jilong, too, although they were smaller than the one in Taipei. The Ministry of Culture and Education in Korea dispatched teachers to these schools in Gaoxiong and Jilong responding to Koreans' request.

At the time, the principal of the school my children attended was Heo Se-uk, who was studying at the National College of Education in Taiwan. Heo returned to Korea later and became a professor at the Department of Chinese and Chinese Literature at Korea University (deceased in July 2010). The problem was that when an elementary school student completed his or her schooling, there was no middle school for Koreans in Taiwan. Hence, I ended up sending my children to an American middle school.

As the educational environment for Koreans was challenging, one of the biggest wishes of the Korean community at the time was building a Korean school. But the Korean embassy could not afford to fulfill their wish. Koreans living in Taiwan had great expectations of me as they knew that I had lived in China for a long time and that I had a special relationship with President Chiang. Honestly, though, I felt uncomfortable asking President Chiang for help on this. In the end, I decided to reach out to Koreans in Hawaii for help, as I had a considerable number of acquaintances there.

The Koreans in Hawaii responded to my request and sent me a sum of money. But it was not enough to establish a school. So, I donated the money to the schools Korean children were attending and asked them to put it to good use.

In the case of Gaoxiong, I visited Mayor Chen Qichuan and discussed with him the question of establishing a school for Korean children. At the time, Koreans mostly lived in the suburbs of Gaoxiong instead of its center, to save on expenses. Zuoying was one such suburb. In Zuoying, there was a promising site for establishing a school, which was near where Koreans were concentrated. The problem was that the site bordered a naval base. Thus, ordinary people did not have access to it. Mayor Chen disapproved of the idea. Later, I brought up the issue with Chiang Ching-kuo, President Chiang's son.

"Koreans in Gaoxiong want to build a school for their children. A small school would do, but there is no site to build one on. Could you please help?"

"Of course, I can. How may I help you?"

"The Korean residents there tell me there is a good site, but it is located in a military zone. I wonder if there's still a way to establish a school there."

"I will look into it."

A few days later, Chiang Ching-kuo called me and asked for the exact location of the prospective site. After I gave him its precise location, he contacted the marine troops there. By his order, they mobilized a bulldozer to level the ground for building a school. Later, I visited Mayor Chen to thank him.

"We could establish a school for Koreans in Gaoxiong thanks to you. Thank you, Mr. Mayor."

"You don't have to thank me. You should thank yourself because you were able to build a school in a place that not many people can access."

When the school was finally built, the Koreans named it Gaoxiong Korean Elementary School. They asked me to write the school name on the school nameplate. The famous Korean actress Choi Eun-hui attended the opening ceremony for the school. She happened to be visiting Taiwan on her way back to Korea from Hong Kong. Upon hearing of her visit, I invited her to the ceremony. Establishing a school was not necessarily a task that I or any other diplomat was charged with, but it certainly was a task no less gratifying.

Taiwan's Stabilization Processes

It is a well-known fact that President Chiang made every effort not to lose mainland China to the Chinese Communist Party. He rallied his demoralized troops to Sichuan and regrouped near Chongqing and Wuhan. As he was deploying his troops across several locations in Chongqing, Chiang was informed that Communist troops were advancing from Xian.

President Chiang became anxious, as all retreat routes would be blocked should Communist fighters bomb air bases where large transport aircraft could take off from and land. He ended up escaping aboard a transport plane to his hometown area, Fenghua, Zhejiang Province. There, he handed over his position as the president to Li Zongren and relegated himself to chairman of the Guomindang.

While Chiang was in Fenghua, the Communist troops crossed the Yangzi River and advanced into Shanghai. Realizing that the war was all over, Chiang took a warship from Zhoushan Archipelago, lying east of Fenghua, for Taiwan in December 1949.

Once resettled in Taiwan, Chiang had several geographic names in Taipei changed. Mt. Yangming was one of them. The original name of the mountain was Mt. Cao. In China, a mountain used as a stronghold by bandits was traditionally called Mt. Cao. Since the Guomindang and Taiwan referred to the Chinese Communist military "Communist bandits," Chiang had Mt. Cao renamed to Mt. Yangming. Another example was Lake Dabei in Gaoxiong. The Chinese character "bei" (貝) is a homonym of the character "bei" (悲), which means "sad." Hence, "Dabei" may well be mistaken for "very sad." Chiang renamed the lake Daming.

Chiang did not stop at just renaming geographic places. Forced to flee to Taiwan, Chiang was determined to start again with an entirely different mindset, if only to survive in his new diminished environment. As a visible reminder of his new resolve, Chiang had the Chinese idiom "wu wang zai ju" (never forget your days in Ju) engraved on a big cliff on Jinmen Island. The idiom comes from an old Chinese tale.

In the Spring and Autumn Period, Prince Huan of the Qi state escaped the corrupt rule of his brother Prince Xiang, and upon fleeing to Ju, encountered much hardship. Once his brother died, Huan returned home and became the king. When he asked his vassals how he should rule his kingdom, Prime Minister Guanzhong replied, "Never forget your days in Ju."

Chiang made thorough military preparations by fortifying Jinmen Island, which is located close to the mainland. At the same time, he also addressed certain Chinese customs that he felt needed amendment. At the time, by convention one would be obliged to serve some twenty dishes when hosting a dinner party. Chiang thought this wasteful, and urged the people to prepare only "four dishes and one soup" or "three dishes and one soup." He also modernized Japanese houses with tatami floors that were used by Japanese soldiers. Thanks to his efforts, the Taiwanese economy grew fast.

Kim Hyeon-cheol, who had been a cabinet minister during the Rhee administration and prime minister in the beginning of the Park administration, once visited Taiwan. When he met President Chiang, he asked,

"How does one eradicate corruption?"

Chiang smiled and said that he had some views on this question as he himself had suffered from the corruption of others around him. He wrote down the following characters:

"*Dao gao yi chi, mo gao yi zhang.*"

Literally, it means righteousness is a foot tall, while evil is ten feet tall. Paraphrasing it, it means that when a Confucian scholar's moral virtue grows by a foot, temptations for him grow by 10 feet. By this Chiang meant however strict the law of the land, rooting out corruption is exceedingly difficult. It requires extraordinary effort. After showing us these characters, Chiang turned to us and said,

"In the end, it is men who make the decisions; hence, good judgment of men and the art of persuasion are imperative."

When I served as the Air Force Chief of Staff, my Taiwanese counterpart was a man by the name of Chen Jiashang. While I underwent flight training in India, Chen had been a chief instructor. Commander Chen visited Korea in the aftermath of the defection by the retired officer of the Chinese air force Zhao Xiyan and the trainee Gao Youzong. The two landed the two-wing airplane AN-2 on Jeju Island and defected to South Korea on September 15, 1961. Although a direct eastward flight from Shandong would have taken them to South Korea, they went further down south for fear of inadvertently flying into North Korea and barely landed on Jeju Island. The Korean government repaired the airplane and exhibited it to the public.

Commander Chen asked me half-jokingly and half-seriously if he could borrow the airplane once the exhibition was over. If he could, he said he would have it exhibited in front of the presidential office. I told him that I would try and reported to President Park that Taiwan wanted to borrow the AN-2.

"What good is it for us to retain an airplane that cannot even take off? Lend it to them," President Park said without a moment's hesitation.

Commander Chen wanted access to the AN-2 because it contained military secrets such as the main routes and radio frequencies which communist Chinese airplanes were using when they took off from and landed at Beijing. Once Korea sent the AN-2 to Taiwan, the Taiwanese Air Force painted over it and extensively propagandized it as if they themselves had captured it. It was to boost the people's

Commander Chen Jiashang's visit with General Park Chung Hee
I introduced Commander Chen to General Park Chung Hee, September 20, 1961.

morale.

The Taiwanese Air Force reported to President Chiang that all this was made possible thanks to General Kim Shin, former member of the Chinese Air Force, as he had made a special request to President Park. Thanks partly to this affair, President Chiang was grateful to me even before I became the Korean Ambassador to Taiwan. Later, the Central Intelligence Agency of the U.S. acquired intelligence on the AN-2 and asked the Korean government to share secret intelligence from aircraft. However, we answered that we could not meet the U.S. request because the airplane had already been sent to Taiwan.

At the time, the U.S. was trying very hard to collect as much intelligence on China's nuclear development activities as possible (China conducted its first nuclear test successfully in October 1964). The U.S. mainly reconnoitered the Xinjiang Province area using the long-distance high altitude reconnaissance plane, U2. There was the sensational episode of a U2 shot down in the sky over the Ural Mountains by the Soviets on May 1, 1960. The U.S. pilot escaped the airplane in a parachute and survived, but was arrested and later freed in a prisoner swap with a Russian spy detained in the U.S.

Due to this incident, the U.S. had a Taiwanese pilot fly the U2 when reconnoitering Xinjiang as a cover in the event the plane was shot down. When the Taiwanese pilot would return from the mission, the U.S. would take the film without sharing it with Taiwan. A U2 flown by a Taiwanese pilot departed from Taiwan, landed on the Gunsan Air Base in Korea, and then took off from there to enter Chinese airspace. It then returned to Taiwan directly without stopping in Korea. The U.S. sought Korea's permission when carrying out such reconnaissance operations.

One day, a key American figure from the intelligence community visited me. Saying that the U.S. needed to implement reconnaissance missions for various reasons, he asked me to report to my boss what he had said verbally. When I reported this to President Park, he accepted the U.S. request and said,

"Why not? Tell him to also share with us any valuable intelligence."

I learned later that the Taiwanese pilots flying U2s included some of my classmates. They reconnoitered not only mainland China but also North Korea by flying over Manchuria. Once I heard this, I visited the headquarters of the Taiwanese Air Force which was across the street from the Korean Embassy. I asked for the Taiwan's cooperation, since Korea was cooperating with Taiwan on the reconnaissance operations. In particular, I asked them to let me know information related to North Korea without fail. Sometime afterwards, Chiang Ching-kuo asked me in confidence,

"Did you know that North Korea is developing a nuclear weapons program?"

According to the intelligence that Taiwan had gathered, equipment related to nuclear weapons development was flowing into North Korea. That was around the year 1965. I immediately reported this to President Park. Taiwan could obtain such intelligence not only because it participated in the U2 reconnaissance operations but also because it was developing a nuclear weapons program itself. Since Taiwan was involved in securing equipment and resources necessary for nuclear development, it was quick to catch on to similar activities by North Korea. It was highly valuable intelligence at the time, as it is even from today's perspective. But our intelligence agencies did not take it seriously. They did not believe that North Korea had the capability to engage in such activities.

The time I visited the headquarters of the Taiwanese Air Force, those who had been my seniors in the flight school stood in line and saluted me. Although I had been their junior in the past, now they were extending me every courtesy as I was visiting in the capacity of an ambassador. The Taiwanese Air Force welcomed me by hoisting the Korean national flag and mobilizing a military band to play the Korean national anthem. I entered the headquarters and gave brief greetings.

"I may be here now as an ambassador, but I feel as if I am still a part of the Chinese Air Force," I said.

People were puzzled, not understanding what I meant by that. I clarified what I meant.

"You guys blow the bugle every morning and evening to signal a daily schedule. I start each day the same way you do thanks to the call of the bugle."

Everyone laughed out loud. The Korean Embassy was indeed directly across from the headquarters. I talked about the U2 reconnaissance operations during a meeting with high-ranking generals in the Taiwanese Air Force. They provided me with pictures of the locations inside North Korea that my government was interested in analyzing, once clearing it with superiors. The pictures included important military facilities such as air fields, ports, etc. It turned out that although the U.S. was unwilling to share military intelligence with its partner, Taiwan, the latter had been tapping into it on its own for some time.

Chapter 14

Shin, You Are Korean Ambassador!

Did You Come to Study Here to Dodge Military Service?

The Korean students studying in Taiwan tended to have poor knowledge of Chinese characters. They could speak Chinese, but their poor knowledge of written Chinese was an impediment to their studies. I fear that Korean students going off to study in China today also face the same problem.

Once, a lady who was the daughter of an independence fighter and had lived in China for many years visited Korea with her husband and granddaughter. Her granddaughter at the time had spare time while she was waiting for the results of the university entrance exam she recently had taken. I presented her with a book on politics, economy, society and culture that was published in Hong Kong. However, since the book was written in traditional Chinese characters, she could not read it properly as she had learned only simplified Chinese characters.

Once a culture goes through change, it is difficult to restore it. Most of the students who go to study in China these days tend to learn only simplified characters. Although simplified characters are quite convenient, I believe that students should learn traditional characters as well in order to fully understand the tradition and culture of China. As China is becoming more and more influential in the world, overseas Chinese are increasingly using only simplified character. At the same time, more than a few people argue that it is no less necessary to learn traditional characters.

In any case, Korean students had a hard time studying in Taiwan as they had not fully learned traditional written Chinese in Korea. Very few Korean students were good at written Chinese in traditional characters as Heo Se-uk was, thanks to having studied them since childhood. As the Korean Ambassador, I had much interest in Korean students. Although there numbers were many, I tried my best to get to know each one and figure out whether they were studying hard. When they visited the Korean Embassy, I pushed them hard thinking that I should take on the role of their parents.

"You wouldn't have come to Taiwan to study just to avoid military service, no?"

"No, no, sir! No way!"

"Then you must study very hard. Studying in a foreign country is a rare opportunity, so do your best each day and try to learn as much as you can while you are here."

I was told later on that Korean students hesitated to visit the Korean Embassy because I would be so stern with them. But I have no regrets. I meant well as I understood well the challenges Korean students abroad faced. After all, I had studied and received flight training in foreign countries far away from my family myself.

I did not just give the Korean students a hard time. The Lunar

New Year's Holiday is called "*chunjie*" (spring celebrations) in China. During the *chunjie*, since school buildings except for dormitories would shut down and most stores would be closed, Korean students would have a hard time finding a place to eat in. Hence, the Korean Embassy provided food for them. The meals were prepared by the wives of the staff members of the embassy who gathered together to make various dishes. The students came to the embassy for meals over the course of two to three days.

Besides the students, Koreans who were without family or were economically challenged also came to eat and sleep during the *chunjie*. When I think of those days, I cannot thank my wife enough. In addition to inviting lots of people over, she would also make kimchi and side dishes as well as purchase basic food like flour and take them to student dormitories. The students appreciated the good will. They would call the days when my wife visited "party day."

In those days, Korean national sports teams visited Taiwan to attend international sporting events not infrequently. At such times, my wife would prepare a good deal of fruits, *kimchi*, and *bulgogi* for the Korean athletes. In particular, she used to provide the athletes with Korean barley tea, as drinking tap water in a foreign country could upset one's stomach. My wife's barley tea was very popular with the visiting Korean athletes. Soon, a rumor went around, that the Korean national team members were so energetic because they drank ginseng tea from the Korean Ambassador's wife.

All this was not part of the Korean Embassy's official job, of course. No one would have complained if the embassy had not done any of this. But my wife gladly went out of her way to do such things.

Some people asked her why she took the trouble to do such things for others. She replied,

"If someday my own children study in a foreign country, wouldn't it be so wonderful if someone occasionally looked after them in this way? I'm happy to help as they are all like my own children to me."

Taiwan's Counterespionage and Bombs over Jinmen Island

President Chiang did his best to eradicate corruption and build a new Chinese society. He also made great efforts to prevent the Communist party from infiltrating his government. For example, he made office colleagues write a report on each other's daily life. While it may seem excessive, it turned out that the chief of staff of General Hu Zongnan was a long-time spy planted by the Communist party. Taiwan's topography was quite mountainous, and many parts of Taiwan's mountains were off limits. This was because the government thought that once Communist infiltrators escaped into the mountains, it would be difficult to pursue them through the mountainous terrain. For this reason, anyone intending to seek entry into restricted areas first needed to obtain the military's permission.

The Taiwanese government was very concerned about the possibility of restlessness on the part of soldiers once they are discharged from the service. In particular, the soldiers who had come from the mainland in most cases had no place to go once they were discharged. Therefore, the government tried to create jobs for them, for example, by putting them to work on paving roads on mountainous areas and construction.

Taiwan's topography is such that its eastern regions mostly feature rough mountains. The government decided to construct a transversal road penetrating through the mountains in Taizhong. Its purpose was to allow military troops to move quickly from one side of the mountain to the other and also provide discharged soldiers with jobs. Chiang Ching-kuo planned and directed the project. He also had a retirement home built for aging soldiers and created a veterans guidance committee which provided care and financial support.

President Chiang ruled Taiwan under martial law from 1949 to 1975. When he died in 1975, Chiang Ching-kuo succeeded him. After a few years, Chiang the younger lifted martial law. Taiwan was still a one-party dictatorship under the Guomindang. Yet, ordinary people did not feel their daily lives were unduly constrained except when it came to politics.

President Chiang had a great deal of interest in the Korean situation and had frequent conversations with me. Due to this close personal friendship, President Park Chung Hee as well as his Minister of Foreign Affairs once warned me,

"Ambassador Kim, you are a Korean ambassador. Don't forget that."

The Taiwanese government itself was also concerned that I might try to get in touch with my former Chinese classmates. It warned my classmates that they should refrain from staying in close touch with me as I was now serving as an ambassador who represented my country. This was an attempt on the part of the government to deter my old friends from complaining to me about the government or revealing sensitive information to me during our casual conversations. But, in reality, no matter how much the Taiwanese government tried, such complaints and information could not but reach my ears from time to time.

Communist China constantly kept an eye on what President Chiang was up to in Taiwan. It planted many spies in Hong Kong, targeting the wives of Taiwanese high-ranking officials who were fond of going on shopping trips to Hong Kong. The spies would become acquainted with them and gather various information from them while accompanying them on shopping sprees in Hong Kong.

The wife of an official who was a close confidante of President Chiang once visited Hong Kong for pleasure. As she was about to return, her friend in Hong Kong held her back, urging her to stay a few more days. But she packed her bags, saying that she had to return home right away.

"Why are you in such a hurry?" asked her friend, curious to know what the rush was.

"My husband will be going on a business trip in a few days," she answered.

That her husband would be going on a business trip almost certainly meant that he would be accompanying President Chiang to some place.

"Where is he going?" asked her friend.

"To Jinmen Island," the wife of Chiang's close aide answered.

In this way, China was able to gather information on when President Chiang would be visiting Jinmen Island. As it turned out, China mounted a large-scale shelling of Jinmen Island the day that

President Chiang was to arrive there. However, Chiang had to return to his presidential office almost immediately upon arrival in Jinmen due to an urgent development back in Taipei. A few high-ranking generals including Defense Minister Yu Dawei who attended him stayed. At lunch, shells fell over them like rain. 440 thousands shells fell on Jinmen Island from August 23 to October 5, 1958. Taiwan fired back, of course. After this bombardment, all the military facilities in Jinmen Island were placed in underground facilities. Fire fights sporadically occurred after this event.

The wife of Chiang Wei-kuo, the younger step-brother of Chiang Ching-kuo, was also a target of Chinese espionage. Chiang Wei-kuo married Shi Jingyi, the younger sister of one of my classmates with whom I had received flight training. The Shi family was a very affluent and renowned family from the Xian and Xibei regions. Since Ms. Shi had been raised in such an affluent family, she lived a very extravagant life. She frequently visited Hong Kong on shopping sprees even after her marriage.

Whenever she went to Hong Kong, both new and old acquaintances approached her and tried to gain her favor by giving her gifts. Once they won her trust, they would dig up as much information from her as possible about goings on in Taiwan and in leadership circles. Ms. Shi would also smuggle goods into Taiwan because as Chiang Wei-kuo's wife, she was relatively free from immigrations procedures in her travels between Taiwan and Hong Kong.

All of this came to the fore due to an absurd event. One time, on the eve of Chiang Wei-kuo's visit to the U.S. as a member of a government delegation, his wife insisted that she go with him as well.

When he said no, she tore up his passport in a fit of rage. As a result, Chiang Wei-kuo was left out of the delegation to the U.S. President Chiang was incensed and ordered a thorough investigation, which revealed all of Ms. Shi's improper activities. Chiang Kai-Shek had his step-daughter-in-law executed in 1953.

Chiang Kai-Shek's Tears

In 1966, during my term as Korean Ambassador to Taiwan, Walter McConaughy assumed his new post in Taiwan as the U.S. Ambassador. The Taiwanese government had some concerns about receiving McConaughy as ambassador. It was said that McConaughy, as U.S. Ambassador to Korea from December 1959 to April 1961, had played a major role in pressuring President Syngman Rhee to step down in April 1960. The presence of this perception in some circles led some in the Taiwanese government to suspect that McConaughy might, under the right circumstance, check President Chiang and somehow force him to step down. For this and other reasons, Taiwanese intelligence agents were planted in the U.S. ambassador's residence as guards and housekeepers.

At the time, there were fewer countries that had posted their ambassador to Taiwan than I had expected, whereas the number of countries that had recognized the People's Republic of China kept rising. Besides Spain, major European countries, such as the United Kingdom, France, and Italy, did not dispatch their ambassador to Taiwan. While I served there, the doyen of the diplomatic corps changed from the Philippine ambassador to the Spanish ambassador. I became the deputy chief of the diplomatic corps in Taipei when the Spanish Ambassador was the head. In reality, the diplomatic corps as a group did not do anything special. We held social meetings occasionally and attended Taiwan's big national events to offer our congratulations. The foreign chiefs of mission did not really socialize together as often as one might think.

After serving eight years in Taiwan, my government suggested that I transfer to another country, specifically, Italy. But rather than continuing to serve in another country as ambassador, I wished to return to Korea. I had accepted the ambassadorship to Taiwan because I thought the job well suited to me in terms of language, personal relationships and so on. It was not necessarily because of a desire to be a diplomat that I had accepted the offer.

There were many others of a military background who had been posted overseas as ambassador: Generals Lee Jong-chan, Paik Sun Yup, Lee Hyeong-geun, Gang Yeong-hun, Ryu Jae-heung, etc. These were all political appointments born of two basic reasons. First, the presence of these senior officers would be somewhat awkward for the young Park Chung Hee military leadership. Second, these elders in the military had given much to their nation and deserved a reward in the form of representing their nation abroad. My case was not that different from the rest, although I was still relatively young at the time.

After eight years in Taiwan, I decided to end my service as a diplomat. I decided to return to Korea. The decision was affirmed all the more strongly because of my children's education. My eldest had

With President and Mrs. Park Chung Hee
During President and Mrs. Park's visit to Taiwan, February 1966.

gone to America to attend college after completing his second grade of high school in Taiwan. The rest of my children had all graduated from an elementary school for Koreans and were enrolled in an American school in Taiwan. I did not necessarily like the idea of my children's studies taking them here and there. Moreover, I thought they had better be educated in Korea, since it was not as if they were going to spend their entire lives living abroad. Apart from my eldest who was already in college in the U.S., I decided to take the rest of my children back to Korea.

My wife was also a big contributing factor in my return to Korea. She was quite close to First Lady Yuk Young-Soo. During my time as the Air Force Chief of Staff, high-ranking generals in the army, air force, and navy would often be invited together with their spouses to dinners and other engagements by the president and first lady. Through these social meetings, my wife became close to the first lady. On my occasional visits to Korea with my wife while stationed in Taiwan, the first lady would invite my wife to the Blue House for tea. The times that the first lady visited Taiwan, the two would also spend much time together.

Thanks to this personal connection, my wife was in a position to bring up casually with the first lady our wish to return to Korea. I gather my wife also mentioned that she hoped to return to Korea all the more because of concerns over our children's education. Soon after my wife had broached the subject, the question of my return to Korea received more attention.

President Chiang Kai-Shek used to invite the entire diplomatic corps to dinner at his official residence once or twice a year.

With President and Mrs. Chiang Kai-Shek   Many of Taiwan's top officials had spouses who hailed from Shanghai, Madam Soong's hometown. My wife, fluent in Shanghainese, enjoyed a close relationship with Madam Soong.

He usually invited everyone during the Chinese Thanksgiving celebrations. The ambassadors would attend with their spouse, and President Chiang would welcome us together with First Lady Soong Mei-ling.

At my last dinner with the diplomatic corps hosted by President Chiang before I was to leave Taiwan, something unexpected happened. By convention the spouse of the doyen of the corps sat to the right of President Chiang, while the head of the corps sat to the right of First Lady Soong Mei-ling. On this day, however, my wife was asked to sit to the right of President Chiang, while I sat to Madam Soong's right. Seeing such a seating order, I realized that this was a farewell party for me. Sure enough, President Chiang, after thanking all the foreign ambassadors for their work, said that he had arranged for this party in part to bid my wife and me farewell on the eve of our return to Korea. It was unprecedented for President Chiang to host a farewell party for a foreign ambassador.

When the final decision regarding my ambassadorship was made, President Park said the following,

"Since President Chiang thought of you more as his own son than a foreign ambassador, he will be missing you very much once you leave Taiwan."

President Park sent me a signed letter to deliver to President Chiang. I gave it to President Chiang during a visit with him prior to informing him of my impending return to Korea.

"Thank you for all the courtesies extended to Ambassador Kim Shin during his ambassadorship in Taiwan over the past several years. It is now time to call him back to Korea and entrust him with a new task. I seek your understanding," Park said in the letter.

President Chiang could not conceal his shock after reading the letter.

"Ambassador Kim, are you really going home? Surely you can stay on longer..."

He could not finish his sentence as his eyes welled up. By then, he was in his eighties, and grown a bit softhearted. At that moment, I conjured up my father, who had been close to Chiang. I felt very grateful to President Chiang for treating me like a son over the years.

"Please do your best to deepen the friendship between our countries even when you're back in Korea," Chiang said, after catching his breath.

My successor was Army General Kim Gye-won. He would be the chief secretary to the president at the time President Park was assassinated in 1979.

I was conferred a medal by the Taiwanese government before I left. Taiwan's *Zhongyang Ribao* (*Zhongyang Daily*) bade me farewell in an editorial. I bade President Chiang farewell at the going-away party hosted by the Chiangs.

"What I focused on most during my eight years of ambassadorship was to play the role of a bridge between Korea and Taiwan. I think that I carried out this task faithfully. I worked on it very hard to the extent that at times I was mistaken for a Taiwanese ambassador instead of a Korean ambassador." I meant by this that I had done my best to deepen the friendship and mutual understanding between our two nations.

During my ambassadorship, I was sometimes tough to my home

government. When Korea tried to import Taiwanese rice during the food shortage situations in the early- and mid-1960s, the Minister of Economic Planning Board blamed me for not taking the trouble to keep him in the loop.

"Give me a full and direct report!" he ordered me.

"If you have something you wish me to do you, please follow the proper procedures through the right chain of command," I replied.

Infuriated by my reply, the minister went to see President Park.

"This urgent matter directly concerns me, and I should be informed of all developments related to it. But the Ambassador to Taiwan is disobeying me."

With a smile, President Park said,

"His response is only too natural, since he has served in the military for a long time. You should not test him and overstep your authority when there is a proper chain of command. It happens that a regimental commander follows a division commander's orders, but not a corps commander's order. That's how a chain of command works."

President Park was defending me as he knew well my personality.

Part 5

Reflections on Our Generation

Chapter 15

My Years as National Assemblyman and Minister of Transportation

Running for the National Assembly and

the Bitter Cup of Defeat

When I returned home from Taiwan and reported to President Park, he told me straight-forwardly:

"I need you to help me now."

"How may I help?" I asked.

"I'd like you to run for the National Assembly in Yongsan."

"I'm sorry sir, but I have no interest in becoming a National Assemblyman."

I declined his request, but the president pressed on.

"The experience will be good for you. Even young lieutenant colonels have become assemblymen. You should give it a try. You can do it, I'm sure."

I declined once again, but he insisted that I help him just this one time. There were several reasons that Park made this request. At that time, the popularity of Park's governing party, Democratic Republican Party (DRP), had hit rock bottom. The party was in crisis, facing the 8th general election on May 25, 1971. Thus, the party felt it needed to recruit notable extra-party figures. In the end, I could not bring myself to refuse the president's request. On January 16, 1971, I was officially nominated as a DRP candidate for the Yongsan district.

Before the official nomination, Mr. Yu Jin-san heard about President Park's request to me to run for the National Assembly. Informed that I was on a trip to Taiwan, he came to meet me Kimpo Airport on the day of my return. He said hello to me, and then proposed that I join the New Democratic Party (NDP).

"Please join the NDP. I will give you the second candidate position for the national constituency, while I take the first candidate position. The Korean Independence Party (KIP) has already merged with the NDP."

The KIP, established by my father, had remained independent until then. However, on the eve of the election, it merged with the NDP. In any case, I could not accept Mr. Yu's offer, because I had already made a promise to President Park. In the end, I ran for the National Assembly as a DRP candidate in Yongsan, competing against the NDP candidate Kim Won-man. My campaign was an endless series of bitter fights, as I had no experience in running for office and hardly knew anything about politics. On the other hand, my opponent, Kim Won-man, was a veteran politician.

At the time, parasitic electioneerers appeared as they did in every election. They peeked around various camps, saying things like, "If you treat me well, I will easily bring at least 1,000 votes to you." Not caring one bit about which party to support, they snooped around both parties and took money from both. Some said they would help as volunteers, but they without fail asked for money once they got their foot in the door.

There were parasitic electioneerers who specialized in spreading groundless rumors that slandered the opposing candidate. Others used dirty methods to hurt the opponent's reputation. For example, the day before the election, they would put about 100 *won* in an envelope with the adversary's name written on it, wrap it around with a rock inside, and throw the projectiles through constituents' windows in the middle of the night. The constituents, after unfolding it to find only 100 *won*, would hurl abuses at the candidate. Still others leaked false information to confuse the opposing camp.

Witnessing such an electoral scene where dirty methods ran rampant, I came to see firsthand the underbelly of politics. I felt I could do nothing in this abyss of foulness. Presumably, such a mindset did not help. I lost the election. The election results showed that only one DRP candidate, Jang Deok-jin, was elected in Seoul. The thing is, he won by offering money to the leader of the NDP Yu Jin-san in exchange for Yu withdrawing from the race. This was the so-called "Jinsan Scandal," which took place in the middle of the election. The young members of the NDP harshly criticized Yu for selling out and giving away a seat in the National Assembly for personal gain. But Yu showed no shame and said with an air of self-righteousness,

"We can win several seats with this money. We can knock down our enemy with their own bullets."

Yu's words ironically came true as all of the DRP candidates except one lost out Seoul. I lost the election not only because I lacked experience but also because I ran too hastily without sufficient preparation. I once complained about this to President Park.

"Isn't it like dropping paratroopers in the middle of the night in the jungles of Vietnam to carry out an operation, sir?"

My complaint was not groundless. I had run too hastily as to have enough time to draw people's attention. After losing the election, I bought a flower bouquet and visited Kim Won-man, my opponent. He was very surprised to see me, for it had not occurred to him that his opponent would actually visit to congratulate him on his victory. I just thought that acknowledging my defeat and congratulating my opponent's victory was good sportsmanship.

The Empty Seat Left by My Irreplaceable Wife

My wife's chronic illness turned for the worse as she toiled away day and night in my campaign shortly upon return to Korea from our long years of living in Taiwan. Since our time in Taiwan my wife had a stomach problem, unable to eat well. Doctors could not figure out the cause. I took my wife whose illness had gotten worse during the campaign to Severance Hospital in Seoul for a comprehensive diagnosis. She was diagnosed with cancer.

The doctors said that hospitalization would not really help and that she would likely not survive beyond six months. I was at a loss for words. The pain of defeat in the election was now overshadowed by the infinitely more painful news of my wife's critical condition. I felt so helpless. The thought of raising our children and caring for them by myself until they all settle down I found daunting, too. I felt so terribly sorry to my wife, guilty that I had put her through helping me in my bid for office. The thought of losing her was painful beyond words.

As mentioned above, I met her in 1947 when I underwent procedures for discharge from the Chinese military and passed through Shanghai on my way to Nanjing. We had our wedding in Korea. She was twenty-three years-old, and I was twenty-seven. My wife was born in Shanghai and had spent her entire life in Shanghai, where there are no mountains. She was most surprised that Korea was so mountains when she finally came to Korea for our wedding.

We had our wedding in December 1948, and we lived with my father in Gyeong Gyo Jang. Since my father passed away on June 26, 1949, the length of time we lived with him was not long. During this short time, my wife always welcomed visitors and served my father as well as any dutiful daughter-in-law could. When she served meals for him, she would place a piece of cloth like an apron on his lap to protect his white traditional shirt. Her thoughtful gesture pleased my father very much.

My wife made considerable effort to adapt to Korean culture and custom, as she had lived only in China. For example, women in China usually wore a relatively simple dress called *qipao*, whereas Korean women wore the elaborate Korean costume, *hanbok*. She adapted well. In particular, she was very thrifty. When she washed grains of rice, any grain from which the hull would not easily peel off she would remove one by one. She was meticulous, careful, considerate, and introverted.

Our family, with my parents-in-law

From left, eldest Jin, third son Hui, youngest Mee, and second son Yang.

After my father passed away in 1949, she gave birth to our first child, Jin, in October that year. Our second child, also a son, Yang, was born in Daegu during the Korean War. Our third son, Hui, was born in Suwon. And our daughter, Mee, was born in Seoul. She knitted our children's clothes out of wool herself. She was so dexterous that she could knit a whole suit for our children in a week. Although thrifty by nature and with herself, with others she was generous. She was always very gracious in helping others who needed a helping hand, never one to turn away from people in need.

I took my wife back home after I was told that hospitalization would do her no good. When she would complain of pain, I gave her a morphine shot myself. Eventually her body grew immune to morphine, and the drug would no longer alleviate her of pain. Until then, I had not shared with her what she was suffering from. Neither had I told any our children.

"Honey, please tell me frankly what kind of disease I'm suffering from," she said, when nothing could relieve her pain.

But I could not bear to tell her that it was a cancer. Saying no words to her, I just administered another shot of morphine. As her pain did not go away even with more and more morphine, she became convinced that she had an incurable disease. One day, she said to me quietly,

"I know even though you don't tell me. Please call all our children in."

When our children all gathered, she spoke, addressing me as well. It was essentially her will.

"My dear children, I haven't told you, but my disease is incurable.

I would like you not to object in the event your father remarries and you live together with your stepmother once I am gone."

She said this because she thought it impossible for me to raise four children by myself. They would not listen to her, telling her not to say such a thing. My wife kept insisting that they should not object to my remarrying. We all wept together, thinking this was her will.

My wife was also very supportive of me when I was the Air Force Chief of Staff. Since I was frequently invited by senior officers at the U.S. Eighth Army, my wife and I also reciprocated with dinners at our house. At such occasions, my wife was a superb hostess, preparing just the right kind of food and also arranging for the perfect table setting. She was also able to maintain close relations with American women, as she spoke English quite well. At U.S. personnel-hosted parties, most of the Korean women congregated by themselves in a corner and talked among themselves, whereas my wife mingled well with both foreign men and women.

The happiest time of my wife's life was when we lived in Taiwan. Among the folks who were close to President and Mrs. Chiang, there were many who were originally from Shanghai and Zhejiang. The dialect thereof was so different from standard Mandarin Chinese used in Beijing that even I could not follow it. Since my wife was a native of Shanghai, however, she mingled well with President Chiang's confidantes. She was also able to speak with First Lady Soong Mei-ling freely in Shanghainese dialect.

Another reason my wife enjoyed her life in Taiwan was that she did not have to worry about me. When I was in the Air Force, she fretted constantly wondering if anything untoward would happen to me, if I would return home safely at the end of the day. In Taiwan, however, she did not have to worry at all. Moreover, in Taiwan I was able to be faithful to my family life because I had the liberty to return home immediately after work. For these reasons and more, she would say every now and then that our time together in Taiwan was the happiest time of her life. She died on November 11, 1971. She was buried near the grave of her parents.

After my wife's death, I frequently drank alone. I also frequently prayed for the repose of her soul. I could not but pray for her, especially at dinnertime, which always reminded me of her. I did not pray because I was a person of deep faith, but because I was driven by absolute loneliness at the thought that I no longer had anyone to count on, consult with, or share life's joys and sorrows with, to laugh and cry together with, any more.

Looking back further into my past, I grew up seeing my grandmother earnestly pray and sing hymns. We had really no one to confide in. Since we were always watched and could be arrested any time, we could count on nothing but the grace of heaven. That's why my grandmother went to church and gave offerings, even though we lived from hand to mouth.

I feel like I still could hear my grandmother singing her favorite hymns, "I Am Trusting, Lord, in Thee" and "Nearer, My God, to Thee." She was especially fond of the former. The lyrics read:

I am coming to the cross; I am poor, and weak, and blind;
I am counting all but dross; I shall full salvation find.
I am trusting, Lord, in thee, Thou dear Lamb of Calvary

Humbly at thy cross I bow; Save me, Jesus, save me now.

Long my heart has sighed for thee; Long as evil reigned within;
Jesus sweetly speaks to me,
I will cleanse you from all sin.
I am trusting, Lord, in thee, Thou dear Lamb of Calvary
Humbly at thy cross I bow; Save me, Jesus, save me now.

Every line seems to capture my grandmother's anguish and longing when we were so poor and lonely.

While we lived in Taiwan, my wife made considerable contribution to establishing three Korean churches in Taiwan. There is bound to be a degree of personal conflicts, feuds, and quarrels in any immigrant community. One might think that the immigrants, facing common problems in a foreign land, would all come together to form a tightly-knit community. But the reality is quite different. My wife put in a lot of effort in establishing Korean churches not necessarily out of overwhelming religious faith but out of the belief that the spiritual consolation and psychological stability that faith brings would deepen the fraternity of the Korean community in Taiwan.

Whenever I felt the big hole in my heart left by my wife's departure, one that could not be filled by anyone, I thought of the hymn "I Am Trusting, Lord, in Thee." Recalling the hymn often gave me a lump in my throat, as it led to memories of my grandmother, my brother, and many others who had passed away before.

Fortunately, my children were all able to complete their studies and settle down on their own. I am really grateful that they all grew up well and were able to take care of themselves even without their mother.

The Iron Horse Wants to Run

After my wife's funeral, my children and I spent each day feeling as if we were sleepwalking, not entirely cognizant of ourselves or our surroundings, so painful was the grief. Confining myself to home, I tried to bring solace to my heart and mind by practicing calligraphy. In the midst of grieving, I received a phone call from Prime Minister Kim Jong-pil, asking me to take up the position of Minister of Transportation. Since President Park knew that I was confining myself to home in the wake of my wife's death, he offered me the position to help me get my mind off the pain of loss and start working once again. I became the Minister of Transportation on November 23, 1971, about two weeks after my wife's death.

The former Minister of Transportation was Jang Seong-hwan, a former general in the Air Force. After serving as the Air Force Chief of Staff, Jang was appointed Ambassador to Thailand. He had returned to Korea earlier than I had, and served as Minister of Transportation for about a year. At the time I ran for office, President Park himself had had doubts about my bid. He thought that even if I lost the election, it would still be helpful if I were able to win a substantial number of votes. In fact, when he asked me to run, he mentioned that even if I were to lose, there would be other

Appointment as Minister of Transportation   President Park Chung Hee appoints me Minister of Transportation, November 1971. Prime Minister Kim Jong-pil is seen in the middle, looking on.

opportunities for us to work together.

As he presented me with the certificate of appointment, President Park went out of his way to offer his condolences. During my wife's struggle with cancer, the first lady called to offer her support and encourage my wife and my family. The moment I was appointed to my new job as cabinet minister, I devoted myself to my new duties and worked day and night. My busy work schedule did help relieve some of the pain of loss. The job of the Minister of Transportation entailed lots of surveys and actual visits to various locations and transportation facilities. I visited all of major ports, railroads, and roads all over the country. Since the Ministry of Transportation was also in charge of tourism at the time, I was responsible for all sorts of government business.

Unlike military administration or diplomatic affairs, transportation affairs involved a lot of licensing-related tasks. For example, when bus companies in other provinces sought to open a new line, it was the central government's job to review each case and issue a license rather than the responsibility of the provincial government, which would have been better positioned for the task. In short, transportation affairs were not organized or implemented systematically. As the central government took care of so much licensing, it was very often the case that the person seeking a new license in a local province would make a trip to Seoul and personally request officials of the Ministry of Transportation to grant him the license, which almost invariably involved treating the officials to meals and other gifts. I brought up this problem in a meeting.

"Should the central government deal with even licensing a bus line in other provinces when the provincial governors themselves can take care of such issues? Transfer licensing authority related to such matters over to the provinces."

But every single one of my subordinates objected. Although they gave various reasons, the real reason was that they did not want to give up any of their vested interests they had stacked up for so long. My proposal did not go through in the end. The wall of bureaucracy was indeed very high.

While I traveled by train to visit railroad stations all over the country, I saw that the station name signs were in Korean and

English only, without any Chinese characters. At the time, President Park was stressing the exclusive use of the Korean alphabet. The Korean names were written large on the signs with small English phonetics below them. I found it unacceptable for these signs and signposts not to contain Chinese characters. Since Korea had used Chinese characters from ancient times, and in view of the fact that there would come a time when Japanese and Chinese tourists would visit Korea in droves, I thought this problematic. Thus, I ordered my subordinates to put Chinese characters on the station name signs.

But they were opposed to this idea as well. They argued that, since there were tens of thousands of station name signs all over the country, the costs of replacing the signs would be prohibitive. I proposed an easy way to solve the problem.

"You don't have to replace existing signs with new ones. All you have to do is put Chinese characters between the Korean and English."

They did as I proposed.

One time, I took a train to the final point of a railway track near the 38th parallel. On a sign was written the "end point of the railroad." I thought that even if it actually was the end point, the railroad would be linked with that from North Korea and run on again someday in the future. The "end point of railroad" seemed to sound too pessimistic. I called in the director of the National Railroad Administration.

"Don't you think that the current name would not be appropriate should Korea be unified in the future? I'd like it to be renamed."

He came back with various prospective names after consultation with many others. The phrase "the iron horse wants to run" caught my attention. I told him to go with it. That was how the sign "the iron horse wants to run" came to be at the end point of the railroad.

The Park administration had already made great efforts to construct highways before my appointment as Minister of Transportation. At the time, besides express long-distance buses, local buses and trucks that ran mostly on local roads were not allowed to travel on the highways. I thought this was not right.

"Highways are the arteries of our nation. The more people and goods travel on them, the greater their contribution is to our nation. It doesn't make any sense to bar local buses and trucks from national highways. Which countries of the world would do this? Why do we not allow other automobiles to run on the highways that were built with taxpayer money? Allow all vehicles to run on the trans-national highways immediately."

When I tried to allow all vehicles access to highways, express bus companies, which had special licenses for exclusive travel on the highway, protested vehemently. They obstinately resisted my policy, insisting that highways were for express buses only. The reason they gave was truly ridiculous.

"Since those automobiles that run on dusty local roads are dirty, they will dirty the newly built highway."

What a preposterous reason. I offered them a solution.

"In that case, we just tell each driver to rinse the wheels of his automobile before entering the highway."

In the end, I was successful in my bid to allow all vehicles access to the highway. Although I was limited in my capabilities and often ran into a wall of bureaucratic inertia, I tried my best to do what I could during my term as Minister of Transportation. I held the post until September 1974, for two years and ten months, which was actually very long for a Minister of Transportation. Most Ministers served for a year or two at most. I did my best, hence, can reflect on those busy times with no regrets.

Why the Chief Secretary to the President for Economic Affairs was a No-Show

Not long after I became Minister of Transportation, I was obliged to give a report to President Park on the general state of the ministry during his New Year inspection tour. Cabinet ministers had to make a report to the president directly during this annual review. Each ministry updated slides from the previous year with new ones in preparation for the report. I worked very hard to prepare my briefing slides. I needed to grasp all the key issues related to transportation affairs in detail since I was to present the material to the president myself and answer any questions he may have.

I went on a business trip after preparing the briefing materials. On my return, I found all of the director generals as well as the vice minister dejected. When I asked what the matter was, they answered that Jeong So-yeong, the Chief Secretary to the President for Economic Affairs, had visited the ministry. He was a young man of about forty years of age who hailed from Daegu and had studied in America after graduating from the college of commerce at Seoul

National University.

He had stopped by to check in advance our preparation for the president's inspection tour. After examining the briefing material, he had told my staff to prepare entirely new materials as they were, he charged, too similar to the data from the previous year. The director generals told me that there was not enough time to prepare a new report. I told them not to fret.

"I will talk to him about this, so you don't need to revise them. I will make the report according to the original version."

My staff, still uniformly worried, repeated that Mr. Jeong was a very influential man in the Blue House. In any event, when Mr. Jeong later inquired with my ministry about the new report, my staff had to tell him that I had decided to use the existing material. He then pushed my staff for new material, saying what we had was unacceptable. Upon being informed of this exchange, I spoke to my staff in a firm tone,

"I was not appointed by the chief secretary for economic affairs, but by the president himself. Should the president find my briefing objectionable, I will resign on the spot."

Taken aback by my words, my staff proceeded to put together the briefing material as planned. When President Park came, I gave a briefing as initially prepared. But I did not see Chief Secretary for Economic Affairs Jeong So-yeong in the room. I found out later that Jeong had not attended the briefing session due to a tipoff from the Director of the Presidential Security Service Park Jong-gyu.

Apparently, Mr. Jeong, upon being informed of my flat out rejection of his directive, went to see Mr. Park, who was from the same hometown as he. Jeong talked to him about my "effrontery," and Mr. Park had advised him not to confront me.

In fact, Mr. Park had had a run-in with me when he escorted President Park on visit to Taiwan in February 1966. Before arriving in Taiwan, President Park had visited Vietnam, Thailand, and Malaysia. At each stop, Mr. Park and his small army of bodyguards had harassed the staff members of the Korean embassy, as presidential security agents were prone to in those days. They were prone to asking the embassy staff to buy gifts for them or to make the staff accompany them to local bars late at night.

They behaved in such a way in Taiwan as well. Since the South Korean president did not have his own presidential airplane, President Park flew into Taiwan on a loaned German Lufthansa plane. The plane landed at Songshan Air Base. In the middle of the night, most of the Korean presidential security guards tasked with guarding the plane, mostly went off to a bar, neglecting their duties and dumping their duties to the Taiwanese guards. The captain of the Taiwanese guards was appalled. Although standing guard around a plane through the night was not the most exciting task, it was unthinkable that the primary security force of a visiting head of state would just leave its presidential plane in the hands of foreign guards and go off to a bar.

Furthermore, the presidential bodyguards tended to treat the embassy staff like their own servants. They even pressured Councilor Yun Ha-jeong to buy presents for them and to tend to them while they went out for pleasure. I told Councilor Yun not to accept their demands.

"Their duty is to protect and assist the president. They should not be extorting you for gifts and carousing at night," I told Yun.

When Councilor Yun refused their demands, some of them even grabbed him by the collar and threatened him, while hurling obscenities at him. Rattled and offended, Mr. Yun came to me and said,

"I will submit my resignation and return to Korea."

As the Korean Embassy to Taiwan at the time did not have a minister appointed to the mission, a councilor was the de facto deputy chief of mission. Yun's indignation was understandable, as the bodyguards who were harassing him with preposterous demands held significantly lower rank as civil servants and were behaving in such a manner only because of their proximity to power. I calmed him down and dissuaded him from tendering his resignation. I was resolved to bring this issue up with President Park the next opportunity I had with him alone. I seized the opportunity when just the two of us were in the backseat of a car.

"I have something I need to report to you sir. Even if it displeases you, I ask you to hear me out."

I told him about all the negligent and shameful misconduct by his bodyguards. Until then, no other ambassador in other missions had told the president of such goings-on before. President Park listened to my complaint without commenting much. That night, around midnight, he called for an emergency meeting and called all of his staff into his room. Some attendants who had gone out carousing had not yet returned to the hotel. Most of those who were conspicuously absent were the president's security guards. President Park was livid.

He became so angry that even the Taiwanese security guards at the hotel rallied forth, thinking there was an emergency.

Sometime after this, the Minister of Foreign Affairs asked me quietly,

"Did you by chance tell the president something that he found disagreeable?"

"Yes, I did. I believed that if we kept overlooking the misconduct of those serving the president, he will be in the dark, and it will come back to bite him. I am sorry for having spoken frankly and upsetting him."

Mr. Park had received more than an earful from President Park in Taiwan because of me. When Chief Secretary for Economic Affairs Jeong had visited him presumably to collude how to punish me, Park told Jeong,

"You're picking a fight with the wrong person. Just let it go."

As a result, Mr. Jeong did not attend my briefing session.

The Tragedy of First Lady and the Opening of Subway Line No. 1

On March 1, 1969, the Hanjin Trading Company obtained the rights to administer the Korean Air Public Corporation and renamed itself Korean Air. When I was Minister of Transportation, Korean Air was in fact a newly-born airline. Since the Ministry of Transportation was the main government agency in charge of overseeing civilian airline, Korean Air personnel frequently visited. So did Cho Jung-hun, the

The Opening Ceremony of Subway Line Number 1
The first subway line in Korea opened on August 15, 1974.

company chief. Mr. Cho's visits were usually related to the short supply of able pilots.

Many pilots and repair men who served in the Air Force entered Korean Air upon leaving the service. Learning how to fly an airplane properly requires extensive training, and the Air Force was the only source of good pilots at the time. Air Force pilots who flew fighters could easily learn how to fly civilian aircraft, as there was no big difference in operating the two. Mr. Cho asked me to help recruit pilots, since I had good connections in the Air Force. But I could not grant his request unconditionally, as recruiting too many seasoned pilots with more than a decade or two of experience from the Air

Force would leave a serious hole in national defense.

Mr. Cho also asked me to draft a legislation that prohibits pilots from switching from one civilian airline to a competitor airline. To fly civilian aircraft one needed to receive training at a flight school established by an American airline and obtain a pilot's license. The flight school taught various flight techniques according to each of the various models of aircraft and issued a pilot's license upon the completion of all the courses. This license allowed a pilot to be employed by any airline in any country. Korean Air, too, hired Korean pilots who had graduated from an American flight school. However, its pay scale was not competitive.

Korean Air pilots were paid only about one tenth of the salary that pilots working for foreign airlines received. Korean pilots knew of this big disparity. Since they all spoke conversational English, they talked to foreign pilots frequently and heard about the number of days of paid leave, the number of hours they had to fly each month, and how much their annual pay was.

Once they realized that they were discriminated against, the Korean pilots asked Korean Air to raise their salary. When the company refused, the pilots took a firm stand, threatening to move to other airlines. This was why Mr. Cho had come to ask me to make a law which would prohibit Korean pilots under contract from moving to a foreign airline. At the time, the pilots also came to me and complained that they were being ill-treated, as they were paid just a small fraction of what pilots working for foreign airlines received.

I thought the pilots had a good point, that their complaint was more than reasonable. Thus, I told Mr. Cho to raise their pay, albeit in stages if he could not raise their pay up to that of the foreign pilots all at once. In the event he agrees, I said, I would also reach out to the pilots and ask them to be patient, as their salary will gradually increase. Fortunately, both parties accepted my arbitration, and the conflict between Korean Air and its pilots was resolved.

Expanding and modernizing railroads was also one of my big tasks. Although I have many happy memories of working on Korea's railways, the one that overshadows them all during my term as Minister of Transportation took place on August 15, 1974. It was National Liberation Day, and, not by coincidence, also the day on which the opening ceremony of Subway Line No. 1 was scheduled. President Park and First Lady Yuk were scheduled to test the subway following their attendance in the National Liberation Day Ceremony held in the National Theater. But a tragic incident broke out before they were to test the subway. Mun Se-gwang, a lone assailant, ran in and fired several shots toward President Park. He missed President Park, but one of the stray bullets hit the first lady, and she died from it that very day. In the end, Prime Minister Chung Il-kwon, representing the president, participated in the opening ceremony of Subway Line No. 1 and rode on the subway.

First Lady Yuk, who was close to my wife, was widely respected and beloved by Koreans. Unlike President Park, who was strong-willed, driven, and overpowered other with his powerful presence, she was warm and motherly to everyone. I think that she was much more than just a wife to President Park. Her death was another tragedy born of the great tragedy of a divided nation.

Chapter 16

The Kim Koo Museum and Library

Becoming a National Assemblyman

After leaving the post of the Minister of Transportation, I became, in February 1976, a member of the *Yusin* Political Friends' Association (YPFA), a floor negotiation group of National Assembly members elected from the national constituency through the president's recommendation. Although the YPFA was a semi-political party constituting a floor negotiation group, it was in fact a party organization under the auspices of the governing DRP. Since I had a military background, I joined the National Defense Committee of the National Assembly.

A serious incident took place during the time I was on this committee. In those days, aircraft were not allowed to fly over the Han River from the south in consideration of the location of the Blue House, which was just north of the river. Antiaircraft guns were placed around the river in case of an emergency. One day, an American civilian airplane crossed the river from south to north by mistake, and the antiaircraft guns fired at it without warning. Fortunately, the aircraft was not hit, but the incident could have blown up into a huge diplomatic crisis.

Since I was with the YPFA, I was thrust into the position of making an excuse for this incident on behalf of the government. However, no matter how hard I tried to come up with mitigating factors, it was an inexcusable incident. At the National Defense Committee hearing on the matter, a person from the ROK-U.S. Combined Forces Command was called in as a witness. Since other national assemblymen had little knowledge of aviation, I ended up asking the majority of questions.

I asked him technical questions about the flying speed, altitude, and direction of the civilian airplane. I also asked him about the possible international implications of the incident had the airplane actually been struck by antiaircraft guns. As I asked him one pointed question after another, the witness from the CFC was soon at a loss for words. Upon seeing me pressure the witness with legitimate questions, the assemblymen from the opposition party complimented me on asking all the right questions. I thought that even as a member of the YPFA, I ought to criticize the government when criticism was due. To this day, I have no regret for my judgment then.

When I was an assemblyman, I used to go to the indoor swimming pool in the National Assembly building to swim about one kilometer each time. One day, Hyeon O-bong, a fellow assemblyman, came to the pool to see me. It was February 1978. Mr. Hyeon had once been a Liberal Party assemblyman during the Rhee administration. He switched to the governing DRP during the Park Chung Hee years and won successive elections, thereby establishing himself as a leading figure in the party.

In the past, I had experienced an unpleasant incident involving Mr. Hyeon. The episode took place when I was the deputy chief of staff of operations in the Air Force. There was a lot of corruption during the Liberal Party years. In particular, illegal campaigning and ballot rigging were rampant. Mr. Hyeon was a powerful politician from Jeju Island at the time. At the start of one campaign season, Hyeon asked me to use a military transport plane to transport his promotional material, leaflets and such, to Jeju Island. It was an unacceptable proposition, asking me to permit a military plane to aid a particular political candidate. For whatever reason, he thought that I would comply with his request. Although I was infuriated, I was not in a position to reject it outright to his face. In the end, his promotional materials were taken aboard the military transport plane headed for Jeju. But I had an idea. I summoned the pilot and told him,

"It is illegal, in fact, to transport promotional materials for an election campaign on a military aircraft. Therefore, you fly the airplane as I tell you to."

The pilot intentionally stopped one of the two engines of the aircraft as he was flying over the sea. Inevitably, the speed and altitude at which the airplane was flying dropped all of a sudden. According to my orders, the pilot then dropped all the promotional materials out of the plane in order to lighten the cargo. Then he was to pretend to fly in the direction of the nearest air base for engine repair. This was a perfect excuse not to carry out Mr. Hyeon's unjustifiable request.

After the engine "breakdown," the pilot restarted the engine and proceeded to fly to Jeju. The transport airplane fulfilled its task of delivering military supplies. Mr. Hyeon must have been extremely frustrated. In spite of this little incident in the past, he and I had no issues during the Park years as we were both in the party.

For Hyeon to come to the swimming pool to see me, presumably he had something important to say.

"President Park orders you to transfer from the National Defense Committee to another committee," he told me.

"Which committee?" I asked.

"You've been nominated for the position of Chairman of the Agriculture-Fisheries Committee," Hyeon answered.

Once I heard what he'd said, I suspected that I was being transferred to another committee because I had embarrassed the government in the previous committee hearing. But Mr. Hyeon told me that I was actually getting promoted from a committee member to a committee chairman. He congratulated me.

I studied very hard for my new job because I did not know anything about agriculture and fisheries. In the end, however, my studies turned out to be of no use. There was a lot of conflict in the Agriculture-Fisheries Committee where complex personal interests were entangled. Assemblymen from opposition parties even grabbed me by the collar, charging that I knew nothing about agriculture and fisheries. When I tried to make a decision on a bill by a vote, some assemblymen would physically take my gavel to obstruct the proceedings. The committee was a place where a power game between the government and opposition parties mattered much more than the expert knowledge necessary to make sound judgment on policies. Other committees were no different. I did not stay in the Agriculture-Fisheries Committee for a long time, because the term of office for assemblymen elected from the national constituency was three years, unlike that for those elected from district constituencies, which was six years.

When I became a member of the YPFA, Lee Jong-chan, a noted former Army general, joined as well. He and I, sitting next to each other, used to commiserate and lament on the state of affairs at the national assembly. We realized that we were witnessing the true nature of Korea's political arena in which machinations, maneuvers, and tricks ran rampant. We had no choice but to remain silent and watch this complete bedlam. In short, we were irrelevant people there.

General Lee and I often asked ourselves why we were sitting there. When I happened to sit next to Mr. Lee during assembly sessions, we passed time taking turns to compose Chinese poems. I would compose a line and hand it to him, and he would compose a couplet and hand it back to me. My awkward time as a national assemblyman, which had unwittingly and unexpectedly started, eventually came to pass.

General Ahn Chun-saeng and the Independence Hall

In the summer of 1982 when I was visiting my eldest son in America, I received a call from the Presidential Secretariat. The government was planning to establish an Independence Hall and asked me to take the chairmanship of the Planning and Promotion Committee. I declined right there and then as I thought it highly inappropriate for me to accept the position, when there were older and more qualified figures, such as, Lee Gang-hun and General Ahn Chun-saeng.

General Ahn Chun-saeng was the most eligible candidate for the chairmanship in terms of both dedication to the independence movement and seniority. Once I turned down the offer, the government nominated Park Sun-cheon for the post. However, many former independence fighters objected to her nomination, when it was revealed that she had encouraged Korean students to volunteer to join the Japanese Imperial Army in her public speeches and through other means during the Japanese colonial period. Moreover, she was at the time eighty-five years-old and was not healthy (she died in January 1983). In the end, General Ahn Chun-saeng became the chairman of the Planning and Promotion Committee for the Establishment of the Independence Hall of Korea in October 1982.

I thought that General Ahn was the right man for the position. A member of the tenth class of graduates of the Whampoa Military Academy, Ahn was shot in the leg while battling the Japanese in the Chinese Army in Shanghai in 1937. Among soldiers of the Korean Liberation Army who were still living, Ahn was the only person to have been injured in battle against the Japanese troops. In fact, many of the people who claimed to have participated in the Korean Liberation Army actually had in name only. When I began my job as Minister of Transportation, I looked over the register of the staff. I found "Korean Liberation Army soldier" written down in the "career" column of Vice Minister Lee Jae-cheol's CV. I was happy to see it and called him in immediately.

"Vice-Minister Lee, you were in the Korean Liberation Army?" I asked.

"Well, actually, I am ashamed to talk about it," he said with a look of embarrassment.

"What do you mean?" I asked.

"In fact, I took care of horses in a cavalry of the Japanese Army up to August 14, 1945," he answered.

In the aftermath of Japan's declaration of surrender on August 15, 1945, Japanese soldiers dispersed through China were put in military prison camps. The Korean Provisional Government asked President Chiang to distinguish Korean soldiers in the Japanese Army and detain them separately since they had enlisted by force. The Korean Provisional Government also suggested to Chiang that it would incorporate them into the Korean Liberation Army and train them before taking them back to Korea. Chiang issued a nation-wide order, including over Taiwan, to this effect. This way, many Korean soldiers in the Japanese military became Korean Liberation Army soldiers virtually overnight.

Against this backdrop, General Ahn Chun-saeng stood out. Most Korean Liberation Army soldiers had little experience in independence activities in China. Since most of the troops of the Korean Liberation Army had been stationed in Xian and Kunming, most soldiers had never even shot a gun in a real battle. General Ahn was a rare exception.

Later, I was contacted by Kim Yun-hwan. He wanted me to take the chairmanship of the board of directors of the Independence

Hall of Korea. He also told me that General Ahn was nominated to be the first president of the Independence Hall. I thought it would be good for me to assist General Ahn as the chairman of the board, and answered in the affirmative. I was to the position at the end of June 1986 and worked in that capacity for about two years. During my time as chairman of the board, I was at time frustrated by the bureaucratic infighting at the organization, but I carried out my duties with a special sense of mission that I was laying a firm foundation for the Hall.

National Division, War, and Pro-Japanese Collaborators

Among the government-recognized independence fighters, many are former soldiers of the Korean Liberation Army. At the same time, there are also many who were active in the Chinese military, such as, General Lee Beom-seok and General Kim Hong-il. Another prominent fighter was General Park Si-chang, the son of Park Eun-sik, who, at the time of the outbreak of the Marco Polo Bridge incident on July 7, 1937, was in Baoding, southwest of Beijing. The Chinese commander at the location was Liu An-qi, who would go on to be the Army Chief of Staff in Taiwan. I met General Liu together with General Park during Army Chief of Staff Liu's visit to Seoul. We reminisced about old days in China, and General Liu all of a sudden mentioned,

"My, General Park made my life in Baoding difficult!"

General Liu explained that when he was the commanding officer in Baoding, General Park, who at the time was the commander of the artillery unit, would fire off at the Japanese troops at the slightest provocation. The situation in Baoding was always tense, with fluctuating escalation and de-escalation, in which General Park played a role.

General Park Si-chang responded strongly to even small provocations, because he wished for an outright war between China and Japan. He believed that a war between China and Japan would be conducive to Korea's independence movement. Besides General Park, Korean soldiers in Manchuria also crossed the border into the Soviet Union and fired at Japanese bases in the Russian Far East, for they wished for an outright war between Russia and Japan as well. As the number of skirmishes between Soviet and Japanese troops increased, Stalin looked into the matter and determined that the Korean independence fighters were a causal factor.

This was one reason that Stalin had ethnic Koreans in the Russian Far East forcibly transferred to Central Asia like Tashkent. Later one day, Yi Chung-mo, the chairman of the Korean society in Tashkent, managed to escape eyes and cross over through Xinjiang to visit the Korean Provisional Government. Mr. Yi asked me where he might go to read newspapers or magazines from the Soviet Union. I led Yi to the library of the Soviet embassy, where he could read Soviet newspapers and periodicals.

The purpose of Yi's visit to the Korean Provisional Government was to seek ways to tell the world of the forcible transfer of the Korean population. The Korean Provisional Government took Yi's exhortation to heart and, upon his recommendation, made an appeal to the leaders of the Soviet Union, China, Great Britain, and the U.S.

In the aftermath of Korea's liberation, Yi was active in protecting the rights of ethnic Koreans in Suyuian Province, which is now part of the autonomous zone of Inner Mongolia.

However, Yi's tremendous efforts were impeded by the constantly changing political situation in China. As hard as Yi tried to address the problem of the forcible transfer of Koreans to Central Asia, progress eluded him. Once the Chinese Communists occupied Manchuria, Yi Chung-mo traveled to Beijing and met up with Mun Jeong-il, a former member of the Chosun Righteous Army, with the view toward ultimately moving to North Korea. However, he died of an illness before he could move to the North. I heard of Yi's travails from Mun Jeong-il during a secret visit to Beijing in 1988.

In any case, thanks to Chiang Kai-Shek's accommodation of the Korean Provisional Government's request to distinguish between Japanese troops and Koreans who had served in the Japanese army, the Korean Provisional Government was able to incorporate those Korean men into the Korean Liberation Army after some basic military training and education in patriotism. Regrettably, however, the plan for the deployment of the Korean Liberation Army was never implemented.

During World War II, the U.S. had as its allies in East Asia a loose coalition of "CBI"; that is, China, Burma, and India. The U.S. commander of the CBI theater was General Joseph Stilwell, who was also the chief of staff of the combined allied forces in China. Although Chiang Kai-Shek was the de jure commander-in-chief, Stilwell had de facto operation command over the Chinese troops. Stilwell advocated the deployment of Chinese troops into Burma and India. However, China lacked the manpower to divert its troops to the region when the demands for Chinese troops deployment all across China were so overwhelming.

Chiang and Stilwell often collided over this. Once Stilwell grew jaded, he started to give some aid to the Chinese Communists, which further drove a wedge in his relationship with Chiang. During this time, Chiang's wife, Soong Mei-ling, visited the U.S. A graduate of Wellesley College, Madam Chiang was fluent in English, and used her command of English to serve as Chiang's special envoy vis-à-vis the outside world. Madam Chiang met with President Franklin Roosevelt and told him why China was not in a position to deploy Chinese troops into Burma and India and also that her husband and General Stilwell had grown apart due to this issue. Sometime later the U.S. replaced General Stilwell with General Albert Wedemeyer, who was not hot-tempered like Stilwell.

In the midst of it all, once Japan surrendered, Korea fell under the command of General Douglas MacArthur, who took up his new post in Japan as Supreme Commander of the Allied Powers. In my view, had Korea been assigned to the General Wedemeyer's command over China, I think the odds are that the Korean Liberation Army, based in China as it was, would have remained as a unit and ultimately become the founding unit of the Republic of Korea Army.

As it turned out, General John Hodge, Commander of the U.S. Military Government in Korea, once disarming the Japanese troops in southern Korea, employed Koreans who had actively collaborated with Japan in security and administrative functions. The division of Korea is certainly a tragedy, as is the subsequent war. But that

South Korea never was able to root out the forces of pro-Japanese collaborators is also a veritable tragedy among greater tragedies.

The Kim Koo Museum and Library Established

During my terms as Korean ambassador to Taiwan, the Kim Koo Commemoration Society had already been created and was engaged in various activities. In 1969, during my time in Taiwan, I had an occasion to chat over drinks with President Park on a visit to Seoul. Although by then four years had passed since the normalization of the diplomatic relation between Korea and Japan (1965), there still was heated criticism of the normalization from certain segments of society and political circles. President Park asked me over a drink,

"The fiftieth anniversary of the March First Independence Movement is approaching. Taking advantage of the occasion of the commemorative ceremony, some people may try to put on a large-scale, organized demonstration. Can you think of any ways to address that possibility? Any ideas on what kinds of commemorative events we should hold?"

I answered with little hesitation.

"Who are the people who actually put into practice the third paragraph of the March First Declaration of Independence, which calls for carrying on the struggle for independence 'to the last person, and to the last moment'? And who are the people who actually fought against all kinds of hardship in China in order to defend the Korean Provisional Government to the bitter end?"

Unveiling of My Father's Statue

The Unveiling of the Statue of Kim Koo took place on Namsan, August 23, 1969. Sun Ke, Sun Yat-sen's son, attended as President Chiang's Special Envoy. President Chiang sent a hand-written scroll commemorating the event.

The Inauguration of Kim Koo Museum and Library
The Memorial Hall finally opened in October 2002, 53 years after my father's death.

President Park was silent for a moment, then replied,

"I will have a bronze statue of your father, Kim Koo, in Namsan."

"How about erecting one in the City Hall Square rather than in Namsan?" I asked.

"People will come to place flowers and pay their respects in front of the statue. But the square area is too crowded. Also, the statue will get dirty from all the vehicle exhaust fumes."

The government decided to build a statue of my father in commemoration of the fiftieth anniversary of the March First Independence Movement in Namsan in 1969. The unveiling ceremony took place on August 23. In fact, President Park made an effort to take care of independence fighters immediately upon coming into power. In his first commemorative ceremony of the March First Movement, he awarded medals to those who had participated in the Korean independence movements. He also helped their surviving family members attend schools and find jobs. To my recollection, few other presidents have made as much effort to recognize independence fighters and their family as President Park.

When President Kim Young Sam decided to pull down the Jung Ang Chung (Capitol Building) in 1995, I proposed to him that we should build a memorial hall commemorating the national independence movement in its wake. My wish was not fulfilled, however. The Kim Koo Museum and Library was established only after many twists and turns. Once the Rhee government fell, public support for building a memorial hall in honor of my father started to grow. But it floundered over the years for various reasons. The idea was brought up again in the Chun Doo Hwan years, but it again floundered. The same thing happened in the Roh Tae Woo government, although President Roh personally spoke of the need for it. It was only in the Kim Dae Jung government that the Kim Koo Museum and Library was finally established. The construction of the museum began in 2000 and was completed in 2002, 53 years after my father had passed away.

Chapter 17

The Establishment of Diplomatic Relation between Korea and China

A Secret Visit to Taiwan

An officer from the intelligence agency reached out to me regarding a highly sensitive matter, as it was said. It was sometime toward the end of January, 1987. I was asked to visit Taiwan as soon as possible and not share with anyone the nature of the visit. It was top secret, they said. On a day when it was snowing heavily, I headed for Kimpo Airport without telling even my family about the purpose of my visit to Taiwan. My task was to seek the good offices of President Chiang Ching-kuo and top Taiwanese officials on a highly sensitive diplomatic incident.

The single largest number North Korean defection since the end of the Korean War had just taken place. Kim Man-cheol and ten others, including children and the elderly, had escaped from North Korea on a 50 ton boat and drifted in the East Sea before being found off the shore of the Mikuni Port, Fukui Prefecture, Japan, on January 20, 1987. The incident made headlines in Korea and all over the world.

The Japanese government found itself in a conundrum. Its relationship with North Korea, which had always been strained, had recently grown even more tense due to the detainment of the captain of a Japanese fishing boat in the North. Japan was of course sensitive about its relationship with South Korea, however, to allow the North Korean defectors to go directly to the South would have strained its relations with North Korea even more. Moreover, the North Korean defectors themselves were in disagreement with each other on which country they sought to go to—South Korea or a third country. Even though they eventually reached a consensus on South Korea, the specific route and means of their travel to South Korea had become a highly delicate matter.

Seoul decided that the best alternative would be for the North Korean defectors first to be extradited to Taiwan, and then be sent to Korea. The Korean government rather than the Japanese government took charge of the negotiations with the Taiwanese government on this. But the Taiwanese government rejected Korea's request out of concerns that it may set a precedent for future defections to the South, which may well put Taiwan in a diplomatic bind. That's when the Korean government contacted me, thinking that I may be the best person to reach out to the Taiwanese government, in view of my close relationships with Taiwan's highest leaders, including President Chiang Ching-kuo.

Diplomacy does not just take place on the official stage, visibly to the outside world. Rather, it often plays out in unofficial channels behind the scenes, and in sensitive last-minute negotiations and decisions away from the spotlight. Only then does the curtain rise and the official performance begins with statements and diplomatic protocol. This is all the more pronounced in the Chinese culture of negotiations, in which apparently irreconcilable issues can often be resolved at the last minute by personal relationships built over a long time.

I did what my government asked me to do. And Mr. Kim and his fellow North Korean defectors were all extradited to Taiwan and stayed there for over twenty hours before they finally came to Korea aboard a Korea Airline plane on February 8, 1987.

I still remember the brief words I said to my family before departing for Taiwan.

"They turn to this old man only when they're in dire need. But I must go, leaving aside everything else, because duty calls!"

Whenever duty calls, one must respond to the nation's call and try his best. It was immensely gratifying that I had a nation that I could call my own, that I had a nation that called on me for help, and that I could be of service when duty called. What greater source of gratification and pride could there be?

An Unexpected Visit by an Official of the Chinese Communist Party

In 1988 when I was chairman of the board of directors of the Korea Independence Hall, a high official of the Chinese Communist Party came to Seoul to visit me. At the time, diplomatic relation between Korea and China had yet to be established. Hence, it was exceedingly rare for an official of the Chinese Communist Party to visit Korea. So, I could not but be curious as to why this Chinese official would wish to see me. He was a Korean-Chinese named Shin Ik-cheol.

The ostensible purpose of Mr. Shin's visit to Korea was to visit his relatives in Korea. But his real purpose was to survey Korea's internal political situation and make an assessment of Korea's foreign policy intentions. Had the real purpose of his visit really been just to visit his relatives, Shin would not have sought officially an extension of stay in Korea. In the middle of his visit, Shin Ik-cheol extended his stay and went around all over Korea for about six months under the guidance of an agent South Korea's main intelligence agency.

Mr. Shin collected a variety of information on Koreans' general feelings toward China, Korea's economic conditions, public opinion on a variety of political and diplomatic issues, etc. Meeting with me was the final item on his agenda. Shin visited me with his wife. After talking with me for a while, he asked his wife to step out of the room. Once Shin's wife stepped out, he and I talked mostly about my past activities in China. I soon got the impression that he had detailed knowledge of my past. It was apparent that he had done a fair amount of research on me.

Soon after our meeting, Shin returned to China. As I came to learn later, Shin's official mission had been preliminary research on prospects, and laying the ground, for the normalization of diplomatic relations between Korea and China. Back in China, Shin reported his findings to the central committee of the Chinese Communist Party. He recommended me as a main point of contact in planning for the establishment of a diplomatic relation between Korea and China.

At the time of his visit, however, I did not know exactly why he had visited Korea or met with me. But, sometime later, an acquaintance of mine in Hong Kong gave me a call, asking me to come to Hong Kong by a certain date.

"For what?" I asked.

"You will see when you get here. It's important," he answered.

I sensed he had a pressing issue he wanted to bring up with me in confidence. I decided to visit him in Hong Kong, as he had requested. I soon found out the issue he wished to discuss with me was the normalization of diplomatic relation between Korea and China. Since China had to take North Korea, its ally, into account, the Chinese government approached this sensitive issue as discreetly as possible.

Going to Beijing via Hong Kong

On September 18, 1988, I left for Hong Kong with my eldest son. It was a time when the entire Korean nation was caught up in the Seoul Summer Olympics. When we arrived in Hong Kong, a Chinese man greeted us at the airport. Since it is still inopportune for me to disclose his full name, I will refer to him as Chester Chung, an English name he liked to use. Chester spoke English well and had an academic air about him. Since Chester was an agent of the intelligence service, he was not at liberty to disclose his true identity and position.

Chester told me that he had been a newspaper reporter during the Guomindang era, and once he was arrested by the Chinese

Communist Party, he was branded a reactionary and expelled with his family to a wasteland in Inner Mongolia. He was assigned to carrying night soil and raising livestock during his exile, before being reinstated as an agent of the intelligence service. It was a common practice of the Chinese Communist Party to cast capable intellectuals out to the hinterland for "reeducation," then reinstate after some time. Chester was one of them.

At that time, Kim Yong-jae, General Kim Hong-il's son, was living in Hong Kong. He advised me not to be seen outside, lest my presence in Hong Kong be revealed and the purpose of my visit come under scrutiny. Although I wanted to change dollars to Chinese *yuan* in preparation for my impending visit to China, there was no official way to convert U.S. dollars to Chinese currency in Hong Kong. With Mr. Kim's help, I exchanged $1,000 to Chinese *yuan* unofficially at a rate of 8.8 *yuan* to the dollar. Soon thereafter, on September 23, I entered China.

In Beijing I checked into Beijing Fandian, a hotel in the capital city. That night a Chinese official invited me to dinner. Toward the end of the meal, he had a cake brought in. On top of it were the words, "Happy Birthday! May you have a long life!" With the cake on the table, I asked my host,

"Whose birthday is it?"

"General Kim Shin, isn't it your birthday today?"

Only then did I realize that my birthday had passed a couple of days ago. While my birthday, September 21, had passed without my realization, my host had seen my date of birth in my passport and had the cake prepared to congratulate me, even if belatedly. About fifty people were present at the dinner. I did not know what kinds of agencies they were working for, but a person named Mao Guohua presided over the dinner. He had been a newspaper reporter and had worked as a correspondent in the U.S. I did not know his exact affiliation or rank, but it was clear that he was senior to Chester Chung. Chester Chung was all ears to anything Mao Guohua would say throughout the dinner.

Chester Chung had come to Beijing with me from Hong Kong and also accompanied me on various trips outside Beijing during my stay in China. On my trips out of Beijing, most of the time I flew and used the VIP room in each airport. VIP rooms remained closed until a special notice was given in advance. But Chester Chung apparently had made prior arrangements. He would show the airport officials a document and everything went smoothly without incident. After a while, I jokingly called Chester "*Shen tong guang da*," which means a man who can solve anything and everything. He just smiled at my words.

I had set foot on Chinese soil for the first time in almost forty years. There was so much personal and national history in China, I could hardly suppress my excitement. I stepped out and went around here and there every chance I had. During my stay in Beijing, I went to see various sites: Tiananmen Square, the National Palace Museum, the Great Wall, Ming Dynasty Tombs, the Summer Palace, etc. I also visited the Anti-Japanese War Museum of the Chinese People near the Marco Polo (Lugou) Bridge. For my visit to the museum, the Communist Party had a Korean-Chinese professor named Kim Jin-gi accompany me as a guide.

With Cheng Siyuan, Vice President of the People's Political Consultative Conference

On September 27, I met with a person named Cheng Siyuan, Vice President of the People's Political Consultative Conference. The Conference, initially created at the time of the Guomindang-Communist United Front, had included other minor parties as well. Mr. Cheng had been the chief secretary for Li Zongren, who became the Acting President in the wake of President Chiang Kai-Shek retirement in January 1949. Once a major figure like Cheng showed up, I thought I had finally met the real power-holder behind the scenes.

In fact, Vice President Cheng Siyuan had met with my father in Chongqing. He knew about my family and the Korean Provisional Government in detail. During our meal together we exchanged mostly pleasantries without broaching the real business at hand. As Cheng did not reveal what he had in mind, neither did I. Back in Korea, when I told Hong Seong-cheol, the chief secretary to President Roh Tae Woo, that I had met with Cheng Siyuan, he was very surprised and told me that I had been received by a really important figure.

The Weeds-Strewn Tomb of Confucius

I had intended to visit Shenyang and Changchun in northeast China after a few days in Beijing. Shortly before I left Beijing, Shin Ik-cheol and his wife came to see me with Wang Zhijian, who was chief of public relations at the Office of Foreign Affairs in Heilungjiang Province. Mr. Wang had escorted Kim Il Sung three times in Harbin before, when the North Korean leader stopped over in Harbin on his way to Moscow by rail.

But I canceled plans to visit Shenyang and Changchun as Mao Guohua dissuaded me from doing so. He was afraid that should I be spotted by someone who knew who I was my undeclared visit to China may be reported to North Korea, it may create a diplomatic problem for Beijing. He was even concerned about the possibility of North Korea abducting me.

So, I changed my mind and visited instead Jinan, in Shandong Province. During my two day-long visit, Jiang Kuisheng, Chief of the Tourism Department, took care of our party. I still remember that Jiang, as a mere director general of a provincial government, referred to Prime Minister Li Peng as if Li were his friend, commenting on Li Peng's personality and character as he pleased. I came to learn that he and Li Peng were indeed old friends, classmates at a university in Moscow. I guess Jiang rattled on like that out of an inferiority complex, as Li Peng had become Prime Minister, while he was merely working for a local tourism department.

Next, I visited Mt. Tai and took the cable car up to its peak. Once back on the ground, I visited General Feng Yuxiang's tomb. General Feng, together with President Chiang Kai-Shek, had led the Guomindang's Northern Expedition and had been Supreme Commander of the Northwest National Combined Forces. Even though he had been a sworn brother of President Chiang, Feng later became estranged from Chiang and did not take up an important position during the war against Japanese. Feng Yuxiang's daughter, Feng Lida, was my classmate at Anhui Middle School.

General Feng had become so completely estranged from President Chiang that in 1947 he even issued an anti-Chiang statement on a visit to the U.S. On his way to China via the Soviet Union to participate in the People's Political Consultative Conference, Feng died when his ship caught fire in the Black Sea. I do not know how his family members collected his remains, but they had built his tomb in Taian, in the foothills of Mt. Tai. In a temple nearby called Rizhaosi, there were many pictures that highlighted his exploits on display. Among them, I found a picture with his daughter's name, Peng Lida, on it. I said to Chester Chung.

"This woman is an alumna of my middle school," I said to Chester.

"Oh, really? She is a high-ranking official," said he.

I later found out that she had studied in Saint Petersburg, Russia, had a successful career in medicine, became a Rear Admiral of the Chinese Navy, participated in the People's Political Consultative Conference, and died in 2008.

My next destination was Qufu, Confucius's hometown. Qufu housed the Confucian Office, Confucian Shrine, and Confucian Forest, where all of Confucius's descendants were buried. At the time in 1988, Confucius was still unfavorably looked upon in China. There still remained the stigma of the degradation campaign against Confucius and Lin Biao in the expression "Criticize Lin Biao, Criticize Confucius" from the Cultural Revolution. Because of this, the Confucian Shrine was left in such a state of neglect that weeds were growing on its roof. Many other parts of the building were left in disrepair.

"This is the tomb of Confucius, a great individual in the history of East Asia. So, let's bow and show our respects to him," I said to my son.

After staying a night in Qufu, I came back to Jinan the next day. I stayed at a hotel named Ji lu bin guan in Jinan, and Jiang Kuisheng hosted us to a farewell dinner.

"You've come as far as Shandong this time and have visited many sites. Please tell me your honest views on how we can make improvements," Jiang said to me.

"Nothing in particular," I answered.

"No, please tell me the truth. Since you've served as Minister of Transportation in Korea, you must have an eye for these things. You must have found something we should address here in China," he said again.

"The roads seem to be well paved," I remarked. I thought it improper for me to make negative comments.

When I mentioned the roads, Jiang said,

"We paved the main road from Qufu to the Confucian Shrine, but there aren't too many cars using it."

"You know, it was the same in Korea, newly paved road being unused at first. But all of a sudden the number of cars on the main roads increased." I mentioned.

It is true that when the Seoul-Busan Highway was completed, few cars used it at first. For this, the opposition party vehemently attacked the government. The press was also strongly critical, sneering whether the government had built the highway for the exclusive enjoyment of a few rich people with cars.

In any case, I kept telling him only good things.

"I found the road to Mt. Tai good and the road to its peak also very good."

But he kept asking me to talk about anything I found wanting. Partly because he kept pressing me and partly because I grew a bit tipsy as the meal progressed, I told him about the problem with the Confucian Shrine.

"Then, let me tell you a piece of my mind, though I fear it may offend you."

After seeking his understanding, I continued.

"Confucius is not only a great man in China alone but also one of the most preeminent men in the history of human civilization. But when I visited Confucian Shrine in his hometown, it was in a state of neglect strewn with weeds. How can it be when even Koreans hold a memorial service for Confucius at the Sungkyunkwan? When I return to Korea and tell Koreans about this, they are bound to be shocked. Should I try to raise funds in Korea for the purpose of properly preserving the Confucian Shrine, I could raise a big sum in no time. May I raise funds and contribute the sum to the Chinese government?"

Jiang Kuisheng was not in a position to answer my question. He turned to Chester and asked him,

"Does General Kim have any opportunity to meet high-ranking people when he returns to Beijing?"

"Yes, he does."

Mr. Jiang said to me after hearing Chester's answer.

"General Kim. Since I am not in a position to answer your question, please raise it again with higher-ups in Beijing."

We then moved on to a different subject, the relationship between Korea and Shandong. I said that since Korea and Shandong are geographically close to each other and historically have had deep ties, there would be vastly increased exchange and cooperation between them once Korea and China improve their bilateral relationship. Mr. Jiang heartily agreed with me.

Chapter 18

Publishing the Chinese Translation of *Paikbum Ilji*

Meeting with Mun Jeong-il of the Korean Volunteers' Army

On September 28, 1988, I returned to Beijing from Jinan. There, Mun Jeong-il (1914-2003) came to see me. Many years earlier, Mun had worked with my brother for the Korean independence movements in Nanjing. He later switched over to the Kim Yak-san communist faction, and in 1940 became a member of the Chinese Communist Party. He even tried to make my brother join it.

Mun also somehow had heard that my eldest son frequently visited the Dongbei region on business and had met up with him in Manchuria. Shin Ik-cheol had arranged for their meeting. Mun had purportedly told my son,

"I have ties with your family over three generations. I knew your great-grandmother, grandfather, and uncle very well. Someday, I'd love to meet your father, too. I am sure there will be many things to talk about with him."

Eventually, that chance came. Mr. Mun had played a role in the creation of the Yanbian Korean Autonomous Prefecture and held

349

fairly high positions in the Chinese Communist Party, including the positions of the vice chief to the National Committee for Ethnic Affairs and a standing member of the National Committee of the People's Political Consultative Conference. His original name was Yi Geun-hyeong, but had also gone by Yi Un-ryong at one point. It was common that those who participated in the Korean independence movements used several aliases to avoid being identified. For example, General Kim Hong-il used to use the alias Wang Il-seo.

As a member of the Korean Volunteers' Army, Mr. Mun fought in the Second Sino-Japanese War in Huabei and Yanan. He also fought in the battle of Mt. Taihang. Thanks to his military records, he was treated by the Chinese as if he had been one of them. He asked me to have dinner at his home. He lived in an apartment for minister-level figures. He had lots of material related to the Korean independence movement at home. Leafing through them, I said to him,

"Do you have plans to compile all these into a book?"

"Three students from Yanbian attending Beijing University are already cataloguing them."

Mr. Mun and I shared meals on two occasions and also talked in my hotel room. Every time we talked, he turned on the radio and set the volume high. The Chinese Communist Party had an agency called the disciplinary committee, which kept track of all party members. Even high-ranking party members could be deprived of their positions if they were caught by the committee in violations of party rules. Mun had once worked in the central disciplinary committee and knew he had to exercise caution. That was why he set the volume of the radio high and also told me to be cautious.

The reason why Mun wanted to see me was that he had thought there was something peculiar about my visit to China. Since there was no official diplomatic relation between Korea and China at the time, Korean nationals who visited China for personal business would often seek Mun out in an attempt to build some connection to the Chinese government. Beijing also regularly went through Mun to contact Korean individuals of influence. Mun assumed that my visit had serious implications when, despite initially hearing of my visit, heard no follow-up report or even gossip about the specifics of my visit. To someone in Mun's position, the silence surrounding my trip to China implied the gravity of my visit.

On October 2, I met with a man named Ye Zhilung. Mr. Ye had worked as one of the closest aides to Mao Zedong for over ten years. The venue for our meeting was the VIP room in the Beijing Fandian. The meeting was not open even to individuals like Mao Guohua and Chester Chung. In the VIP room were five elderly men. At that time, the Premier of China was Yang Shangkun. Unable to take up the sensitive matter of political normalization himself, Yang had retired elders stand in his place. Yet, Mr. Ye did not talk about politics with me. Instead, he asked me the same sort of questions that Jiang Kuisheng had asked me.

"Mr. Kim, it's been a while since your last visit to China. Please give us your advice on anything you think we need to make improvements on."

I brought up the problem of the Confucian Shrine again. Mr. Ye smiled and remarked,

"The central government already has made plans to look into it."

Later when I was visiting America, I received an invitation from Jiang Kuisheng to attend a country-wide event to celebrate the renovation and reopening of the Confucian Shrine. But he told me that even as his government had renovated the buildings and cleaned up the surroundings, it did not know how to conduct the memorial service for Confucius in the traditional Confucian way. Hence, I advised him to go to Korea and learn how to do it. Officials in the Shandong government then went to Sungkyunkwan University and learned all the rituals and protocols.

Anyways, for senior former statesmen like Ye Zhilung to meet with me was sort of a test for them to gauge how trustworthy I was. As the Chinese government made plans for the normalization of diplomatic relations with Korea, it was proceeding in such a roundabout way rather than taking up the matter officially itself. The Chinese were very cautious so as to minimize potential complications.

Lost in Memories in Xian and Chongqing

After meeting with the elders in Beijing, I made my way over to Xian. I stayed at a hotel called Renmindasha, which was built by the Soviets to celebrate the founding of the People's Republic of China. I went to see the Terracotta Army exhibition first and then went sightseeing toured around the city. The most notable places in Xian were the museums and castles. The castles and city walls were built during the Ming dynasty and were heavily fortified as Xian was close to the "barbarian" peoples in Xibei.

After visiting Xian, I flew over to Chongqing on a twin-engine propeller plane. After a night's sleep in a hotel, I made my way to Tanzishi to revisit the Mt. Heshang graveyards. I tried to look for the graveyard from the car, but not only the graveyard for Koreans but the entire cemetery was nowhere to be seen. I jogged my memory and tried to find the graveyard for Koreans, but the topography had changed too much. I eventually gave up trying to find the spots by car, and decided to look for them by walking from the Sunjia Flower Garden just as I did a long time ago.

Fortunately, while travelling along the old roads, I remembered the location of the graveyard for Koreans. At that time, I was the only person that knew where it was. For what it's worth, the site which Professor Jo Dong-geol found with the assistance of a Chinese guide sometime ago was not the correct place. What he found actually was the Mt. Guanyin cemetery, which was newly built. The Mt. Heshang graveyards had disappeared with the construction of roads in the area. All the gravestones were used as materials for the road construction.

After visiting the graveyards, I went to Tuqiao where Koreans had congregated and formed a small community. This place, too, bore little resemblance to how it was in the past, with many of the old buildings gone. There once had been a big zelkova next to a waterfall in Tuqiao, but it too had been cut down. Across from the waterfall was Qinghua Middle School, which a small number of Korean students had attended. Eom Gi-seon, the daughter of Eom Hang-seop, had attended this school, too. I visited the school. The former principal had gone off to Beijing, and a man who had worked for the school for a long time welcomed me. He remembered so much of the old days.

I then dropped by the South Hot Springs, which used to be hard for ordinary people to access. Here, Madam Soong Mei-ling's old villa still remained intact. From here, I visited the Chaotian Gate and the Wushiye Port and then the school in Qingmuguan I had attended. I also visited the Hongyan Revolution Memorial Hall and the Mt. Pipa Museum, located atop the highest hill in Chongqing.

Another Line of Communication

When I returned to Korea, I met with chief secretary for the president Hong Seong-cheol and told him all about my time in China. The Chinese, in inviting me amid all the secrecy, actually wanted me to convey to my government what I had seen and heard in China. They tested me in various ways in order to gauge if I would, like many Korean politicians who visited China, use my visit and the relationships I formed in China for my own political gain. Before my return, they said to me emphatically:

"If you go back to Korea and say that you've met this person or that person for your own political advantage, we will deny every claim you make."

"Don't worry. Such a thing will never happen," I assured them.

Mr. Hong reported everything I told him to President Roh Tae Woo. At the time, the Korean government itself was making its own overtures to China. The government's point man to carry out this task was Kim Bok-dong, President Rho's brother-in-law. Kim, through a man with business interests in China, at the time was trying to establish a link to Tian Jiyun, Vice Prime Minister for Economic Affairs. Mr. Hong suggested that I meet with Mr. Kim. So, I went to his office in Gangnam, Seoul, and told him about my visit to China. His reaction was quite guarded and not particularly friendly. He seemed to be wary of me, thinking that I was interfering with the work he was doing.

One time, on one of his visits to Seoul, Chester Chung arranged for a meeting among Kim Bok-dong, me, and himself. Seeing Kim come alone to the meeting without his aide, I got the impression that he was trying to monopolize this task. So, I voiced my thoughts to Chester Chung after the meeting.

"Since Kim Bok-dong is working on this already, I think we should drop it. I think it's time for me to bow out of all this."

But Chester was adamant against it.

"If you pull out now, the whole thing could collapse. Let's keep on with this for as long as we can."

I gather Chester Chung tried to dissuade me vigorously since his own interests were intertwined in working with me. While the talks between the two countries were progressing steadily, Mao Guohua reached out to me through several intermediaries. He wanted to see me in Bangkok. He told me that a Chinese cultural group was to visit Bangkok for goodwill performance, and Mao was to be the head of the delegation. When I proposed that we meet in Hong Kong instead, he replied that it was not a good place to meet, as there were many eyes and ears in Hong Kong.

I went to Bangkok with my third son to meet with Mr. Mao. When we arrived there, Chester Chung was waiting for us. Mao came to see me in the middle of the night. We talked about various subjects, and I also told him the same thing that I had told Chester.

"When I returned to Korea I conveyed to the Blue House my visit to China. But I learned that the government already had a point man tasked for the job. Since redundancy could create a conflict of interest, I think I'd better take myself out of this."

But all of sudden Mao said that a party secretary in the North Korean Embassy in Beijing wanted to see me. Finding the proposition very odd, I said to him in a somewhat irritated tone,

"Why are you talking about a North Korean party secretary when we are discussing issues that concern our two nations? What does he have to do with this matter?"

Mao responded calmly,

"Nothing much, really. I just happen to be close to this person and once mentioned that I was in communication with you. He said that he wanted to meet you, too, and wished to join our next meeting."

I thought that this was not right, and made it clear to Mao.

"This is an entirely different matter. I am trying to advance the relations between China and Korea. Once North Korea becomes even slightly involved in this, things will become complicated and even uncontrollable. I will never get involved with a North Korean."

I met with Chester Chung once more after that. By then, Kim Bok-dong had taken full charge of the task of establishing diplomatic relations between Korea and China, and many people were involved in the job. I told Chester again that I wished to opt out of the matter completely. He replied resignedly,

"I see. But please be sure to contact me if you need to."

After that, I did not involve myself in the matter again.

Celebrating the Publication of *Paikbum Ilji* in the Great Hall of the People

After my visit to China in 1988, I frequently revisited for personal reasons. Altogether, I travelled to China nearly fifty times and visited almost all the provinces, autonomous prefectures, and the major cities. I felt different emotions and took away different impressions with each visit, but the one memory that stays close to me is my visit in 1994 on the occasion of the publication of the Chinese translation of *Paikbum Ilji*, my father's autobiography.

The Chinese translation of *Paikbum Ilji* was published on June 26, 1994, on the 45th anniversary of my father's passing. The book was translated by the married couple Xuan Dewu and Zhang Minghui, specialists in Korean language, under my supervision. With the introduction written by Professor Ji Xianlin (1911-2009), who was a giant in the field of humanities in China, the 292-page book was published by the Democracy and Construction Publishing House. It was the product of two years of work following the initial discussions with our counterparts in China in 1992.

At the time of the publication, many Chinese as well as Korean-Chinese were under the impression that the existing North Korean ruling forces had led Korea's anti-Japanese struggles. The publication of the Chinese translation of *Paikbum Ilji* was a significant event in that it played a role in correcting the Chinese public's misunderstandings regarding the Korean independence movement. As China had been the land where my father, the Korean Provisional Government, and countless independence fighters had shed so much of their blood, sweat, and tears, the publication of the Chinese translation itself was an occasion of great significance.

I wished to hold the book publication ceremony in the Great Hall of the People in Beijing. But the Korean authorities were entirely pessimistic about the prospect. An individual from the Korean intelligence service assigned to the Korean Embassy in China flat out said that it would be impossible to have such an event in the Great Hall of the People. The Korean Ambassador to China, Hwang Byeong-tae, took the same view and said so. They all believed that as it had been only two years since the establishment of diplomatic relations between Korea and China in 1992, holding such a ceremony in the heart of the Chinese capital would be difficult. But I thought it was quite possible, since I was well acquainted with Zhu Muzhi, former Minister of Culture and President of the China-Korea Friendship Association. Mr. Zhu was at the ceremony.

I heard later that the Chinese were also mindful of the sensitivity of the event, and, in consideration of their relationship with North Korea, had sought the opinion of the North Korean embassy. They were pleasantly surprised by the response.

"We have deep respect for Kim Koo, too. We will send some of our people to the publication ceremony as well."

Publication Ceremony: *Paikbum Ilji* in Chinese

The ceremony took place in the Great Hall of the People, Beijing, on July 12, 1994.

Thus, the ceremony was held on July 12, 1994. The *Renmin Daily* and *Guangming Daily* came to cover the event. China Central TV had also registered to cover the event, but canceled as the news of Kim Il Sung's death on July 8 drew the station's full attention.

The ceremony was an emotional experience for me. I could not help but think about my father who had made his way all through China, totally committed to fighting for our nation's independence. I look back Korea's modern history and, again, ask: Who fought for Korea's independence "to the last person and to the last moment," as the third paragraph of the March First Declaration of Independence calls for?

There were many patriotic martyrs who gave it all, who risked their personal safety and who risked their lives to fight for Korea's liberation under the harshest conditions in Korea, Manchuria, Shanghai, Chongqing, the Maritime Province of Siberia, and the Americas. Among the noble and proud heroes stands my father. He would now be watching over from the sky the splendid prosperity of our country, the Republic of Korea, which has inherited the "legitimacy of the Korean Provisional Government of the Republic of Korea established by the March First Movement." He would also be watching the tragic reality of the ongoing division between the South and the North.

Throughout the ceremony, I could hardly take my hands off *Paikbum Ilji*. For it was not simply a book but my father's breath and spirit itself.

Afterword

This book is a compilation of an extensive set of tape-recording sessions on my recollection of my life. In my attempt to structure the book around a central storyline and make it relatively concise, I have had to leave out much of the recorded material. I plan to have all of the tape-recordings transcribed as a resource for the further study of modern and contemporary Korean history. I have approached the recording sessions with the view that it is my obligation to history to leave my recollections as a historical record.

In this book, many individuals are mentioned; some briefly, some at length. It would not be an egregious exaggeration to say that almost all the key figures in the history of Korea's independence are mentioned in this book. I considered adding a brief description of each in footnotes or endnotes, but decided against it, for background information on these individuals are readily accessible and an oversized notes section may impede the flow of the narrative. In some cases, I've added the briefest annotation; but for the most part have left the figures unintroduced. For this, I seek the reader's understanding.

This book ends in the mid-1990s. Since then, I've mainly worked with the Kim Koo Memorial Association and the Kim Koo Museum and Library. I have also spent time participating in ceremonies and events related to the ROK Air Force and various independence movements as well as compiling and organizing the many photographs and records accumulated over the years. I have also welcomed many distinguished guest visitors to the Kim Koo Museum and Library and given them a tour myself. I have also enjoyed being in the company of children and young visitors.

In late October 2010, I attended the inauguration of the Kim Koo Forum at Beijing University in China. This forum was established by the Institute of International and Strategic Studies at Beijing University, with support from the Kim Koo Foundation, which is headed by my daughter, Mee. The forum hosts regular seminars on various issues related to Korea-China relations and the international politics and history of East Asia. Before the inaugural seminar of the Kim Koo Forum, Luo Haocai, President of the Chinese Foreign Friendship Association and former Vice Premier of the National Political Consultative Conference, presented me with the "Ten Contributors to Korea-China Friendship Award."

Through times both busy and more leisurely, I occasionally reminisce about the mountains and streams in An-ak, where I lived with my grandmother when I was a boy. While I was born in Shanghai, I consider An-ak my hometown. I wonder if my childhood friends are still living and how the town has changed today. In retrospect, when I dropped the evacuation message by a parachute over the town during the Korean War was the last time I saw An-ak. Since more than sixty years have passed, I often think I will no longer remember where everything is even if I were to visit again.

When in reminiscing about my hometown like this, I cannot but be reminded of my father who fought so hard against Korea's division and believing that division would entail a war between the South and the North. While Korea's reunification will be difficult to achieve in the near future, I only wish that the day will come soon when the South and North come to seek genuine reconciliation and cooperation and establish peace in the Korean peninsula. I have no doubt that what my father, from up above, regrets the most is the split and the tense standoff between the South and North and that my father's most ardent wish is the reconciliation and cooperation between the two sides. When the true era of South-North reconciliation and cooperation begins, I am certain that the beliefs my father held and the actions he took will come to be reevaluated in new ways.

I once again reflect on the meaning of my father's admonition to me in the wake of Korea's liberation to defer return to Korea and instead go to America for further pilot training. I once again reflect on the promise I made to myself witnessing Japanese planes' indiscriminate bombings of Nanjing and Chongqing. It was a summons to fly Korea's skies in a plane flying the Korean flag and defend Korea's freedom in the post-liberation period. It was a pledge that I would fly a warplane at the forefront in the struggle against the Japanese oppression.

The exuberance and joy brought by Korea's liberation was short-lived. The overflowing joy I felt when I flew freely over the skies of my country on an aircraft with Korea's national flag painted on its body was also short-lived, for I had to fly the skies of my country beset by the tragedy of an internecine war. I had to bomb the mountains and rivers of my own country, even if it was in defense of freedom. The tragedy of using the aviation skills acquired under such harrowing conditions against my own compatriots was certainly not just my own personal tragedy. The times and history of our lives drove us all into this great national tragedy.

We must never again repeat this tragedy. Hence, we must all become masters of our own time and history and, with wisdom and courage, step forward to achieve our nation's reconciliation and cooperation. All these wishes and meanings are embedded in the title of this book, *To Fly Korea's Skies*.

Chronology of Kim Shin's Life
(Kim's corresponding age in parentheses)

1922 (1)

Born to Kim Koo and Choi Jun Rye in the French Concession of Shanghai, China, on September 21 (August 1 by the lunar calendar).

1924 (3)

Choi Jun Rye, mother, dies in Hongkou Hospital, Shanghai.

1925 (4)

Returns to Korea with grandmother, Kwak Nak Won, in November.

1927 (6)

In, brother, returns to Korea in September. Attends Anshin School in An-ak, Hwanghae Province. First dreams of becoming a pilot on a school trip to Mirim Air Base, run by the Aviation Corps of the Japanese Army.

1934 (13)

Flees to China with In, brother, on March 19. In April arrives in Jiaxing by train from Shanghai and meets father for the first time in nine years. Moves to Nanjing via Shanghai with grandmother.

1935 (14)

Attends Dazhongqiao Elementary School in Nanjing. Changes name to Guan Shin.

1936 (15)

Attends Chiang Kai-Shek's 50th Birthday Celebrations as a Boy Scout. Watches air show and the "presentation of airplanes" to Chiang at Minggugong Airport.

1938 (17)

Kim Koo is shot by Yi Un-hwan in Nanmuting, May 7. In July, departs Changsha with the Korean Provisional Government for Guangzhou, settles in Foshan. Acts as a liaison between Guangzhou and Foshan. In October, relocates with the Korean Provisional Government from Guangzhou to Liuzhou, Guangxi Province.

1939 (18)

Departs Liuzhou with the Korean Provisional Government in April. Arrives in Chongqing, Sichuan Province, with grandmother and settles in Sunjia Flower Garden. Enrolls in Zhongyang University Middle-High School in Qingmuguan as a second-grader. Changes name to Kim Shin Gang. Grandmother dies in Chongqing on April 26.

1943 (22)

Graduates Zhongyang University Middle-High School. Enrolls in Xinan Lianhe University, Kunming. Suffers from severe typhoid and moves to Chongqing.

1944 (23)

Works for the Ministry of Internal Affairs, the Korean Provisional Government. Completes basic flight training at the Chinese Air Force Academy in Kunming, Yunnan Province.

1945 (24)

Travels from Kunming to Indian-administered Lahore to receive flight training. In, brother, dies in Chongqing in March. In August, during flight training in Lahore, hears news of Korea's liberation. In December, departs Lahore for the U.S. for further training.

1946 (25)

Enrolls at Randolph Air Base in San Antonio, America.

1947 (26)

Meets Dr. Syngman Rhee and Dr. Lin Yutang in Washington, D.C., in January. In June, departs Randolph Air Base and travels to Shanghai, graduates from the Chinese Air Force Academy in Nanjing. In September returns to Korea by sea with niece, Kim Hyo-ja.

1948 (27)

Departs for Pyongyang with father on April 19. Brings back to Korea the remains of Yi Dong-nyeong, Cha Ri-seok, grandmother, mother, and brother. On August 23, joins the ROK Army Air Force. On December 18, marries Lim Yoon Yeon at Namdaemun Church.

1949 (28)

Kim Koo killed by Ahn Du-hui, on June 26. Father buried at Hyochang Park following a State-National Funeral on July 5. Moves to Geum Hwa Jang on August 23. First child, Jin, born on October 30.

1950 (29)

Graduates Military Staff Academy in May. Korean War breaks out on June 25. Flies back with U.S. jets to Daegu from Itazuke Air Base, Japan. Attacks North Korean forces crossing river into Chungju, first sortie. Based in Gyeongju with the First Division of the Army.

1951 (30)

Appointed Commander of Air Base 101, First Combat Air Wing, on August 1. Appointed Deputy Commander of the First Combat Air Wing and Commander of the 10th Combat Air Wing on November 10.

1952 (31)

Appointed Commander of the 15th Aviation Training Corps, First Combat Air Wing, on June 16.

1953 (32)

In July enrolls in a program at the U.S. Air Force Academy. Appointed Director of Operations, Air Force Headquarters, on July 15. Appointed Commander of the 10th Combat Air Wing on September 10.

1956 (35)

Appointed Deputy Chief of Staff of Administration, Air Force Headquarters, on September 15.

1959 (38)

Completes graduate program at the National Defense University in June. Appointed Deputy Chief of Staff of the Air Force, on July 25.

1960 (39)

Appointed the sixth Chief of Staff of the Air Force, on August 1.

1962 (41)

Discharged from the Air Force, August 1. Presents credentials as Republic of Korea Ambassador to the Republic of China, on October 9.

1970 (49)

Leaves post as ROK Ambassador to the Republic of China in December.

1971 (50)

Returns to Korea in early 1971 and runs for office of the National Assembly in Yongsan District, Seoul, to no avail. On November 11, Lim Yoon Yeon, wife, dies. On November 24, appointed Minister of Transportation.

1974 (53)

Ends term as Minister of Transportation, on September 17.

1976 (55)

National Assemblyman, *Yusin* Political Friends Association.

1986 (65)

First Chairman of the Board, Korea Independence Hall.

1988 (67)

In September, visits Beijing via Hong Kong. Meets Cheng Siyuan, Vice President of the People's Political Consultative Conference, on September 27. China regards Kim Shin unofficial partner in dialogue in planning for the normalization of diplomatic relations with Korea. Visits Jinan, Qufu, Xian, Chongqing, Shanghai, etc. and returns to Korea in October.

1994 (73)

Ceremony on the occasion of the publication of the Chinese translation of *Paikbum Ilji*, in the Great Hall of the People, Beijing, on

July 12.

1999 (78)

Senior Advisor to the ROK National Unification Advisory Council, in July.

2000 (79)

Chairman, Kim Koo Memorial Association, in February.

2002 (81)

Director, Kim Koo Museum and Library, in October.

Awards and Decorations

1951	Gold Star Chungmu Distinguished Military Award
1952	No Star Eulji Distinguished Military Award, Presidential Medal
1953	Presidential Medal, Gold Star Eulji Distinguished Military Award
1954	No Star Eulji Distinguished Military Award, UN War Medal, U.S. Bronze Star
1956	No Star Hwarang Distinguished Military Award, No Star Chungmu Distinguished Military Award
1957	U.S. Bronze Star
1958	Commendation by the Minister of National Defense for Distinguished Service
1960	Taiwanese Order of the Cloud and Banner, Taiwanese Order of Brilliant Star, Taiwanese Order of Propitious Clouds
1961	Philippine Meritorious Service Award
1962	Thai First-Grade Crown Medal, First-Grade Order of Service Merit, Gukseon Medal of the Order of National Security Merit
1963	Heungin Medal of the Order of Diplomatic Service Merit
1974	Blue Stripes Medal of the Order of Service Merit
1976	Gwanghwa Medal of the Order of Diplomatic Service Merit
1990	National Medal of the Order of National Foundation

index

H

Han Gap-su 한갑수
Han Gyeong-jik 한경직
Heo Jeong 허정
Heo Se-uk 허세욱
Hong Seong-cheol 홍성철
Hwang Byeong-tae 황병태
Hyeon Ik-cheol 현익철
Hyeon O-bong 현오봉

I

Im Byeong-jik 임병직
Im Yeong-sin 임영신

J

Jang Deok-chang 장덕창
Jang Deok-jin 장덕진
Jang Do-yeong 장도영
Jang Dong-chul 장동출
Jang Du-cheol 장두철
Jang Seong-cheol 장성철
Jang Seong-hwan 장성환
Jeon Myeong-seop 전명섭
Jeong Jeong-hwa 정정화
Jeong Seong-won 정성원
Jeong So-yeong 정소영
Jeong Tae-hun 정태훈
Jeong Yeong-jin 정영진
Ji Cheong-cheon 지청천
Jo Jae-cheon 조재천

Jo So-ang 조소앙
Jo Wan-gu 조완구

K

Kim A-ryeo 김아려
Kim Bo-yeon 김보연
Kim Bok-dong 김복동
Kim Bung-jun 김붕준
Kim Chang-ryong 김창룡
Kim Cheol 김철
Kim Cheol-nam 김철남
Kim Dae-eon 김대언
Kim Deok-mok 김덕목
Kim Deok-ryang 김덕량
Kim Do-yeon 김도연
Kim Dong-su 김동수
Kim Du-bong 김두봉
Kim Du-man 김두만
Kim Eui-han 김의한
Kim Gye-won 김계원
Kim Hak-gyu 김학규
Kim Hong-il 김홍일
Kim Hong-ryang 김홍량
Kim Hong-seo 김홍서
Kim Hyeon-cheol 김현철
Kim Hyeong-uk 김형욱
Kim Hyo-ja 김효자
Kim Hyo-suk 김효숙
Kim Ja-dong 김자동
Kim Jang-heung 김장흥
Kim Jeong-pyeong 김정평

Kim Jeong-ryeol 김정렬

Kim Jeong-suk 김정숙

Kim Jong-hang 김종항

Kim Jong-pil 김종필

Kim Jun-yeop 김준엽

Kim Jwa-gyeong 김좌경

Kim Ki-nam 김기남

Kim Kyu-sik 김규식

Kim Man-cheol 김만철

Kim Mu-jeong 김무정

Kim Sang-yeop 김상엽

Kim Seon-ryang 김선량

Kim Seong-eun 김성은

Kim Seong-ryong 김성룡

Kim Seung-hak 김승학

Kim Si-yeol 김시열

Kim Sun-ae 김순애

Kim U-jeon 김우전

Kim Won-man 김원만

Kim Won-yeong 김원영

Kim Yak-san 김약산

Kim Yeong-hwan 김영환

Kim Yong-dae 김용대

Kim Yong-jae 김용재

Kim Yong-je 김용제

Kim Yong-jin 김용진

Kim Yong-u 김용우

Kim Yun-hwan 김윤환

L

Lee Beom-seok 이범석

Lee Eung-jun 이응준

Lee Gang-hun 이강훈

Lee Geun-seok 이근석

Lee Han-rim 이한림

Lee Hyeong-geun 이형근

Lee Jae-cheol 이재철

Lee Jong-chan 이종찬

Lee Sang-su 이상수

Lee Seong-ho 이성호

Lim Hak-jun 임학준

Lim Yoon-Yeon 임윤연

M

Min Pil-ho 민필호

Min Yeong-ju 민영주

Min Yeong-su 민영수

Mun Jeong-il 문정일

N

Na Tae-seop 나태섭

Na Wol-hwan 나월환

No Deok-sul 노덕술

O

Ok Kwan-bin 옥관빈

Ok Man-ho 옥만호

Ok Sung-bin 옥성빈

P

Paikbum 백범

Paik Sun Yup 백선엽

Park Byeong-bae 박병배

Park Byeong-gwon 박병권

Park Byeong-rae 박병래

Park Chan-ik 박찬익

Park Chang-se 박창세

Park Chung-hun 박충훈

Park Dong-yeop 박동엽

Park Eun-sik 박은식

Park Hui-dong 박희동

Park Jong-gyu 박종규

Park Si-chang 박시창

Park Sun-cheon 박순천

Park Yeong-jun 박영준

R

Ro Baek-lin 노백린

Ro Tae-jun 노태준

Ryu Dong-ryeol 류동렬

Ryu Jae-heung 류재흥

Ryu Won-sik 유원식

S

Seonu Jin 선우진

Shin Geon-sik 신건식

Shin Gyu-sik 신규식

Shin Hyeon-sang 신현상

Shin Ik-hee 신익희

Shin Seong-mo 신성모

Shin Sun-ho 신순호

Shin Yong-ha 신용하

Song Byeong-jo 송병조

Song Myeon-su 송면수

Y

Yang Gi-tak 양기탁

Yang U-jo 양우조

Yi Cheong-cheon 이청천

Yi Chung-mo 이충모

Yi Dong-hui 이동휘

Yi Dong-nyeong 이동녕

Yi Gi-bung 이기붕

Yi Ha-yu 이하유

Yi Hae-pyeong 이해평

Yi Jae-hyeon 이재현

Yi Jun-sik 이준식

Yi Seong-gu 이성구

Yi Si-yeong 이시영

Yi Su-yeong 이수영

Yi Ui-sik 이의식

Yi Un-hwan 이운환

Yi Yeong-mu 이영무

Yu Jin-dong 유진동

Yu Jin-san 유진산

Yuk Young-Soo 육영수

Yun Bo-seon 윤보선

Yun Cheon-ju 윤천주

Yun Ha-jeong 윤하정